427760

D1611121

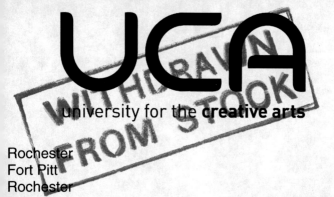

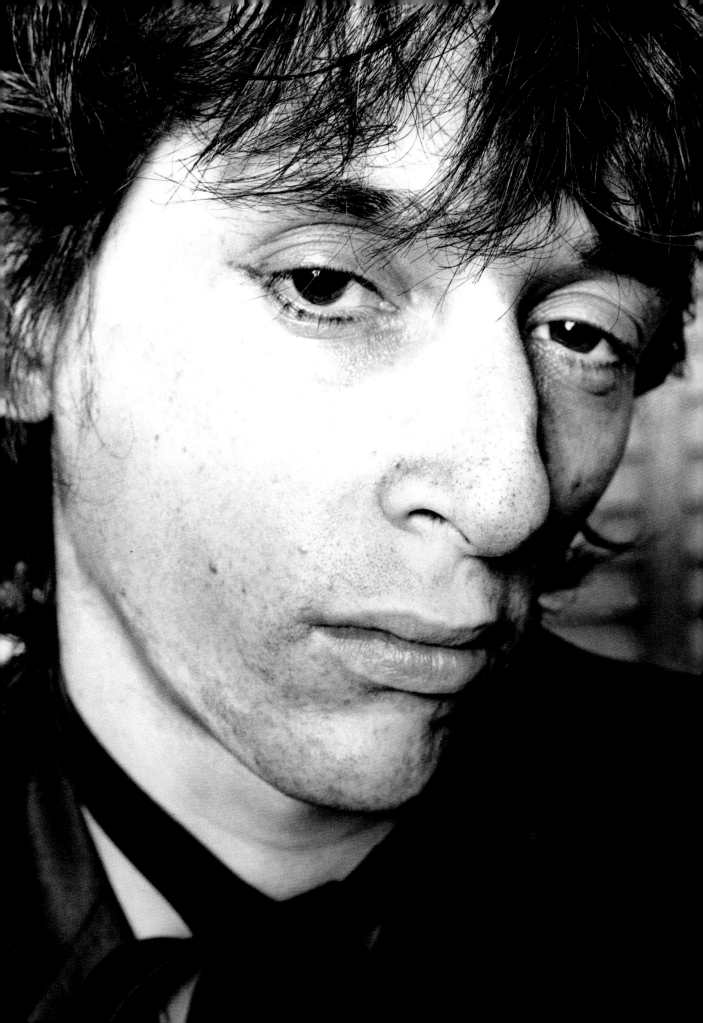

# CONTENTS

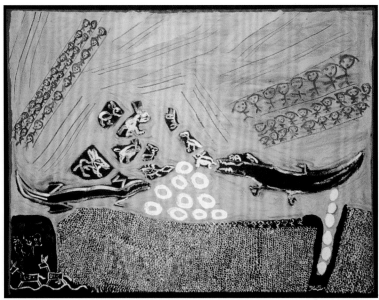

**DEDICATED TO HIROYA AKIHAMA . . .**

It was his destiny to
reach out to the world
after his own time.
He was always worried in life.
He fixated on death in life.
He feared it, then embraced it.
Plagued by obsessive concern
about the future, he often attempted
to obliterate it, knowing that
I was there to cushion the fall.
It was my job to calculate his risks.
The responsibility was overwhelming.
I was responsible for two lives,
his and my own.
One day I wasn't there
and it was over.
It was his destiny
to meet the world
as a rōnin, a samurai
tossed out upon the waves.

—Marcia Resnick

7

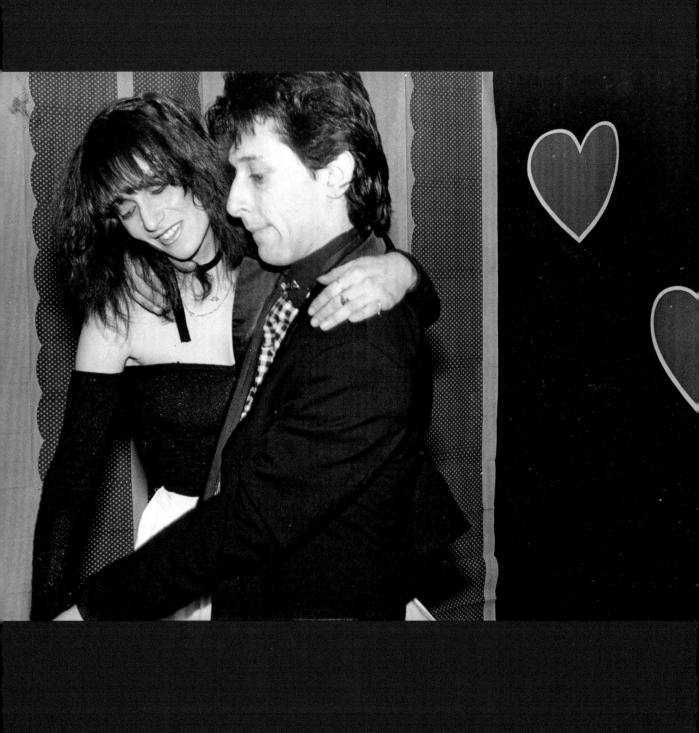

# PREFACE

BY MARCIA RESNICK

*What men they were! There were giants in those days!*
—Lester Bangs, *Psychotic Reactions and Carburetor Dung*

PUNKS, POETS & PROVOCATEURS documents Bad Boys—men who, in the words of Jack Kerouac, are "the mad ones, the ones who are mad to live, mad to talk, mad to be saved, desirous of everything at the same time, the ones who never yawn or say a commonplace thing, but burn, burn, burn like fabulous yellow roman candles exploding like spiders across the stars." Bad Boys can be at once formidable and endearing. Being "bad" also makes people attractive, especially to the opposite sex. "Playing rock and roll makes a person handsome," states Richard Hell in his autobiography, *I Dreamed I Was a Very Clean Tramp*. They live life on the edge. Some, like John Belushi, Lester Bangs, and Johnny Thunders, fell off that edge way too soon.

Journalist Mason Inman writes in *New Scientist* magazine that such people embody "a nasty suite of antisocial personality traits known as the 'dark triad'": narcissistic self-obsession, psychopathic thrill seeking, and Machiavellian exploitation. At their extreme, Inman explains, these traits have exigent cultural costs—but in moderation, the attributes set certain people apart, investing them with singular force, a burn.

After reading William S. Burroughs's *Junky* at seventeen in 1968, I asked a school friend to inject me with heroin every day for about a week. At first I got sick, a usual occurrence for a first-time user. After a week I stopped and got very sick for a couple of days. This was my first "chippie" (small habit) and my introduction to hard drugs. That summer, I traveled to Paris for a couple of months and hung out with the growing community of American draft resisters and draft deserters who'd settled there. Many of the deserters had become addicted to opium in Vietnam. They often sent me to the local pharmacy to buy paregoric (camphorated tincture of opium), supposedly for my grandmother to use as an antidiarrheal medicine. To do this, I was to show up as an innocent little girl in a cute dress. When I delivered the paregoric, they would begin the tricky process described in *Junky* of boiling it down, straining it to remove the camphor, and eventually mainlining it into the bloodstream. This was my introduction to Bad Boys.

Years later, on an overcast spring day in 1976, I totaled my Chevy station wagon on the corner of West Street and Jane outside the Jane Hotel in New York City's West Village. I was knocked out for a couple of hours. When I came to, my mind was streaming with vivid images. During my two-week hospitalization, I photographed the outlines the doctors drew on my body to indicate where they planned to treat my internal injuries. After the medical procedures, I began attempting to face my life by recording its events, employing descriptive texts and pencil sketches. Back in my studio, I revisited my adolescence with staged photographs; the sister of one of my students, seventeen-year-old Laurel Rubin, played the part of me. The character I created was a combination of the girl I had been in Paris and my much younger self. I paired the photos with third-person literary observations.

The result was my book *Re-visions* (Coach House Press, Toronto, 1978). I recounted the "crimes" of my girlhood and the quirks of puberty: sticking chewing gum under my chair in school, being unruly in class, avoiding eye contact with adults, sharing an intimate kiss with my Howdy Doody puppet. A pair of jacks placed on my model's eyelids became the stars that were in her eyes. An image titled "She was always told that her eyes were her greatest asset" revealed Rubin hiding behind a large blanket cut with two holes, from which her wide-open eyes peered. "She was often gripped with the desire to be elsewhere" showed Rubin from the waist down, clutching a hastily packed suitcase and running away from home in a short skirt, knee socks, and saddle shoes. Situating myself in my own history by writing words and making photographs helped me demystify my past.

"*A Bad Boy doesn't have to be the prototypical James Dean character. Or like Marlon Brando in* **The Wild One***. A Bad Boy is someone who has a special magic, who has charisma, and who braves living on the edge. Quentin Crisp was subversive, elegant, and valiant. Johnny Thunders was so bad that he was self-destructive. But in a glamorous way. Or so people thought.*"

—MARCIA RESNICK

Johnny Thunders (PAGE 2)
Johnny Thunders with Resnick (OPPOSITE)

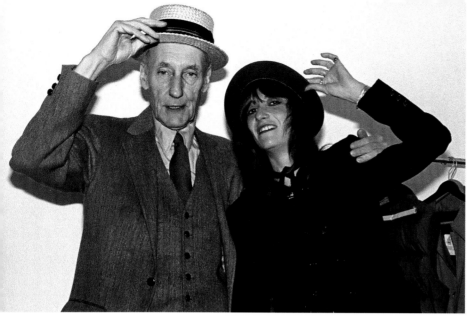

William Burroughs with Resnick

After working on *Re-visions*, I was "gripped with the desire to be elsewhere" once again. This time, I traveled to Egypt on my own and became the virtual prisoner of a deranged Arab soldier who didn't know I was Jewish. Good out of bad, this abrupt exposure to ungovernable maleness led me to my next and greatest subject, Bad Boys. In an attempt to understand the barriers between men and women, I was compelled to record the emotional geography of the male face. For the next five years I submerged myself in portraiture. The fact that I was a woman photographing men was crucial to the dynamic of my project. It seemed like that girl from *Re-visions* had traveled on to explore a world where boys called the shots.

In the early 1970s, photography was emerging as a fine art. From 1967 to 1972, I'd studied art and photography at New York University and Cooper Union, then explored conceptual art as a grad student at California Institute of the Arts. I was discovering the world through my camera. I moved back to New York City in 1973.

The times crackled with energy. Punk attitude was gaining momentum. Punk was about doing whatever you did the best you could and willing things to happen. Punk was about industry, not virtuosity. Punk was about being young and adventurous. Everybody was collaborating. Rock musicians and artists were graduating from art schools. Painters were making films. Writers were doing performance art. Sculptors were creating environments. Artists were acting in films and making music. It was in this milieu that I taught photography for several years at Queens College, Cooper Union, and NYU. Each night, though I was serious about my daytime obligations as an educator, I went out to hear music at CBGB, Max's Kansas City, and the Mudd Club. The latter was also a venue for film showings, readings, and theme parties. Guilty about spending so much time in clubs, to find my subjects and photograph the scene, I convinced myself that my photographic forays into the night constituted my art.

Music was always important. First came Bob Dylan and folk music; then, in the 1960s, rock 'n' roll permeated my life. I loved the Beatles and saw them at Shea Stadium in 1965. The raw audacity of the Rolling Stones excited me even more. During the late '60s, I worked in the ticket booth, designed posters, and ran errands for the rock 'n' roll musicians who performed at the seminal Anderson Theater on Second Avenue in NYC. Chuck Berry and the Animals performed there. Across the street at the Fillmore East, I saw the Doors, Jimi Hendrix, and Janis Joplin. I also went to jazz clubs, listened to regional music while on independent study in Mexico, and sat under Charlemagne Palestine's piano while surveying world music at CalArts.

When I first heard the punk bands at CBGB, I was intrigued by their eclecticism. The Ramones were as spare and repetitious as the hypnotic minimalism of Philip Glass. Blondie blended '60s pop, disco, and rap to create a danceable new music. I embraced the in-your-face lyrics and attitude of the Sex Pistols, the New York Dolls, and the Heartbreakers. Rock 'n' roll was investigating its own history and experimenting with both lyrics and form. It was art school all over again! Hearing James Chance and the Contortions, I was mesmerized by the dissonant sounds James spurted from his saxophone; he danced like a hyperkinetic James Brown. This alternative music made the mainstream rock 'n' roll that bubbled from the radio sound like yesterday's papers.

Punk, believe it or not, was a hugely nurturing scene. Robert Quine, the unique lead guitarist in Richard Hell and the Voidoids, supplied me with tape mixes of his musical influences: the Velvet Underground, Syd Barrett, Miles Davis, J. J. Cale, the Byrds, the Stooges, Frank Sinatra, and an array of rhythm and blues, jazz, and early rock. The brilliant rock writer Lester Bangs lent me records and taught me about the roots of punk. Both Lester and Robert became portrait subjects and close friends.

I jumped on opportunities to get to know people I had met at clubs. Pushing my way through crowds to get backstage at concerts was routine. When I encountered my subjects, I tried to simulate the look of a studio portrait, always attempting to isolate my subject from other people. After taking quick, candid pictures backstage or in dressing rooms, I would often invite people to my studio for photo sessions.

My fifth-floor loft on Canal Street had two thousand square feet of mostly open space with windows that looked upon the Hudson River. It was bathed in sunlight by day and the light of a punk club by night. The studio part was situated against a wall. My bed was nearby and served as a resting place for people who were tired because of the late night–early morning hours when many sessions took place. The bedroom area was chock-full of personal paraphernalia, clothing, books, art, and photographs that could be examined by anyone who visited. In the studio, atmosphere could be generated with music, lighting could be manipulated, and props could be employed. Experiments with lighting and distance from the subject resulted in a range of vantage points, from above to close up. I liked the intimacy and loosening of time restraints in the studio, where photographs were the product of prolonged conversation and interaction. I embraced the give-and-take, the confrontation and collaboration of picture taking.

I had many memorable experiences meeting my subjects. In May 1977, *Rolling Stone* included some pictures from *Re-visions* in an article about twelve up-and-coming photographers. Among the questions we were asked was "If you could be in any one situation anywhere, at any time, with anyone and any camera, what would it be?" My answer, which was used as a headline for my work, was "I would like to be in bed with Iggy Pop and a Polaroid." The result was an invitation to meet Iggy backstage at a Stooges concert. Thus I came to know the rocker to whom I had given a candid shot of publicity.

In 1978, the writer Victor Bockris was working for Andy Warhol's magazine *Interview*; he brought me to the Factory to meet Andy, who had been a hero of mine since high school. I had seen Warhol many times outside my apartment on Houston Street near Ballato's, an art-world restaurant he liked. He looked like a ghost and appeared to have a pink aura. Though there was a flurry of activity around him, he was approachable and engaging. Victor and I hung out with him on several occasions at Studio 54 and the Mudd Club, where he was always taking pictures and making pointed observations.

Also in 1978, Victor introduced me to William Burroughs at the Tropicana Motel in Los Angeles; I subsequently met William several times at the Bunker, his apartment at 222 Bowery, which had been the men's locker room of a gymnasium. In late 1978, I was given carte blanche to take photographs of the Nova Convention in downtown NYC. This multimedia retrospective of Burroughs's career featured readings and performances by counterculture figures and rising avant-garde musical personalities, including Terry Southern, Allen Ginsberg, Philip Glass, Timothy Leary, John Cage, Patti Smith, Frank Zappa, Laurie Anderson, Chris Stein, and Debbie Harry.

On New Year's Eve in 1979, I had a raging case of the flu. Liz Derringer, an interviewer and the wife of musician Rick Derringer, phoned me. She asked if I would like to meet Mick Jagger so that he could decide if he wanted me to photograph him for her cover story in *High Times*. I said "Of course," then fiendishly searched for

David Byrne with Resnick

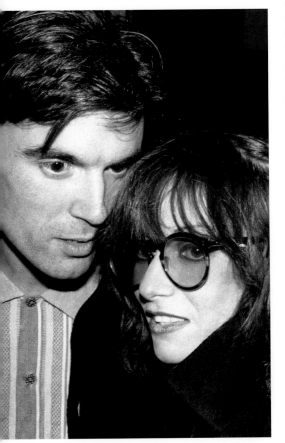

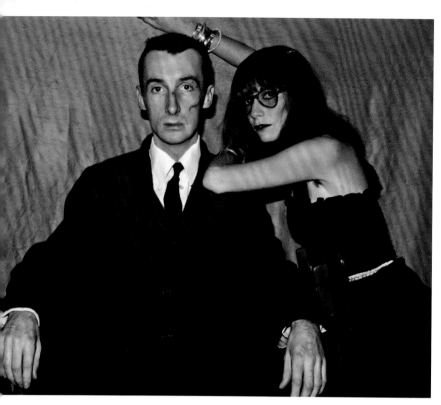

any cocaine I could find lying around my loft. Fortified with cocaine and a prodigious determination, I grabbed my camera and a small portfolio of my work and ventured out. Mick had just shaved off the full beard that he'd grown in Paris, and his complexion appeared uncharacteristically ruddy. He felt self-conscious and didn't want to be photographed. My flu sapped my energy and caused me to seem atypically calm and relaxed. Mick thought I was really "cool" (though my fever made me very hot) and chose me to photograph him two weeks later for Liz Derringer's article. Several days after our initial meeting, I read on the *New York Post*'s Page Six that Jerry Hall and Mick Jagger were vacationing in the Caribbean, recuperating from what was probably my flu.

Victor was working on his book *With William Burroughs: A Report from the Bunker*. In March 1980, after my photo session with Mick, Victor and I pooled our contacts and invited Andy Warhol to dinner with William and Mick at the Bunker to record a talk. That dinner was a meeting of three counterculture kings. At first, William and Andy were chatting, mostly about attractive boys. "Someone should invent a sandwich with a drink in it," Andy suddenly said. He seemed to have a new idea every second. When Mick arrived, the conversational dynamic changed. Though they all were obliging, those three egos in one room were so large that it became uncomfortable—there was no subject they could all agree upon. Not wanting to add stress to the already complex situation, Victor impeded my picture taking. I took only one roll of film during the whole event.

There were many times when I was told not to take photos. When Brian Eno escorted me to a David Bowie concert at Madison Square Garden, we went backstage. Brian told me not to take out my camera. My fingers were literally itching, but I complied. Then there was the time backstage when Iggy Pop beckoned me into a little room where he, Keith Richards, and David Bowie were sitting, comparing coincidentally injured thumbs. Again, I was told not to take pictures. But it was so funny to see these three simultaneously wiggling thumbs I couldn't help myself and lifted my camera. Two large bouncers stopped me, and I was bodily removed from the dressing room.

In my studio, I was amused by the antics of such provocateurs as Abbie Hoffman and Brion Gysin; the latter decided to suck on the big toe of his four-toed left foot. Charles Ludlam could manipulate his face as if it were made of putty. I solicited most photo sessions, but was also solicited by people to photograph them. I sometimes softened my subjects with drugs. Gregory Corso comes to mind. Trying to elicit responses from the men I photographed, I moved, posed, wore provocative clothing, and behaved seductively. When I showed Joseph Beuys "a little leg" after walking alongside him down the

Victor Bockris with Resnick (ABOVE)
Mick Jagger with Resnick (OPPOSITE)

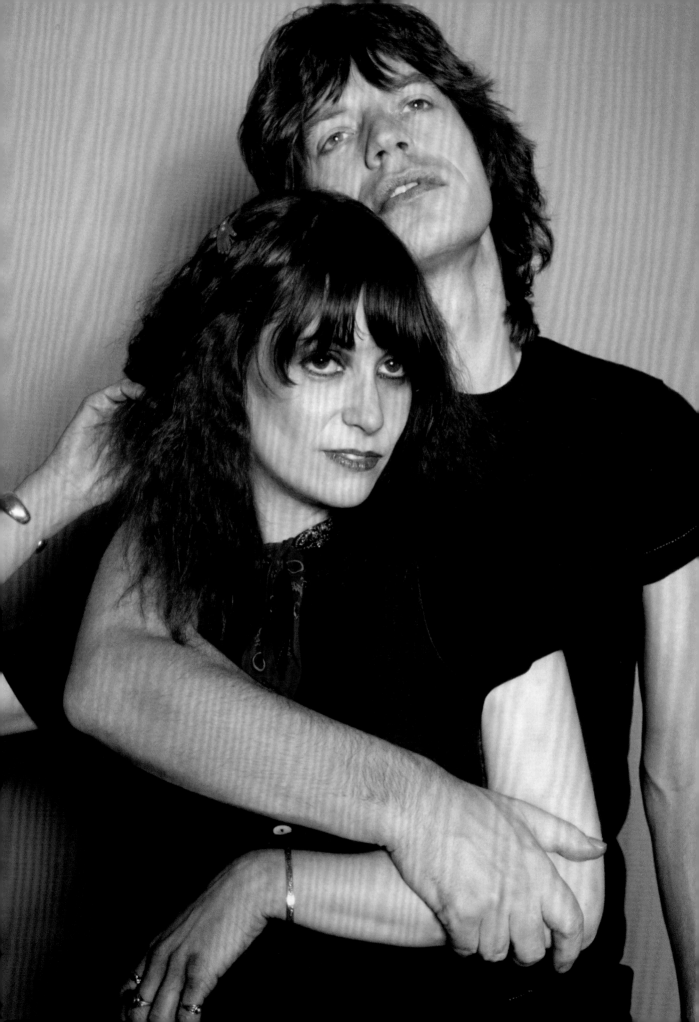

spiral ramp of the Guggenheim Museum toward the portable studio I had set up, I got an iconic shot of the usually stoic artist. The photograph of Beuys cracking up with laughter became a cover of the *Soho Weekly News*.

I had first met Johnny Thunders in 1972, at a party where the newly formed New York Dolls played. I met him again in 1977, when he was in the Heartbreakers. My boyfriend Steve Shevlin, who was in a band called the Senders, worshipped Johnny's unique guitar prowess. I wanted to meet Johnny again and went to his room in the Gramercy Park Hotel with two friends, the punk rockers Joy Ryder and Avis Davis. Johnny and I connected immediately, and I photographed him posing bare-chested but otherwise clothed in the bathtub. *too fast to live too young to die* was tattooed over a cross on his upper left arm; *mom* was tattooed between the wings of a skull and crossbones on his upper right arm. He wore cutoff sleeves to cover his forearms, hiding track marks acquired from shooting dope.

Over the next few years we developed a friendship. Johnny was charming, street smart, and insightful about people. I thoroughly enjoyed watching him perform and loved to photograph him as much as he loved to be photographed. He styled the photographs I took of him with impeccable taste. He had an intuitive understanding of photography and helped me select the images, which I used to get an NEA grant in 1978. Our penchants for innovative clothing styles and mutual indulgence in drugs further cemented our relationship. He was like the brother I never had.

From 1979 to 1980, Johnny played in Gang War with the great MC5 guitarist Wayne Kramer, who had recently left prison after serving two years of a four-year sentence for selling cocaine. (I wound up marrying Wayne in 1982 for one fateful year.) From 1981 to 1982, Johnny was homeless and even sold his guitar. Heroin had menaced his life and career. He stayed with me in my loft until I introduced him to Christopher Giercke, a German-born film producer. Christopher was entertaining friends around a large table and passed around lines of cocaine on a mirror. When Johnny was handed the mirror, he scraped his lines into a spoon and ran to the bathroom to shoot them. Christopher was so shocked and intrigued by Johnny he endeavored to resurrect his foundering career by managing him while patiently fostering his health and sobriety.

In early September 1981, I spotted John Belushi in the New York after-hours club AM-PM. Jane Fire, the drummer in the Erasers, had introduced me to him a couple years earlier, and I would frequently encounter him at clubs. I asked John when he was going to do a photo session with me for my Bad Boys series. He said, "How about now?" I didn't believe he was serious, so I remained at the club for a while. Returning home at 6 a.m., I saw a limousine waiting in front of my building. I turned on a mix of my favorite music as John and his entourage filed into my loft. Directing John to an area lit by strobe lights, I began shooting.

John paced around like a caged animal, fidgeting incessantly. He had been on a drug bender for a few days. He seemed unable to sit still for my camera, uncanny for someone known for being deliberate and fluid when performing. "Where are the props?" he queried. I first gave him sunglasses, then a scarf. He requested a beer, then a glass. After donning a black wool ski mask that he took off a nearby mannequin, he settled into a chair. Only his eyes and mouth peeked through the openings in the mask. The large, ominous, anonymous "executioner" had finally reached his comfort zone. I didn't know he was executing himself. When we were finished, he promptly fell on my bed and went to sleep. A half hour later, his friends woke him up to travel to the Hamptons to attend Lorne Michaels's wedding. When everyone was gone, I noticed he'd left a videotape of *On the Waterfront* on my bed. I couldn't help thinking of how much John resembled Marlon Brando's heroic but emotionally spent character.

On a Sunday at the beginning of March in 1982 I went over to Christopher Giercke's loft to show John the results of our session. As he descended a stairway to take a limo to the airport, I handed John the two contact sheets. In the sixty little images, John appeared to have crossed a line between reality and an emotional netherworld. I wondered whether the vulnerability that could be plainly seen in the shots might make him uncomfortable. He stated flatly that they were terrible and quickly handed them back to me. Later that week, on Friday, March 5, John Belushi died of a drug overdose in a bungalow at the Chateau Marmont in West Hollywood.

In 1982, I was photographing the Psychedelic Furs while they were recording at Todd Rundgren's studio in Woodstock, New York. I took a walk in the woods with Richard Butler. We talked about the classes I taught in school. He was in love with Bebe Buell and told me that she had just broken his heart. I handed him the tiny silver gun charm I'd been wearing around my neck and reassured him that he would either renew his relationship with Bebe or fall in love with someone else. Shortly thereafter, he wrote the song "Only You and I" on the *Forever Now* album.

> yeah I fell in love
> like all good dreamers do
> finally in anger I
> gave it all to you
> I never shouted it
> like we do in school
> knee-jerk negativity
> just never got me through
> and Marcia said so carefully
> you don't get a vote
> this is not a five and ten
> this is not a joke she said
> it's only you and only I
> bang bang
> bye bye.

If you look up the lyrics on the Internet, "Ma she" is substituted for "Marcia." The Internet is wrong.

The people from the extraordinary New York milieu in which I lived and worked had no way of knowing that the years between 1977 and 1982 were enchanted, endangered, and unrepeatable. Back then, the city streets and punk venues buzzed with life. No one predicted that by 1983 AIDS would've begun killing off the era's unstoppable vagabond gregariousness and its raw, honest sexuality. I spent great swaths of time schmoozing with brilliant, erratic, wildly talented men while conceiving and developing *Punks, Poets & Provocateurs*. Some diplomatic skills were required. Bringing the book's ship into harbor sometimes meant slipping into the persona of a Bad Girl. Well, nobody was twisting my arm. I sensed kindred spirits in the faces of the men I photographed. I believe they also recognized the enfant terrible in me. I hope these photographs have captured and preserved some of the intricate dynamics of the time. I hope that my journey through this world of remarkable men will give a sense of what it was like to be alive among them. As for the divide between male and female behavior, that, thankfully, will remain a delicious mystery forever.

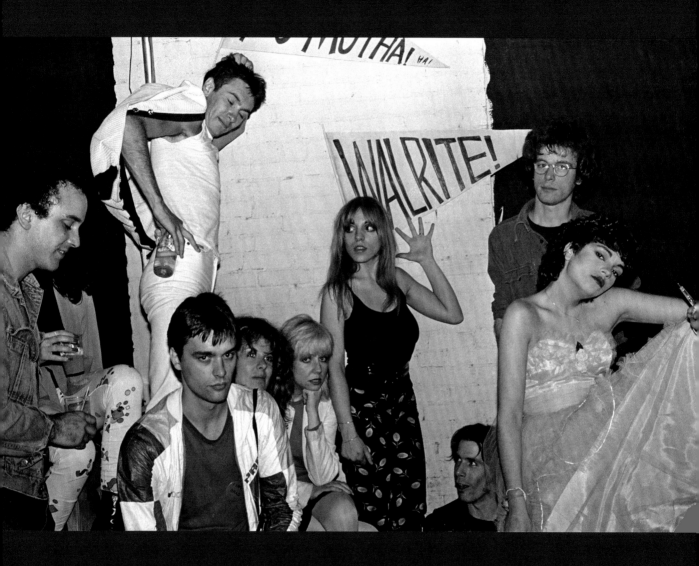

# INTRODUCTION

*Norman Mailer stood on a tiny cocktail table at CBGB just in front of and to my right. Joey Ramone leaned into the audience on half-bended knee in ripped jeans with the microphone cord wrapped around the arm of his black leather jacket, making love to the microphone: "Oh oh oh oh oh oh and I luv her"—injecting passion and myth with the thick beauty of his keening voice—"And it'z trew, izz treww . . . ah, oh oh oh . . . " Norman stuck his mouth in my ear and yelled, "Heroic!"*
—Victor Bockris diaries, 1979

PUNKS, POETS & PROVOCATEURS is a book of photographs of the culture heroes of the 1970s and early 1980s. They were taken in New York during the period of the counterculture's final climax, which played a large role in transforming the crime-riddled, drug-plagued city into a palace of light. These men have never been presented as a group before, and therein resides the book's particular strength. In 1977 the twenty-six-year-old conceptual photographer was rocked out of her controlled studio environment and into the milieu of downtown's avant-garde landscape by the punk rock music that was electrifying New York. That fall, when Resnick began this book, the Rolling Stones' *Love You Live* was the season's soundtrack, and the Ramones, Television, Blondie, and the Talking Heads were all playing at CBGB.

Punk was an extremely appealing movement to the artists of the New York underground. It drew inspiration from the beat generation writers Allen Ginsberg and William Burroughs, who lived among us; from the music and aesthetic of the nearby Warhol Factory; and from the poetry of our neighbors at the Poetry Project at St. Mark's. To Resnick, New York punk was an art project she needed to photograph. Punk was a visual and sensual style feast, with a gloss of newness making it shine extra bright. Many photographers descended on punk as if it were a goldmine. Resnick seized upon her own angle. In her previous book, *Re-visions*, she had confronted her passage through puberty. Now, she decided to confront the mysteries that separated men from women, by taking portraits of these vibrant young rockers.

This book was created in a time when punk changed everything. If you don't know what I mean, trust Glenn O'Brien, whose "Beat" column in Andy Warhol's magazine *Interview* was one of the most accurate chronicles of New York punk. "Punk changed the world," O'Brien wrote. "It made it faster, louder, simpler, skinnier, smarter and less full of bull. You could dance to it. You could fight to it. You could stay up all night to it. It was the perfect soundtrack for quitting your job, redecorating your apartment, thinking about pop art or group sex or robbing a drugstore."

Resnick's project took off on the tidal wave of punk music and art that poured out of New York when it was the cultural capital of the world, and she soon found herself including a wider spectrum of subjects than punk rockers. It turned out the city was full of artists from both earlier and contemporary eras who were united by their roots in the counterculture; after all, in their youth Mick Jagger, Muhammad Ali, and Andy Warhol were the biggest punks on the scene. Resnick put together a unique group of culture heroes whose like would never be seen again. Consequently, the publication of *Punks, Poets & Provocateurs* is a historic occasion.

Bad Boys date back to the beginning of time, but after World War II, with the arrival on the world stage of James Dean and Elvis Presley, the Bad Boy became a counterculture icon. From Muhammad Ali and Chuck Berry through William Burroughs and Andy Warhol to Allen Ginsberg and Mick Jagger, he towered over the counterculture's global population. In the early '70s, after women's lib, gay lib, and black lib had pushed the white man off the stage, punk brought the Bad Boy as counterculture icon back front and center. It was this testosterone-charged punk rocker—a rolling pin in his pants and

*"Marcia Resnick, who took the photographs on these pages, was and remains the scene's memory, living the life even as she chronicled it."*

—LUC SANTE, "THE PARTY," *NEW YORK TIMES MAGAZINE,* OCTOBER 5, 2003

Puberty Party at the Mudd Club

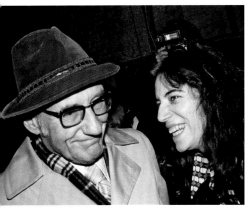 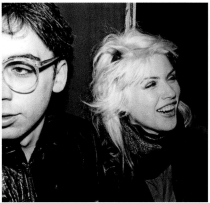 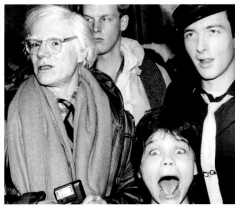

William Burroughs and Patti Smith
at the Nova Convention

Chris Stein and Debbie Harry
at the Mudd Club

Andy Warhol, Harley Davidson, and
Joe Strummer backstage at a Clash
concert at the Palladium

a scar plastered on his face, playing real rock 'n' roll music right in your face—who became the new beauty. It was this image Marcia Resnick confronted in September of 1977 when she began to investigate what most distressed her about men through the lens of her camera.

The joy of the collection is in its locating a tribe of artists, living and working in New York. The promise of the '60s actually blossomed in the '70s. This was America's high civilization period, which Jack Kerouac had foretold in the '50s. It marked the time in which the largest population of a unified art community of players from the '40s onward thrived. They shared in common a passionate commitment to what was called "the unspeakable visions of the individual." Resnick's book is an homage to these culture heroes, whom she saw forming a beat-punk generation.

Its catalyst was the new, raw sexual dynamic born out of the combination of the recently unleashed gay population, a new generation of sexually liberated young women who rejected the bondage of the nuclear family, the hip-hop and graffiti artists, and the counterculture's latest iconic Bad Boys, the punk rockers. Punk music gave everybody the opportunity to relive their adolescence. "Punk may have expressed a nihilistic point of view, but there was a whole lot of life-affirming stuff going on," recalled Deerfrance, a singer in John Cale's band. "There was still passion, but mainly there was a whole lot of sex. Everything was just oozing sex. If you had one room with no heat you would not be alone at night. The juices were flowing, and it made the bands and everyone want to go out and meet each other. It was real life."

Phoebe Hoban put it best in her biography of our favorite painter, Jean-Michel Basquiat:

> A new bohemia was in the making, a wild nexus of music, fashion, and art that created a distinctive downtown aesthetic. Punk and the subsequent new wave movements that quickly took over were a welcome antidote to the sterile conceptual and minimalist art that had numbed the art scene during the post-pop decade [of the early seventies]. . . . Like the sixties, this was a multimedia event, amplified by an English invasion of fashion and music that crisscrossed the Atlantic and was transmuted in Manhattan.

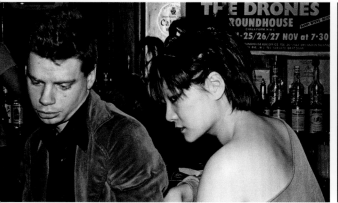
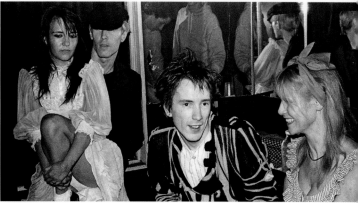

James Chance and Anya Phillips
at CBGB

Jeannette Lee, John Lydon, and Nora
Forster at the Ritz before a PiL concert

Above all, *Punks, Poets & Provocateurs* is about personal transformation. Punk was a society of people who were not in control of their lives until they transformed themselves into who they wanted to be: from Andrew Warhola to Andy Warhol, from Jeffrey Hyman to Joey Ramone, from Richard Meyers to Richard Hell. "There was a conscious decision among the core people that went to the [Mudd] Club to be in something different from everything else," VJ and graffiti artist Fred Brathwaite (aka Fab 5 Freddy) explained to Tim Blanks in the *New York Times*. "You would wake up tomorrow morning and say, 'I'm an actor' and you'd be an actor, or 'I'm a musician' and you'd be a musician, and everyone would accept you as that. Just doing it in that little realm for that little audience was enough."

"We were so sure of ourselves, we never doubted anything," movie actor and Lounge Lizards saxophonist John Lurie wrote in his memoir. "We were powerful, smart, energetic, confident, egocentric, astoundingly naïve. Nothing outside of our fourteen-block radius mattered."

*Punks, Poets & Provocateurs* is a tour de force of photographic skill. Resnick has a strong intuitive sensitivity about capturing her subjects. As she explains, "I was trying to turn the tables on men by turning the man into my object, but I soon became aware that in order to seduce a man into playing the role of object I was compelled to turn myself into an object. I was very conscious of myself as an object. I dressed extremely provocatively, with a girlish flair. The clothes I was wearing, and the way I stood and moved, informed the kinds of exchanges I had with my subjects. I was posing on my side of the camera as much as the Bad Boy was on his."

Her coy style echoes the primordial boldness of punk and new wave music. "I was into picture taking as a 'let's see what happens next' kind of game," she says. "As soon as a subject entered the lens of my camera, he was coming into a relation-ship with me and becoming part of what I wanted to say about the world. I always wanted to make beautiful photographs, and I wanted to make photographs that got close to people. As I was taking the pictures, I was dancing closer and closer to my object. I enjoyed playing with the distance between me and the sitter. Some men did not know how to handle posing when I was practically sitting on their lap. On occasion, I found myself throwing people 'up against the wall' and kicking them into place."

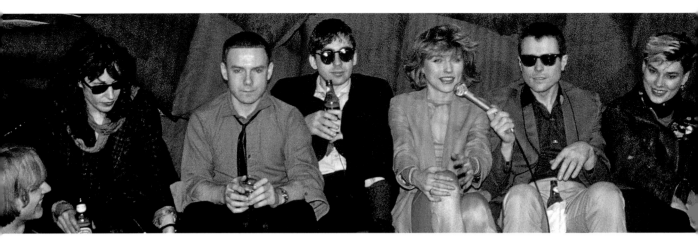

Walter Steding, Kate Simon, Robert Fripp, Chris Stein, Debbie Harry, Glenn O'Brien, and Edwige in Glenn O'Brien's *TV Party*.

*Punks, Poets & Provocateurs* is a record of one of New York's lost civilizations. The cross-pollination and collaboration between these artists created a kind of magic universe of the arts. William Burroughs and Brion Gysin gave us *The Third Mind*. Tom Verlaine and Richard Lloyd created Television. Rene Ricard klieg-lit Jean-Michel Basquiat with his "Radiant Child" profile. Johnny Thunders and Jerry Nolan delivered the Heartbreakers. Chuck Berry influenced John Lydon, while Charles Ludlam's Ridiculous Theatrical Company revolutionized theater and influenced Jackie Curtis. Richard Hell and Bob Quine dreamed up the Voidoids. Legs McNeil launched punk literature with his Famous People Interviews in *Punk* magazine, and the incomparable Lester Bangs captured the music world in *Creem* and other periodicals. Glenn O'Brien and Walter Steding gave us our own variety show on *TV Party*. Victor Bockris wrote books with William Burroughs and Debbie Harry and about Muhammad Ali and Andy Warhol. John Cage and Philip Glass mesmerized us with new musical forms. James White (aka James Chance) danced and sang faster than James Brown. David Byrne and Brian Eno ventured into the Bush of Ghosts. Spalding Gray and the Kipper Kids revitalized performance art with downtown humor. John Waters gave us Divine in *Pink Flamingos*. Klaus Nomi spirited us to the heavens with his divine operatic voice. Nicholas Ray and Jack Smith paved the way for the new wave directors Amos Poe, Eric Mitchell, James Nares, Nick Zedd, and Jim Jarmusch. Julian Schnabel painted with and on broken plates. Mick

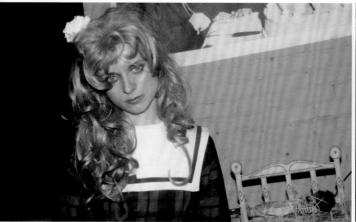

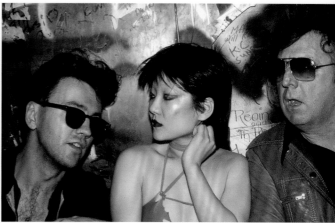

Girl dressed as Christina Crawford with cake for
Joan Crawford Mother's Day party at the Mudd Club

Diego Cortez, Anya Phillips, and Terry Southern
at Max's Kansas City

Jagger delivered the Rolling Stones primer on New York City *Some Girls*. Danny
Fields managed the Ramones, while Malcolm McLaren unmanaged the Sex Pistols
to death. Andy Warhol changed the world. The three kings of the counterculture,
Jagger, Burroughs, and Warhol, had dinner at the Bunker, where their clashing egos
resulted in a profound silence. Fab 5 Freddy taught Debbie Harry how to rap. John
Belushi achieved the remarkable feat of having the number one rock album, number
one movie, and number one TV show in the United States at the same time. Brian
Eno devised *No New York*; Ed Koch took a bite out of the Big Apple; Steve Rubell's
uptown Studio 54 and Steve Mass's downtown Mudd Club fascinated everybody;
and lots of guys got black eyes.

Resnick is the book's continuity. Between 1977 and 1982, her Bad Boy sessions were the emotional engine of her life. She *was* a beat punk, accepted and
at times adored by her subjects as an artist for whom the collaboration of a photo
session was a key to life. In their pursuit she was a fearless adventurer, going deep
into the toxic night where only wolves and heroes survived. Her intrepid nature was
essential. One minute she would be dancing up a storm in the Mudd Club; the next,
she would be slipping through the darkness to emerge in somebody's hotel suite
taking photographs in the bathroom. At her best she was a savage artist, operating
from the deepest heart of darkness and trembling.

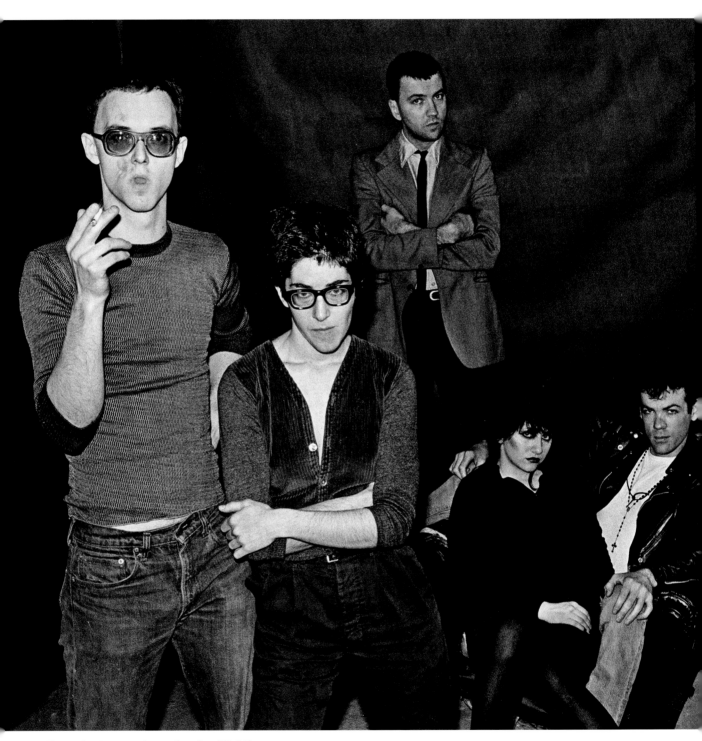

The royalty of no wave cinema: Scott B and Beth B,
Diego Cortez, Lydia Lunch, Johnny O'Kane, Bill Rice,
and Adele Bertei

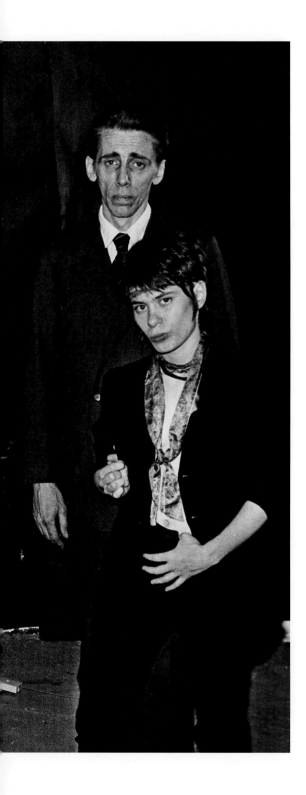

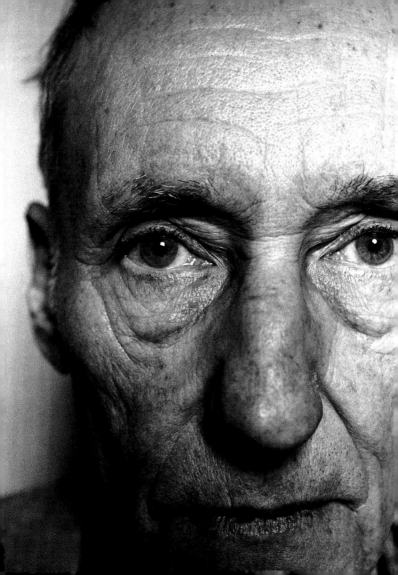

# THE BEATS GO ON

"The Beatles changed American
consciousness, introduced a new note
of complete masculinity allied with
complete tenderness and vulnerability.
And when that note was accepted in
America, it did more than anything
or anyone to prepare us for some
kind of open-minded, open-hearted
relationship with each other and the
rest of the world."

—ALLEN GINSBERG,
BEATLES ESSAY, ROLLING STONE, 1984

William Burroughs

THIS CHAPTER BLENDS photographs and texts about the beat writers, with three key players—Terry Southern (literature), Andy Warhol (art), and Mick Jagger (music)—acting as bridges between the Beats and the 1960s. All these men possessed the requisite characteristics of the dark triad (self-obsession, thrill seeking, and exploitativeness).

Jagger led the Stones through the late '70s and early '80s. The band put out the double live album *Love You Live* (1977) and the studio albums *Some Girls* (1978), *Emotional Rescue* (1980), and *Tattoo You* (1981). Andy Warhol published *The Philosophy of Andy Warhol* (1975) and released his last film, the punk classic *Bad* (1977). He painted his punk trilogy *Oxidation Paintings* (aka *Piss Paintings*), *Skulls, and Shadows* in 1978 and 1979. In 1979 he published *Andy Warhol's Exposures*, photo portraits of '70s stars with humorous text, and had his *Portraits of the Seventies* show at the Whitney. In 1980 he published his chronicle of the 1960s, *Popism*. Allen Ginsberg published two books of poetry, *Mind Breaths* (1977) and *Plutonian Ode* (1978), his collected correspondence with Neal Cassady, *As Ever* (1977), and his *Journals: Early Fifties, Early Sixties* (1977). Penguin Books released William Burroughs's unexpurgated *Junky*, which became a staple of everyone's library. In 1981 Burroughs published the first in a trilogy of novels, *Cities of the Red Night*. Burroughs and Warhol were seized upon as godfathers of punk.

Resnick plays with the dichotomy of the hard image and the tender center. Her first three Burroughs portraits were taken in the Bunker session of 1981, when she also photographed Allen Ginsberg and Gregory Corso. Burroughs's face, though formal, is open and tender to her camera. Then your eyes meet his double-page-spread portrait with shock. The face is closed, almost hostile. It is the first portrait she ever took of him, three years earlier, in 1978. Her Warhol sequencing is similar. The odalisque of Warhol captures his beauty and his sense of humor. Yet how much harder he looks in the double-page black-and-white portrait.

Resnick's portraits of Mick Jagger are also remarkable achievements. As they got into the session she got the impression that Jagger was not sure of his identity, yet she pulled out of the world's reigning Bad Boy three distinct portraits that show a mastery of the iconic image.

Many photographs reveal the unexpected. When Bad Boys pose for portraits they rarely smile, but the laughing picture of Bill Burroughs and Terry Southern is one of my favorites. And fresh-faced, sparkling-eyed Allen Ginsberg is a real blast of joy. Marcia's portrait of Gregory Corso may be *the* classic Bad Boy image in the book. Confrontational behind sunglasses and a cigarette, Gregory just had "it." Look further into the panorama of seven laid-back Bad Boys sitting on a couch. Look at their faces, look at Allen Ginsberg and William Burroughs's quite different smiles, then look at the pain in Peter Orlovsky's eyes. Her portrait of Andy Warhol and William Burroughs together stands as a historic coupling of two of the greatest romantic visionaries of their times.

These men were supportive of each other. When Warhol's Factory was put down as a place of perversion in the 1960s, Ginsberg said, "I always thought the Factory seemed like a good project. There were people taken in to work with Andy, to work with their neurosis and work with their colorfulness and maybe turn it to artistic advantage and value and maybe get therapy that way."

This chapter is also rich in scenes recorded in the period when the pictures were taken. In this first scene, John Giorno is the poet and owner of Giorno Poetry Systems, which released classic recordings of the times—Burroughs's *Nova Convention* album, and records featuring Giorno, Burroughs, Jim Carroll, and various other Bad Boys. Stewart Meyer was Burroughs's protégé, a young novelist whose first book, *The Lotus Crew*, is about the heroin epidemic that had begun to devour so many people in the downtown scene.

Peter Orlovsky, Allen Ginsberg, Gregory Corso, and William Burroughs

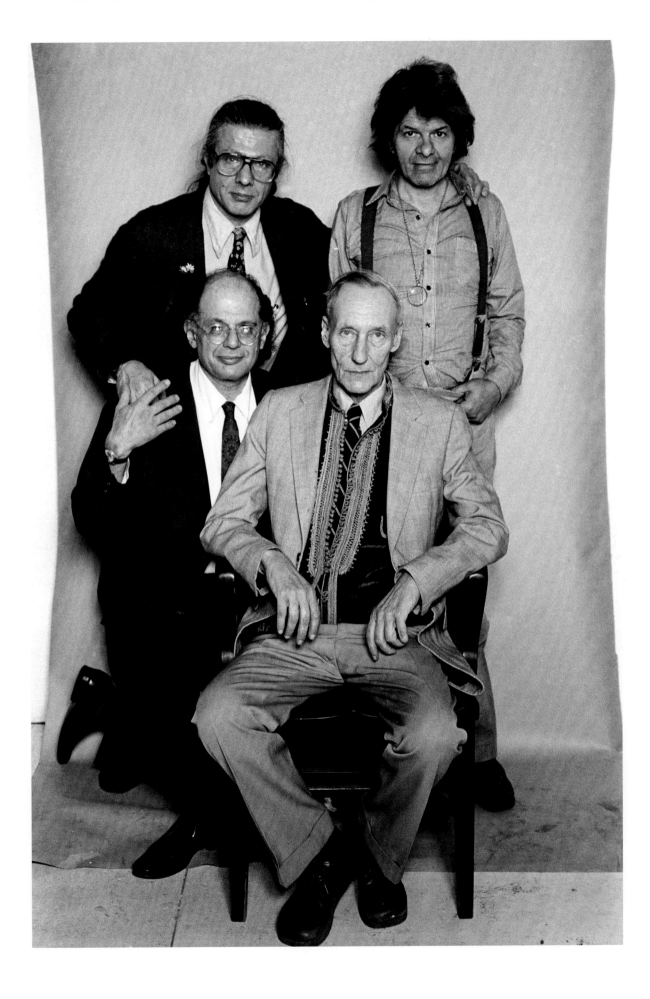

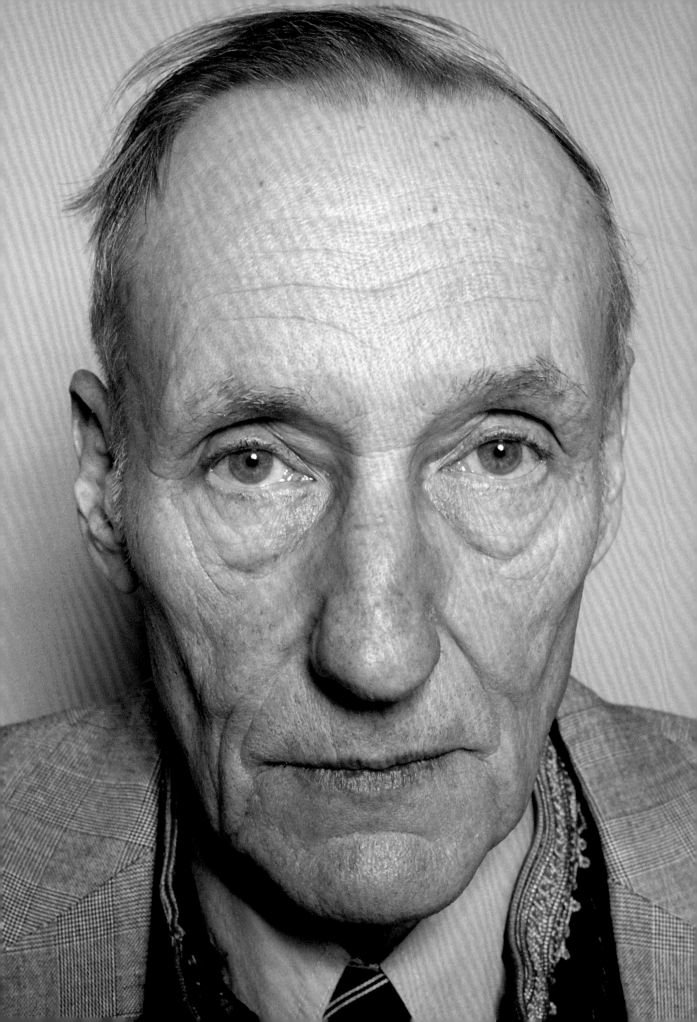

# WILLIAM BURROUGHS
## NEW YEAR'S EVE, 1979

***It was a very literary scene. Burroughs wrote the script and
we all adhered to it and attempted to create* Interzone*.***
–Mick Farren, author and singer in the Deviants from Legs McNeil
   and Gillian McCain, *Please Kill Me: The Uncensored Oral History of Punk*

WE WERE SITTING up in John Giorno's loft above Bill Burroughs's Bunker in their
landmark building at 222 Bowery. I told Bill that Marcia had called in the morning
to tell me she could not, under any circumstances, see me tonight because she
was very sick in bed, but then had called back in the afternoon to explain that Liz
Derringer had summoned her to Mick Jagger's apartment that night to discuss
Marcia's *High Times* cover shoot for Liz's interview with Mick. She had to go, she
told me. She knew I would understand.

"Little Marcia, she never hesitates," Bill chuckled.

During a dinner of lamb roasted on the spit in John's fireplace, we discussed
myriad topics. At the time William was using heroin again, and its use had spread
through the punk community to such an extent that my first question was not as
outrageous as it might sound.


VICTOR BOCKRIS: What do you think, William? Should one be able to use heroin
a couple of times a week or once a week or whatever without getting too fucked up
on it? Do you think that's true?

WILLIAM BURROUGHS: No, because you may use it once a week, but then you
get the habit that you need it that often, and that's going to lead to twice a week. You
take two more days to recuperate or come down on methadone, so no, it's not easy.

WILLIAM: [In an aside to his protégé, novelist Stewart Meyer] I guess Victor might
need some fudge [majoun, a very powerful combination of marijuana in fudge I'd
never previously taken] now.

STEWART MEYER: William, that fudge has taken my head off.

WILLIAM: I need a little more!

VICTOR: I need a lot.

STEWART: It's in the fridge, right?

WILLIAM: Yeah, sure. You'll find it.

STEWART: Can you use a bit more?

JOHN GIORNO: Later, actually. I'm fine right now.

WILLIAM: I'll take some.

STEWART: I'm bouncing off the walls here.

WILLIAM: [Looking at the TV] What is this going on here?

VICTOR: Is it two girls fucking!? Jesus, look at that man in shorts! Isn't that a strange
ritual . . . what channel is this you have on, John?

JOHN: CBS.

WILLIAM: I heard the story about how some hardcore porn went on one of the major
channels before anyone could stop it.

VICTOR: They had a guy sticking a lightbulb up his ass . . .

WILLIAM: This looks like an underwear comedy.

VICTOR: [Switching the subject to a recent interview Bill gave] Well, Bill, does the
very worst interview you had to give under the most unpleasant circumstances stand
out in your memory?

WILLIAM: I've had lots of interviews where the questions were so bad it was boring. John, if you ever see that fucking Mr. Joe Blow, ask him where in the hell he got the idea that I'm sixty-nine years old. I mean, it's ridiculous. All my bios say how old I am.

JOHN: When did this happen?

VICTOR: The interview you were at.

WILLIAM: He asked some of the stupidest questions I ever heard. . . . He said they're gonna fuck us up, they're gonna have the police in here, well, so he just wouldn't–

[John shows us the lamb roasting in the fireplace.]

WILLIAM: That's great.

VICTOR: Terrific. God, it looks good. Well, don't you think that next time they ask you for an interview, you should say, "Over dinner at Lutèce"?

WILLIAM: Usually neither of us wants to put out the time, and I don't know if it would get any better. They do have some awfully stupid questions. "Do you believe in individuality?" and all that, just this same old stupid thing. "Oh, do you think this is a good thing?" Things like that, you know, and "Do you feel that nirvana is a good thing?" I got quite grumpy. John was there. John! Didn't I get quite grumpy during the interview with Joe Blow? You were there.

JOHN: Oh yes, I know–it was hooooorrible.

WILLIAM: And wasn't I grumpy?

JOHN: Yeah. It got worse, and the more stoned we got, the worse it got.

WILLIAM: John said, "That's the flattest interview I ever heard," and it was. I feel it was his fault, didn't you? I thought he wasted it. What he was saying was just awful.

JOHN: Sometimes the questions were the antagonistic picky kind that bring no result.

WILLIAM: Yeah. The antagonism that produces nothing.

[We talk about the Watergate scandal of 1974.]

WILLIAM: There was a terrific shift in America for the better after Watergate. The whole incipient police state was just shattered.

VICTOR: But authority is still a physical force.

WILLIAM: I never said it wasn't. I'm just saying that a lot of the particularly malignant powers it was gaining then could have led to a 100 percent police state, and that was just exactly where they intended to take it. . . . This "under arrest" business is so watered down now from what it was in the '60s, when a man could be framed and have people coming in and stripping him naked in his own apartment. Well, this just doesn't happen anymore. People don't come into a gentleman's apartment and strip him naked. There is this terrific change and the real shift was at Watergate. Watergate debunked the whole attitude of authority and knocked the whole bunch of people out who were out to frame people on drug charges based on their political or intellectual opinion.

[I go downstairs to get the ticket the Ramones had sent for their concert at the Palladium on nearby Fourteenth Street later that night, then return to John's dinner.]

WILLIAM: All is cool. Got your tickets?

VICTOR: Yeah.

WILLIAM: Good. Good. Take a little more.

VICTOR: Tickets for the show.

WILLIAM: That's right. Tickets for the show, tickets for the show.

VICTOR: Is Allen [Ginsberg] coming over later on tonight?

JOHN: Yeah, yeah.

VICTOR: What's he doing?

JOHN: He's having dinner with Lucien [Carr] and Fernanda [Pivano].

WILLIAM: Is he coming?

JOHN: Yeah, in a few minutes. With Fernanda and [Herbert] Huncke.

WILLIAM: Good. Excellent, excellent.

VICTOR: I heard there was a big article about Jack Kerouac in the *New York Times*.

WILLIAM: Yes. I haven't seen it, but someone said there was a picture of me in 1957. Imagine that. I was good-looking in those days. I had all my teeth.

VICTOR: I'm imagining away.

WILLIAM: Yeah, you shoulda seen me. Well, anyway, you can see me in this picture.

VICTOR: I will. I'll rush out and buy it.

WILLIAM: You must, you must, you must. I must have a copy myself. John, did you see the picture of me in the paper? I want it, I want it, I want it. I must have it immediately. Me in 1957. All me teeth was me own.

After dinner, around 9 p.m., I left to go to the Palladium to see the Ramones. About half a block up the street I encountered the writer Udo Breger, with magazine editor and art collector Carl Laszlo, walking toward the Bunker. We exchanged ecstatic greetings and marched on. About two blocks before the Palladium, the majoun I'd taken an hour earlier began to take effect. It was like twenty joints hitting me at once. It was as if I had two bodies. My arm jerked unexpectedly forward as my shoulder suddenly moved backward. It was a very odd sensation, as if I were trying to walk out of my body. My mind was moving in and out of itself, and I did nothing to coordinate my movements. By the time I got inside the Palladium I was jousting wildly with a thick cane Bill had given me for Christmas. Two guys began giving me a lot of trouble, so after the first four songs I left, unable to meld with the crowd. Apart from the extreme effect of the majoun, the rest of my evening was inconsequential, although many bizarre things happened.

Back at John Giorno's, events were taking a different shape. Carl Laszlo choked on a piece of meat that got stuck in his esophagus, contorting and gasping "Ich sterbe, ich sterbe" (I'm dying, I'm dying) for several long panicky minutes. Finally, one of his two burly German boyfriends managed ("with great presence of mind," William assured me) to hug Carl in the Heimlich maneuver, dislodging the piece of meat. Everybody was so stoned that it quite upset the artistic ambience of the evening. Bill took Carl downstairs to the Bunker to recover. Carl returned, sheepishly, twenty minutes later. At midnight Bill grabbed the *I Ching*, and his friend, the poet Anne Waldman, read out the lines. They said that the worst thing was going to happen now. According to Udo, who was there throughout the evening, as 1979 ended the atmosphere was muted.

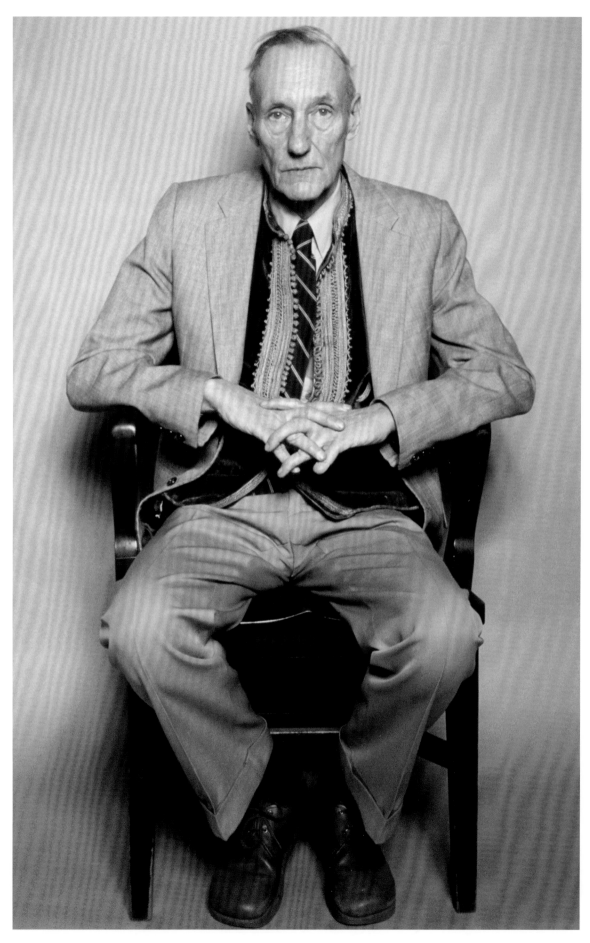

William Burroughs (ABOVE AND FOLLOWING PAGES)

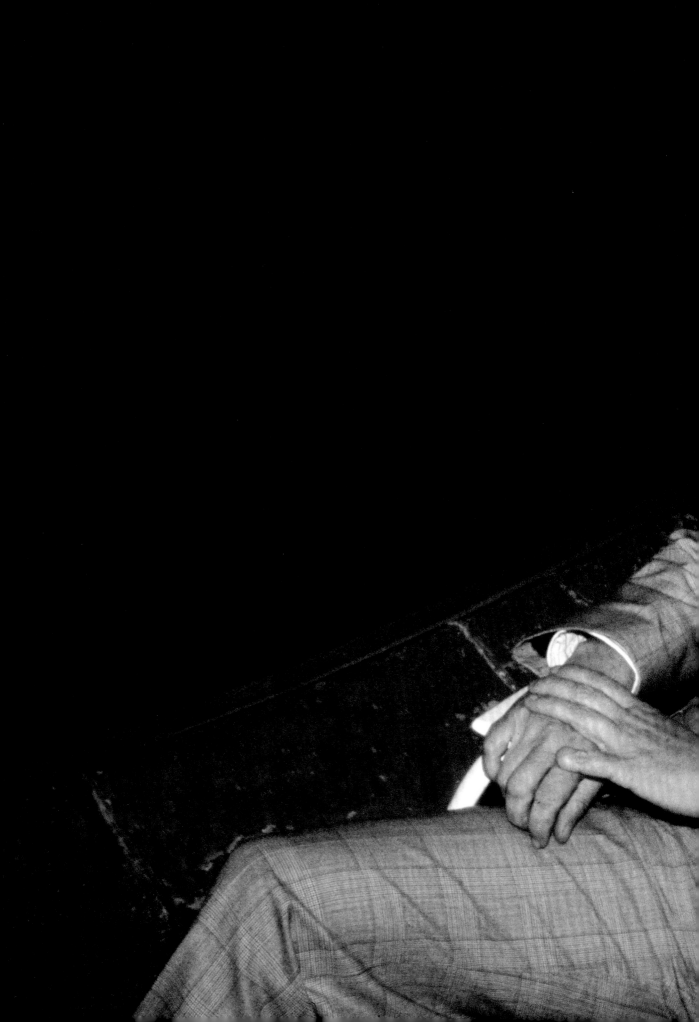

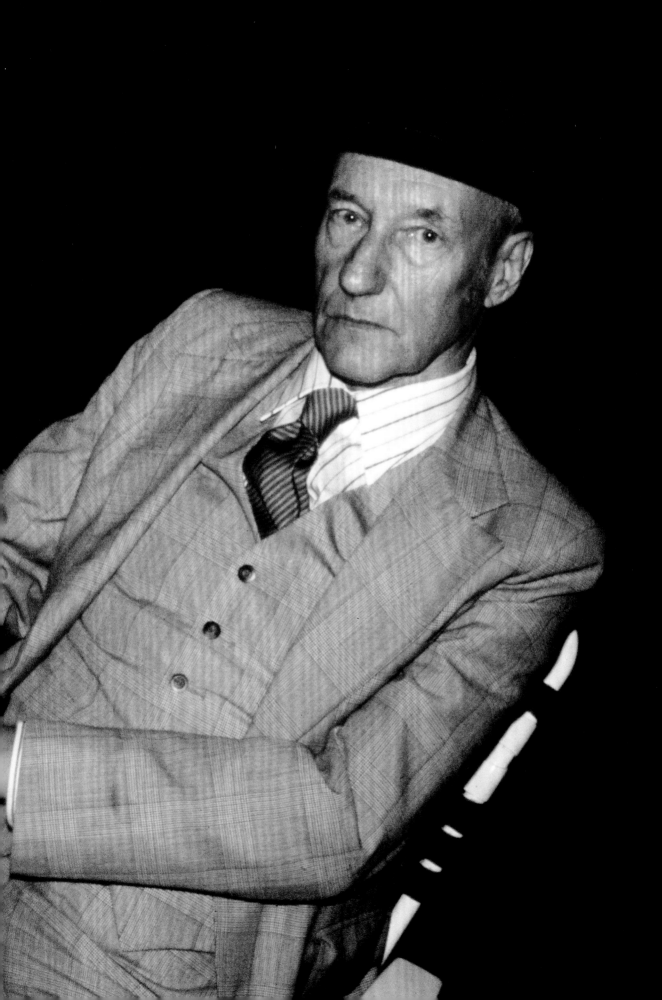

# ALLEN GINSBERG
## GOLD MEDAL

*I dare your reality, I challenge your very being!*
–Allen Ginsberg, *Plutonian Ode*

TEN MONTHS EARLIER, on February 11, 1979, I accompanied William and his assistant James Grauerholz to dinner at the National Arts Club in Gramercy Park to commemorate its award of the gold medal in poetry to Allen Ginsberg. New York School poet Ted Berrigan was the emcee. I invited Marcia to join us. While she took pictures, I recorded the speeches excerpted here.

NORMAN MAILER: I don't truly have in my own mind credentials of a normal order for introducing Allen Ginsberg. Except, as I sat here wondering what these prefatory remarks might come to, it occurred to me that mountains tend to be immensely self-centered. They're concerned with their own works. They try to notice how a particular plot, how a particular patch of forest, is doing down below them, and how the snow fields are doing this year, and they feel the profound stir of the earth beneath their seat and they're tremendously concerned with themselves. If a mountain can, it takes its pulse. Now weather is quite obviously bad at the summit and mountains rarely have anything to see. Occasionally there is a little clearing and the mountain looks out two hundred miles and "My God!" Annapurna says, "There's old Everest!" And it says, "You know, Everest is really impressive when you get down to it."

Well, I can only say–I'm famous for my vanity–but I can only say that when I pick up a book of Allen's, I can crack it anywhere, start reading a few lines, and I say, "My God, I'm not Everest, I'm Annapurna!"

And Allen took the totality of his experience and said, "I believe there's finally only going to be virtue. And I present it to you–the American people–in that fashion, because I believe that if you can come to understand me, you will come to believe, as I believe, that the totality of my actions will represent virtue, that you'll all be larger and more interesting and more imaginative as a nation, and greater."

JACQUES STERN: Allen is famous because of "Howl," but also because of his famous poetry readings. I attended a couple of those readings in San Francisco in 1957, and he was hugely popular. Ginsberg's reading was incredible because it was literally attended by the whole of San Francisco's elite group. The audience was not just other writers, poets, and musicians–yeah, it was those, too–but the reading was also attended by society people and bankers. Because in those days, you have to remember, there was a tremendous amount of influence from the man who founded the Bank of America, a guy called [Amadeo] Giannini, who happened to be interested in intellectuals and in avant-garde writing. So he brought in all these people to listen to Ginsberg.

Now, Allen has great qualities, too. He is one of the greatest friends one could have. He is very good and very loyal to his friends. Allen is also a good critic–one of the best that ever lived. As a matter of fact, in my opinion, in terms of embracing and understanding literature Allen is probably one of the greatest critics of all time. Burroughs is the only person Ginsberg ever looked up to. Allen is absolutely oblivious to anybody telling him any critique. You have to remember Allen is a tower of life. . . . First of all, as far as he is concerned, the beat generation is his because he publicizes it every month. He is the only one who pulled it together.

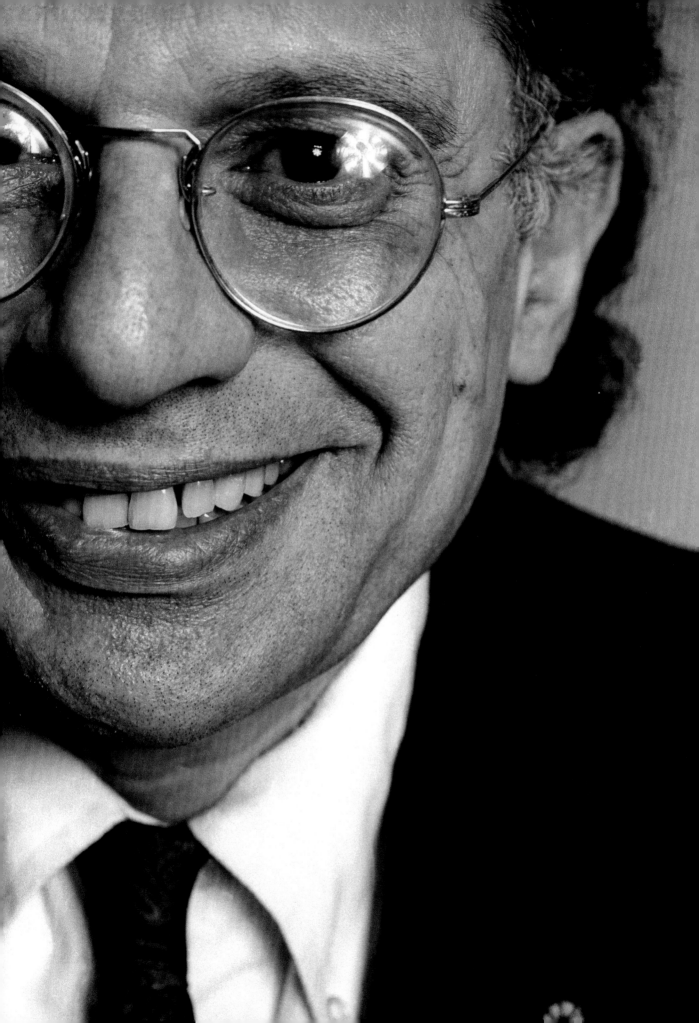

JOHN ASHBERY: Another repercussion that Allen would have on poetry is that I think he was one of the first poets who was able to make a living from writing poetry. Not by publishing it, because he's always published with small presses, but from public readings of his work, which is indeed the only way a poet can make a living these days. He also gives away most of the money he makes to other people: friends, poets, people he doesn't even know who need money, and to causes. He has devoted incredible amounts of time to the things he believes in. I was a visitor at the Jack Kerouac School of Disembodied Poetics at Naropa in Colorado for a couple of summers while Allen was teaching there, and I was amazed that all day long poets, who might not even be involved in that school, would come along, knock on his door, and ask advice about their poetry—how they should get it published and this and that. Allen spent, it seemed to me, almost twenty-four hours a day helping these people. And that, I think, is something not too many people are aware of. It's something I would very much like to do myself, but I just don't have the time. Allen is the only person who does have the time. He takes the time.

I was talking today with a poet who's a good friend of Ted Berrigan's, Ron Padgett. They both lived in Tulsa, Oklahoma, when they were in high school. They were putting together a high school poetry magazine in about 1958, and they wrote to Allen and asked him for a poem for their magazine. He not only sent them a very long poem, an important one, but a long letter wishing them well with their publication. Ron said that this made him feel that "for the first time I was in contact with literature and lives and poetry in America, and I had this wonderful feeling for many years after that." Very few poets, I think, would be willing to go to all those lengths.

Anyway, that's why Allen Ginsberg is here tonight. Except that I don't think the establishment is embracing him, so much as I think his embrace has eventually included it.

I think he's changed the role of the poet in America so that now everybody experiences poetry. I think it's much closer to us now than it was twenty years ago. And I think that is due not only to Allen's poetry, but to his truly exemplary way of living, which is a lesson to me, and for many of you here, and for many people in America.


HENRY GELDZAHLER (commissioner of cultural affairs for the City of New York): Allen announced to the world that you can be homosexual and be included in the culture. He is a poet of human sexuality whose truths are described so feelingly and tellingly that their particularities become universal. We all feel as we read Allen Ginsberg what Allen Ginsberg feels. It is easier and more palatable for me to be an American and to be a homosexual because Allen has stood and spoken out. His eloquence allows us to share his victory . . .

In my name, and in the name of the City of New York, thank you, Allen Ginsberg!

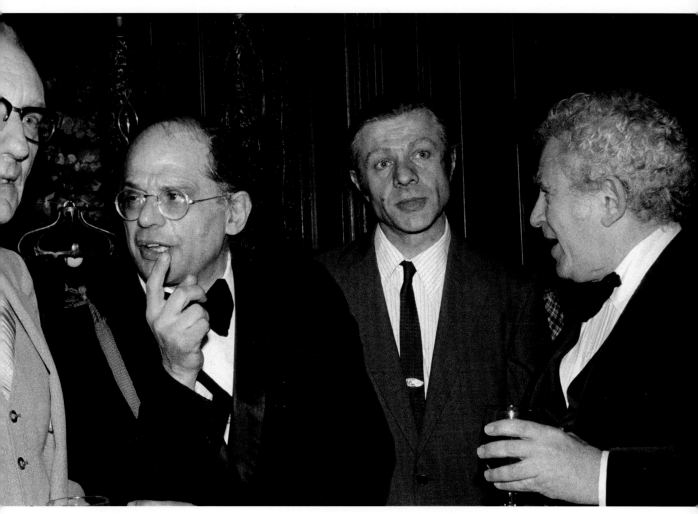

William Burroughs, Allen Ginsberg,
Peter Orlovsky and Norman Mailer (ABOVE)

Peter Orlovsky, William Burroughs, Allen
Ginsberg, Victor Bockris, John Giorno,
Sylvere Longtrin, and James Grauerholz
(FOLLOWING PAGES)

WILLIAM S. BURROUGHS: To my way of thinking the function of art is to make us aware of what we know and don't know that we know. . . . Allen's openness, his writings, and his outspoken attitude toward sex and drugs were once thoroughly disreputable and unacceptable, and now have become acceptable and in fact respectable. And this occasion is an indication of this shift of opinion. You remember that it was once extremely unacceptable to say that the earth is round. I think that this shift whereby original thinkers are accepted is very beneficial both to those who accept them and to the thinkers themselves. Somerset Maugham said the greatest asset any writer can have is longevity, and I think that in another ten or fifteen or twenty years Allen may be a very deserving recipient of the Nobel Prize.

ALLEN GINSBERG: It is my turn to respond and give some sense of my thinking on being the center of attention upon this occasion . . . and the stamp of the city's approval on cocksucking by the commissioner of cultural affairs . . .

Obviously I am Allen Ginsberg. I am the person that these people have been talking about, and I am positively everything they have said. I boldly acknowledge with friendliness and accuracy the situation. On the other hand it also is an acknowledged fact that I don't know who I am and nobody here is sure precisely of what they have been saying and I'm not sure of what I'm saying, and even the gold is questionable. . . . Who knows, perhaps the universe itself is an illusion. In fact, it really is, so that I am completely empty, as you all are, so we can all relax because nothing depends on our being real.

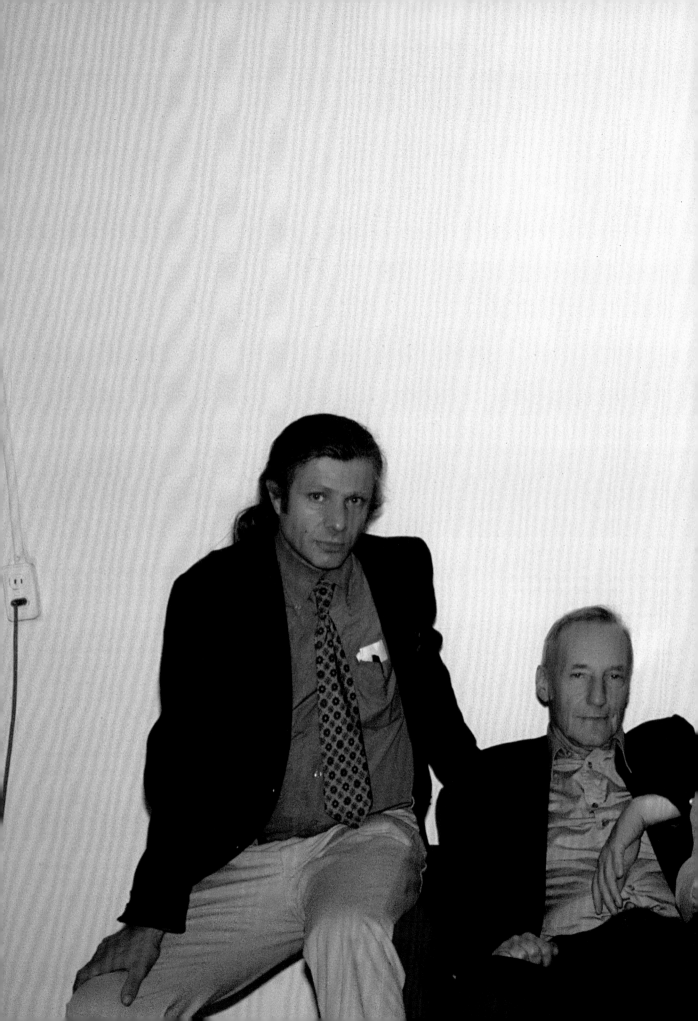

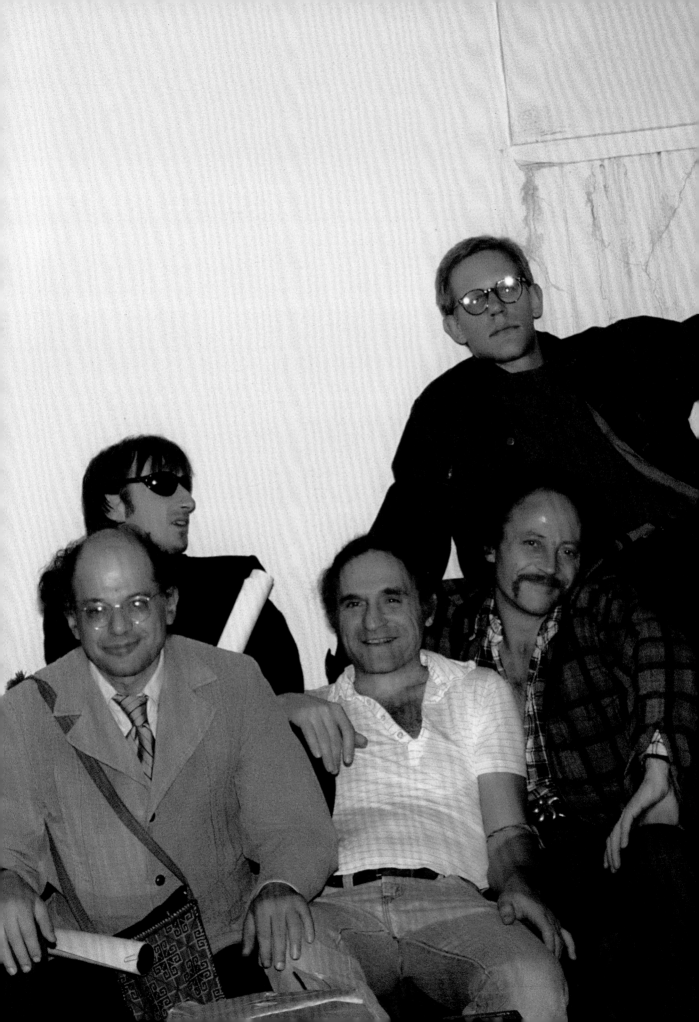

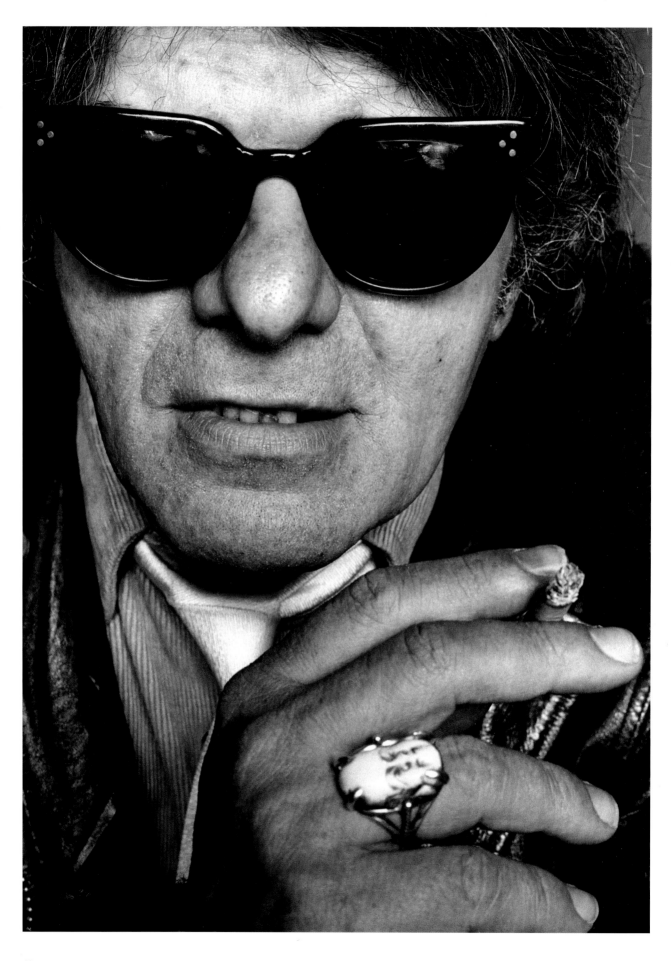

# GREGORY CORSO
## THE HAPPY BIRTHDAY OF DEATH

*he came with his wrists taped & he carried his own coat hanger–i could tell at a glance that he had no need for Sonny Rollins but i asked him anyway "whatever happened to gregory corso?"*
–Bob Dylan, *Tarantula*

GREGORY CORSO was one of the four beat writers who made a tremendous impact on American culture from the late 1950s to the present.

Jacques Stern, a classic Bad Boy in his own right, was a close friend of Corso, Ginsberg, and Burroughs in Paris from 1957 to 1962, when they were living at the Beat Hotel and Corso was writing his greatest book, *The Happy Birthday of Death*. Jacques was independently wealthy but disabled for life and in a wheelchair. A charming, sympathetic man, he was a sounding board for these writers at a crucial time in their development.

JACQUES STERN: They all believed that they were part of a group and they all depended upon each other, because they really did believe that there was a new generation in their writing. Bill had a real fondness for Gregory, but I don't think he appreciated his talent. . . . Allen Ginsberg was a very, very ambitious character, which Corso wasn't. Allen, being a poet, had a great fondness for Gregory, and yet kept him in his subordinate role. For one thing, Allen considered himself the discoverer of Corso, which to a certain extent he was, but let's face it, that gave Allen the position of being the boss.

As far as I'm concerned, Gregory Corso is probably the most talented poet the beats ever had. And during that small period of time, 1957 to 1962, he was the best poet in America, although America wasn't Corso's subject. His subject was literally the pit of the stomach of the poet. The what-is-happening-to-me kind of poetry–what kind of anguish is forcing me to just fall about? . . . . What Corso divulged in his poetry was the innards of Corso in the context of everything around him, but subjectively swallowed and then regurgitated. And I would say he is the great regurgitator in American poetry.

VICTOR BOCKRIS: What was the difference between Gregory's relationships with Allen and Bill?

JACQUES: Burroughs told me implicitly he thought that Corso was a better writer than Ginsberg, but he made me promise I would never tell. You gotta realize, Allen Ginsberg was always publicizing Burroughs, himself, and Kerouac, but just leaving Corso out, although he himself admired Corso. The difference was that William would let Gregory talk, would converse with him and would laugh at his jokes, whereas Allen wouldn't let him talk.

Burroughs was much more attentive to the human side of Corso, but Corso was always scared to say anything against Bill. Of that bunch Bill was the only great character who spoke to him, was never mad at him, and never criticized him. But remember, Bill was not a poet, so Gregory was not competition. Meanwhile, Gregory depended hugely not only on Bill and Allen, but on their approval. And Corso was so unbelievably fragile in that sense. . . . When the Beats stopped living together and traveling together in 1962, Gregory disappeared . . .

We would often meet at Café [de] Flore in Paris–it's a very famous café in which I had a corner table for about twenty-five years. Corso used to jump up on the table at the Café Flore and recite his poetry. The point is, at the Flore at the table next to you is sitting Camus; across the way is Sartre. In those days, when you saw who was sitting there, you didn't jump on the fucking table and start spouting. Now, contrary to what he thought, everybody applauded it, even those who didn't know English. They were applauding the gall, the guts, whatever he had . . .

> "*What do you know about the Beat Generation? Great works of art to stand beacon like Statue of Liberty naked and courageous, individual statement of private actual, uncensored individual perception.*"
>
> —GREGORY CORSO

Gregory Corso

41

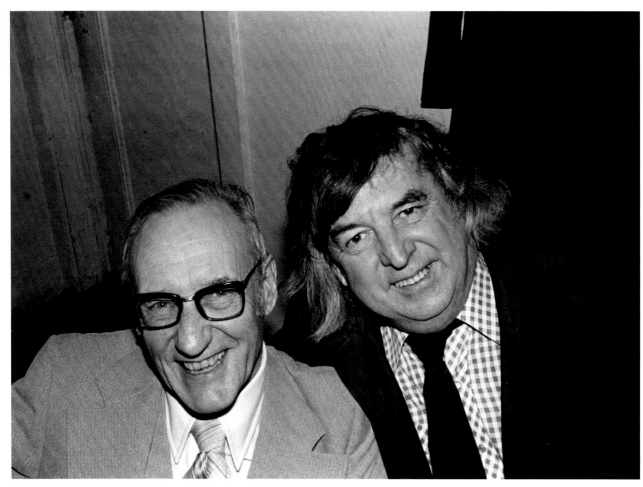

William Burroughs and Terry Southern (ABOVE), Brion Gysin (OPPOSITE)

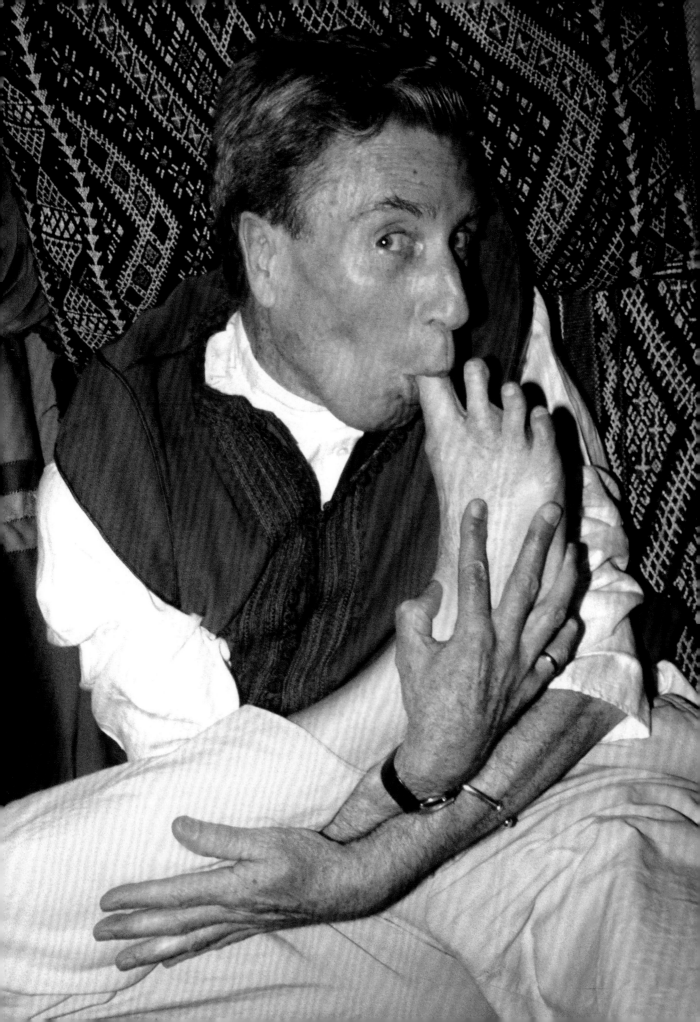

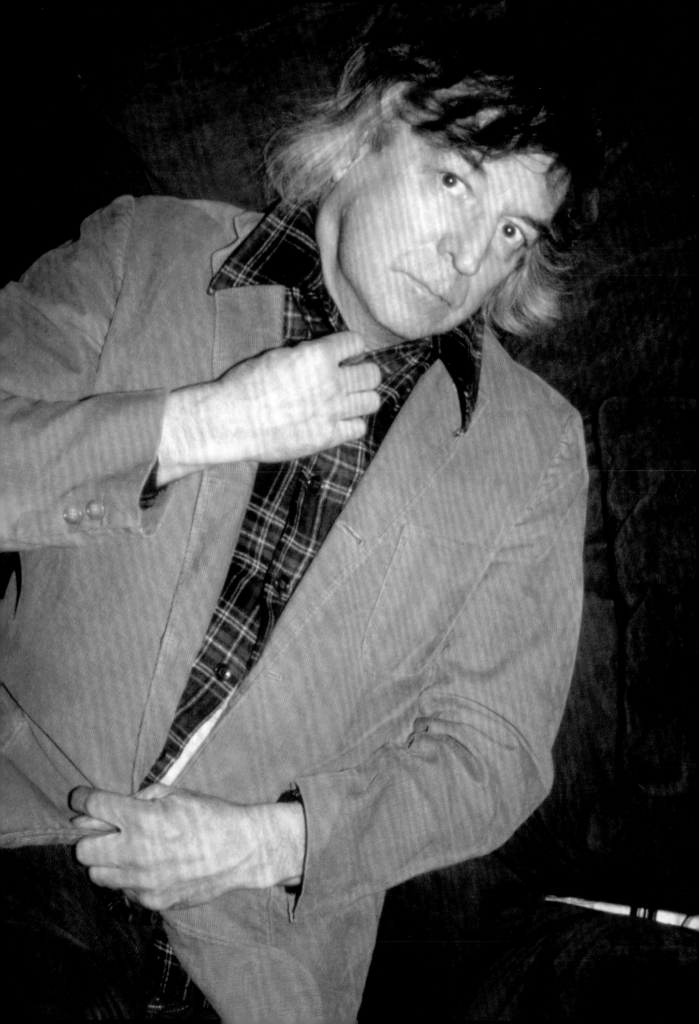

# TERRY SOUTHERN
## THE GRAND DAYS
From *Gadfly*, January–February 2000

*In 1967, the Beatles put Southern on the famous album cover of*
**Sgt. Pepper's Lonely Hearts Club Band,** *along with others, alive and*
*legendary, of the Alternative Establishment. Terry is tucked behind*
*Edgar Alan Poe and in front of Lenny Bruce. What a fortuitous and telling*
*placement—next to the master of the macabre on the one hand and the*
*great practitioner of black humor on the other.*
—George Plimpton, writer, editor of the *Paris Review*

TERRY SOUTHERN was a blessing to those of us who ran into him at the Mudd Club and other venues. He was constantly working on films and books. For one glorious moment it looked as if he was going to get Bill Burroughs's *Junky* made into a film. Naught came from this, but he was a good example to us of a man who committed himself completely to the life of an artist. He was published alongside Burroughs in Paris in the 1950s, but became famous in America in the 1960s. Terry was equally at home in the milieu of Hollywood, the Rolling Stones, the Beatles, and the beats. Readers are encouraged to seek out his classic books (*Red-Dirt Marijuana and Other Tastes*, *Candy*, *Blue Movie*, *The Magic Christian*, and *Flash and Filigree*) and see the films he wrote, from *Dr. Strangelove* in 1964 to *Easy Rider* in 1969. He straddled that decade and came roaring into the '70s aboard the Stones' lapping-tongue-painted plane on their 1972 tour of America.

In the halcyon days of 1964, Terry Southern was the most famous writer in America. *Candy* was number one on the *New York Times* bestseller list. *Dr. Strangelove* was number one at the box office. He was appreciated by his peers: "Terry Southern is the most profoundly witty writer of our generation," wrote Gore Vidal. "Terry Southern writes a clean, mean, coolly deliberate and murderous prose," attested Norman Mailer. "Terry Southern is the illegitimate son of Mack Sennett and Edna St. Vincent Millay," added Kurt Vonnegut. "Terry Southern was one of the first and best of the new wave of American writers, defining the cutting edge of black comedy," concluded *Catch-22* author Joseph Heller.

Profiled in *Life* magazine in 1964, Terry came across as a determined crusader for the counterculture. "The important thing in writing is the capacity to astonish," he said. "Not shock—shock is a worn-out word—but astonish. The world has no grounds for complacency. Where you find something worth blasting, I want to blast it." (A classic punk attitude.) Asked if he was for or against America's intervention in Vietnam, and how he thought the conflict could be resolved, Terry gave an example of what he meant: "'Intervention' would seem to me rather weak semantics for the bombing of civilians— the use of napalm and herbicides . . . the destruction of villages, schools, hospitals, roads, bridges, crops . . . the massacre of women and children. I should have thought a somewhat stronger term—like 'barbarism,' 'rape' or 'pillage'—more correct.

"As for how would I 'resolve the conflict,' there is only one conceivable way— and that is, with President Johnson at the fore, quickly, silently, and with great stealth, to slither out, on our stomachs. Anything less would hardly be in character with our grotesquely reptilian behavior, and our very sick motives."

Terry began his last great run in 1967, during the Summer of Love. First he published *Red-Dirt Marijuana*, one of his funniest and longest-lasting books—a classic of the new journalism that would lead to the work of Hunter S. Thompson.

In his introduction to Lenny Bruce's *How to Talk Dirty and Influence People*, British critic Kenneth Tynan wrote that "Terry Southern once said that a hipster was someone who had deliberately decided to kill a part of himself in order to make life bearable. He knows that by doing this he is cutting himself off from many positive emotions as well as the negative, destructive ones he seeks to avoid; but on balance he feels that the sacrifice is worthwhile."

Terry Southern

# ANDY WARHOL
## NAPOLEON IN RAGS

*Andy Warhol has constructed a body of ideas which in themselves make a literary contribution . . . of the same order as Rousseau, Jarry, or Duchamp. Its rawness (a dispensing with taste that becomes almost a form of American taste for the raw) obscures Warhol's miraculous nature. If he were French our universities would have embraced him in innumerable thesis. As it is, his apotheosis is taking place in Germany . . . Just as Wilde's epigrams were repeated by his contemporaries in drawing rooms, Warhol's are retold in gossip columns, the drawing rooms of the masses.*
–Mary Josephson, *Art in America*, 1971

SO MANY OF THE MEN profiled in this book were writers. Andy Warhol is a good example: during his life, and in the aftermath of his premature death in 1987, Warhol published fourteen volumes, four of them classics. Many of Warhol's books were translated into several languages; they received copious attention in the international press. Yet to this day, few people think of Andy Warhol as a literary figure.

Over twenty-five years have passed since Warhol's death. During these years, research into his life and work has become an industry, evidenced in a whole museum of books, articles, films, documentaries, symposiums, retrospectives, interviews, lectures, CDs, and spectacles. In this arena of interest, little exists about Andy Warhol as a writer. I asked a well-known critic at the Whitney's symposium on Warhol's legacy, shortly after Warhol's death in 1987, why there had been no mention of Warhol's writing; he replied that the body of work was beneath consideration. And when Penguin recently republished three of Warhol's books in its Classics series, the jacket copy described him as a painter and filmmaker, not a writer. This resistance to the idea of Warhol as a writer is strange, because his writing is so integral to the rest of his work that to ignore it is to ignore the essence of his contribution.

The first person to pin Warhol as a man of words may have been Bob Dylan. His 1965 single "Like a Rolling Stone" is thought, by some critics, to be about the relationship between Andy Warhol and his superstar Edie Sedgwick. In one famous verse Dylan describes Warhol as Napoleon, but the key point is his recognition of the power of Warhol's language. The way he spoke was so seductive his followers simply could not refuse anything he asked them to do. Before he was shot, Warhol's presence and voice were so strong they dominated and shaped everything and everyone around him. Two months after the song was released, Warhol started writing the novel *a*.

At the Factory, writing was the third arm of Andy Warhol Enterprises. Andy wrote the majority of his books in trilogies. The first came in 1967 and 1968, with the publication of *Andy Warhol's Index (Book); a: a novel*; and the "telephone book" (the thick 1968 Swedish catalog of his Stockholm retrospective). These three books introduced the world to life at the Factory, in words and photographs. The best of them, and the root of all Andy's writing, is *a: a novel*–the transcript of Warhol's tape-recording of twenty-four hours in the life of *Chelsea Girls* star Ondine. With literary roots in James Joyce's *Ulysses* and Jack Kerouac's *Visions of Cody*, Warhol's 1968 book can also be read as part of a trilogy with the 1966 film *Chelsea Girls* and the 1967 album *The Velvet Underground & Nico*. The three works–all products of the Factory collective–break with traditional form to make something beautiful and new. The novel's broken language mirrors the sound of the album and the look and sound of the film. *a* is equally powerful on its own; when it was published in 1968, the *New Yorker* and *Newsweek* hailed it as a work of genius.

The next trilogy of publications, published after Warhol was shot, goes deeper into experimentation: *Blue Movie* (1970); *Transcript of David Bailey's ATV*

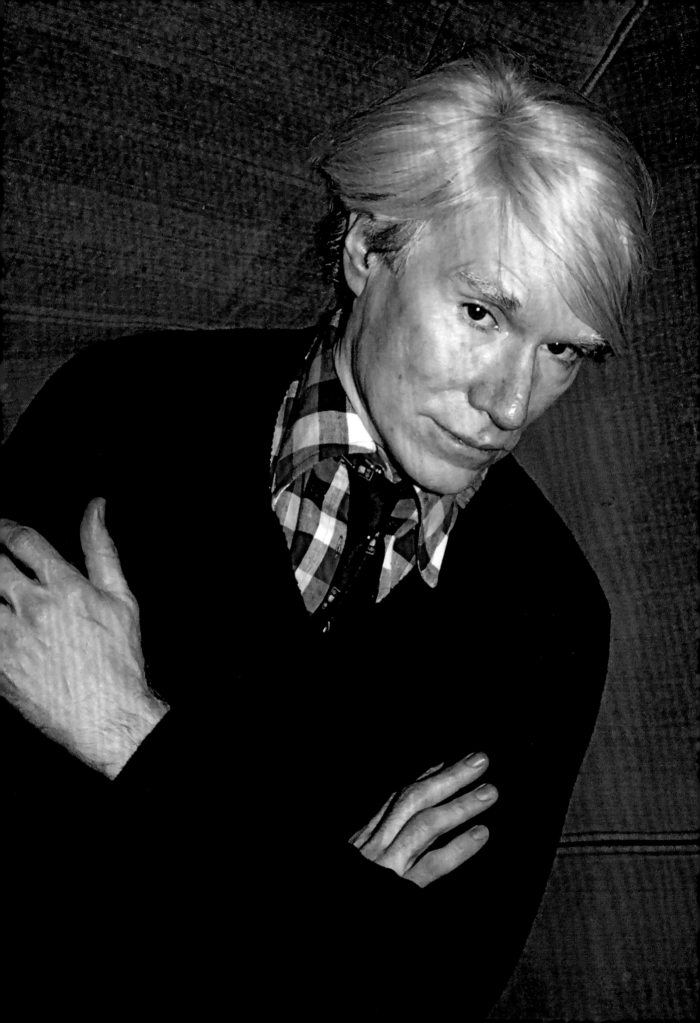

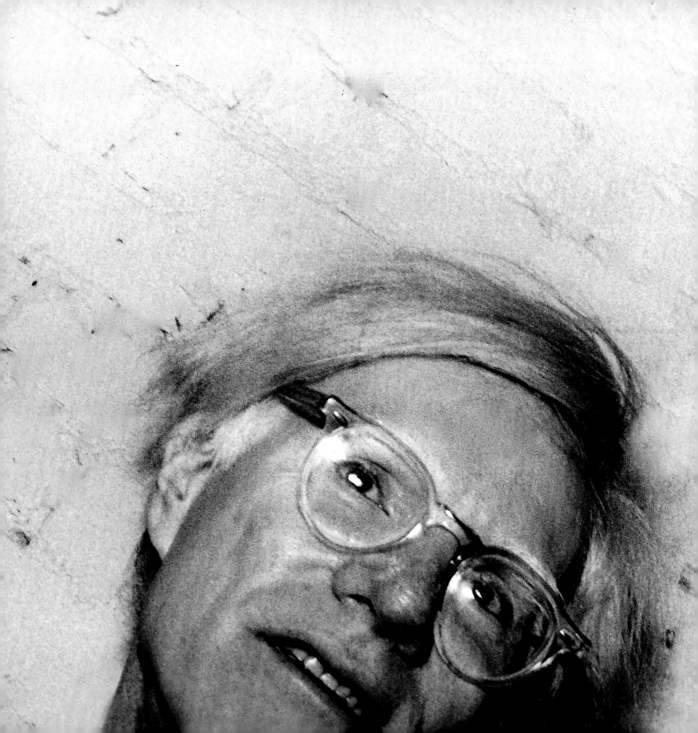

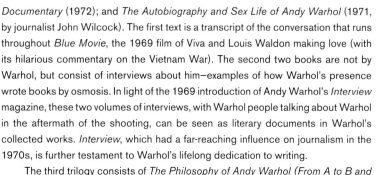

Documentary (1972); and *The Autobiography and Sex Life of Andy Warhol* (1971, by journalist John Wilcock). The first text is a transcript of the conversation that runs throughout *Blue Movie*, the 1969 film of Viva and Louis Waldon making love (with its hilarious commentary on the Vietnam War). The second two books are not by Warhol, but consist of interviews about him—examples of how Warhol's presence wrote books by osmosis. In light of the 1969 introduction of Andy Warhol's *Interview* magazine, these two volumes of interviews, with Warhol people talking about Warhol in the aftermath of the shooting, can be seen as literary documents in Warhol's collected works. *Interview*, which had a far-reaching influence on journalism in the 1970s, is further testament to Warhol's lifelong dedication to writing.

The third trilogy consists of *The Philosophy of Andy Warhol (From A to B and Back Again)* (1975); *Andy Warhol's Exposures* (1979); and *Popism: The Warhol Sixties* (1980, coauthored with Pat Hackett). These three books are aimed at the mainstream, in line with his mid- to late-'70s oeuvre, but they hold up well today—particularly *Philosophy*, which reveals Warhol's Zen positions. The text of *Exposures* is a decorative account of the high '70s, in a style that would take full bloom in the Warhol diaries. An idiosyncratic account of the 1960s, *Popism* is a must-read for anybody interested in the era.

After the initial financial failure of all these books and the collapse of his publishing company in the 1980s, Warhol appeared to draw back from his commitment to writing at least a trilogy of books per decade. His final production was the anemic *America* (1985); it was poorly designed and received disappointing reviews, but its text was amusing. After his death, though, came two surprises. *Andy Warhol's Party Book*, again coauthored with Pat Hackett, was an intriguing look into Warhol's desire to turn everything into a party. *The Andy Warhol Diaries* was, at last, the blockbuster he had hoped for. It dominated the best seller list in the U.S., and did very well in countries including France and Germany. However, despite being compared to the Goncourt journals and firmly putting Warhol on the list of the great diarists, it too failed to establish him as a writer.

Warhol was the recording angel who never stopped trying to use words to distinguish and define the human comedy. A singular, brave, lonely man, he poured as much passion and reality into his books as into everything else he made. From childhood to death, Andy Warhol's first line of defense and attack was in words. He even claimed that he married his tape recorder.

What more evidence do we need to show that this man was a committed writer? I beg you to demand an anthology, *The Andy Warhol Reader*, to present his writing in the same context as his paintings and films—leading at last to the *Collected Writing of Andy Warhol*, annotated in twelve uniform volumes.

Andy Warhol (LEFT AND FOLLOWING PAGES)

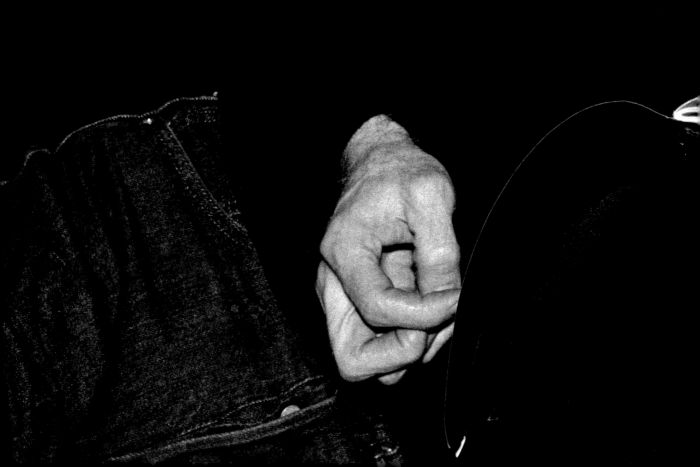

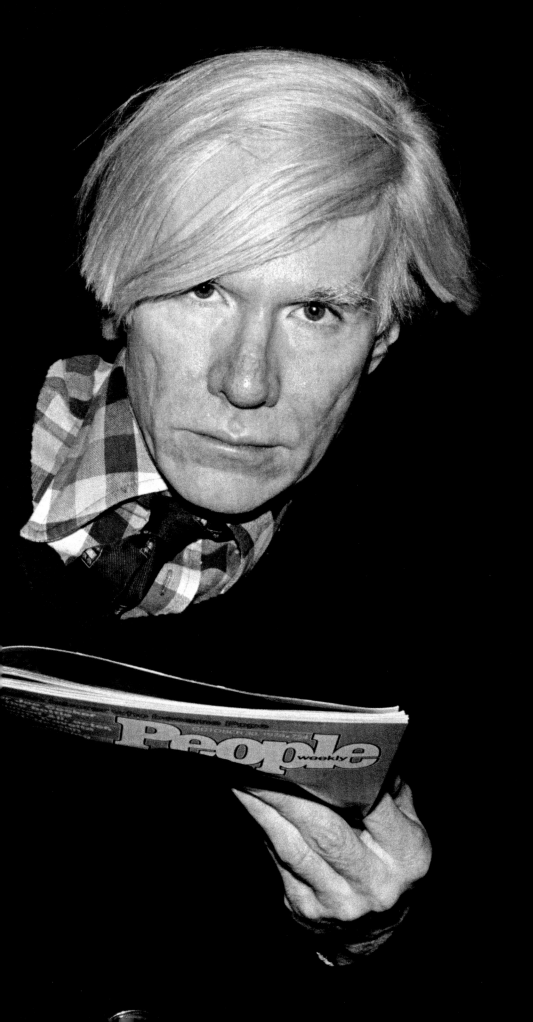

# MICK JAGGER

IN NOVEMBER 2014 the *Village Voice* put together a list of the sixty best songs about New York City. The Rolling Stones came in at number six with "Shattered," off their best-selling album *Some Girls*. The song's "lyrics are spot-on in their pointed observations, snottily talk-sung by Jagger," the list's authors wrote. "Maybe Mayor de Blasio can use a lyric as the city's motto: 'Pride and joy and greed and sex / that's what makes our town the best.'"

Mick Jagger has long been an intimate observer and partaker of life in New York, and a friend of more of Marcia's subjects than any other contender. He met and became influenced by Andy Warhol on the Rolling Stones' first U.S. tour in 1964. He befriended William Burroughs, Allen Ginsberg, and Terry Southern in London in the late 1960s. In 1971 Warhol did the iconic cover of the Stones album *Sticky Fingers*. From 1972 onward, Mick and his first wife, Bianca, were celebrated in Warhol's *Interview* magazine. In 1975, the year *The Philosophy of Andy Warhol* was published, the Stones rented Warhol's Montauk compound to rehearse for their U.S. tour, and Mick collaborated with Andy on a series of Mick Jagger portraits. The Stones began announcing their U.S. tours from New York in 1975. Mick began living in New York City in 1977. In the interim, Jagger has worked with Kenneth Anger, Chuck Berry, James Brown, Dr. John, Andy Warhol again, Jim Carroll, and Todd Rundgren. Jagger and Keith Richards took part in Paul McCartney's Concert for New York City after September 11, 2001, playing "Salt of the Earth."

## NEW YEAR'S EVE AT MICK'S PLACE, NEW YORK, 1979

BY LIZ DERRINGER

THE NIGHT LIZ AND MARCIA dropped in on Mick so Liz could do the *High Times* interview, Mick lived one block north of John Lennon, just off Central Park West on Seventy-Third Street. He had just finished recording the Rolling Stones album *Emotional Rescue*. The atmosphere was warm and convivial. Champagne was passed around.

LIZ DERRINGER: How do you get around to writing an album?

MICK JAGGER: Writing a song is like—you're writing a song all the time. It's not something that you suddenly do. It's always there. Suddenly it's in the right mixture inside you to come out and it just pops out. Usually when you're writing on the piano or a guitar, you don't write in lyrics, on their own. . . . But the whole idea of the song should come in the best way, together. . . .

LIZ: It's really hard to come up with something original.

MICK: There is nothing new under the sun, dear. . . .

LIZ: Are you a Catholic?

MICK: No. We're very staunchly anti-Catholic. We're very much so. But I couldn't believe—I used to go into people's houses in South America and Brazil, they'd have these statues of this wooden saint. They collect them, you know. The women particularly. And . . . you go into a room dominated by this huge table with big—they're quite big, a foot tall—and they name them and tell about them. It's absolute bullshit, I mean, all these saints. It is. Everyone knows it. . . . Most of these saints—that particular religion turns me right off.

LIZ: I think religion starts trouble.

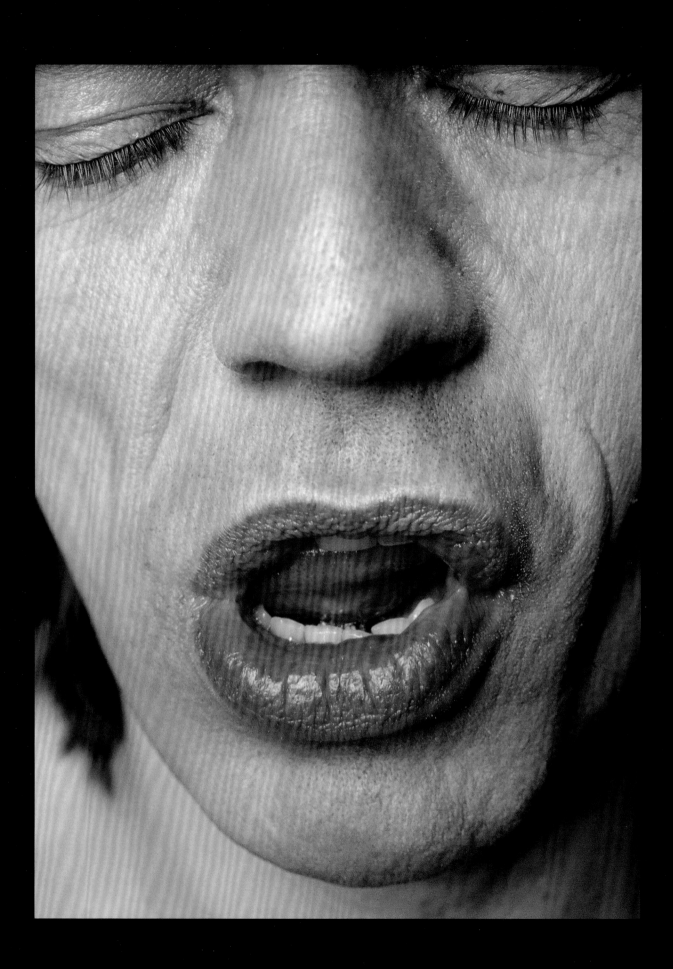

MICK: Well, everyone knows that, you know, killing for ideas is the most dangerous form of killing at all. Being willing to die for your ideas rather than your country is another concept, but dying for an idea, like in religion, is absurd.

LIZ: Do you love being on stage?

MICK: . . . I think schizophrenia is the main problem there because you can see yourself playing this part. 'Cause it's going on the stage with your act. It's all an act, obviously. You don't want to be really like that in real life. It's very dangerous if you find yourself looking at yourself. But you can't help . . . examining what you're doing. The other thing is, you get the feeling after a while that it's a perfectly normal thing to do. Which in reality it's not. It's abnormal, because it's abnormal psychosis you're putting yourself through. . . . You're becoming another character. Not only that—it's worse than being an actor because people don't think you're playing a part, they actually think you're like the guy on stage. That's the whole illusion in rock 'n' roll music. That you're really like that, that's you. . . .

LIZ: People have this image of you as being like a somewhat evil, sullen type character . . .

MICK: . . . Rock 'n' roll stage performance is obviously a very limited form of entertainment. Obviously it's got a lot of appeal 'cause it's lasted a long time. . . . Nothing's changed, you know, not really. Four blokes with guitars running about the stage, I mean, really, in two lines, that's it, isn't it? . . .

LIZ: Yeah, but I just get so sexually turned on by seeing a rock star.

MICK: Well, that's what it's about. It's getting sexually excited. Why do all these boys get sexually turned on who are not homosexuals? . . . I've never been able to discover the reason because at least half the audience has always been boys. At some points in my life, it's been more.

LIZ: Do you rehearse a lot before a tour?

MICK: . . . The music's rehearsed a lot. You see, all people think about is, they think, in rock 'n' roll, they get the music off right and they think it's okay standing there looking macho. Well, it's not. That's boring. . . . People think it's enough just to stand there, and for most it is enough. I think it's amazing that people put up with it. . . . Do you get a hard-on just watching the guy standing there? I just think—I don't mean it too sexually, I must admit. I forget about that, you know. I don't think about the sexual part of it very much. I mean, not when I'm on stage. I just start rubbing my cock. . . .

"The essential ingredient for any successful rock group is energy—the ability to give out energy, to receive energy from the audience, and give it back to the audience. A rock concert is in fact a rite involving the evocation and transmutation of energy. Rock stars may be compared to priests."

—WILLIAM BURROUGHS, *CRAWDADDY*, 1975

Mick Jagger

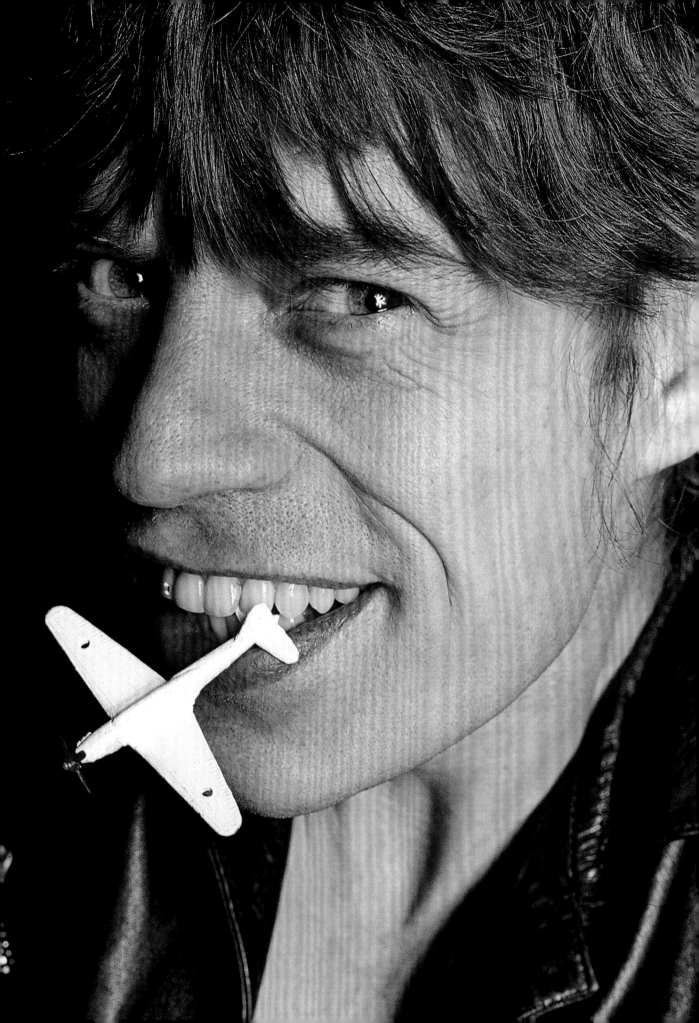

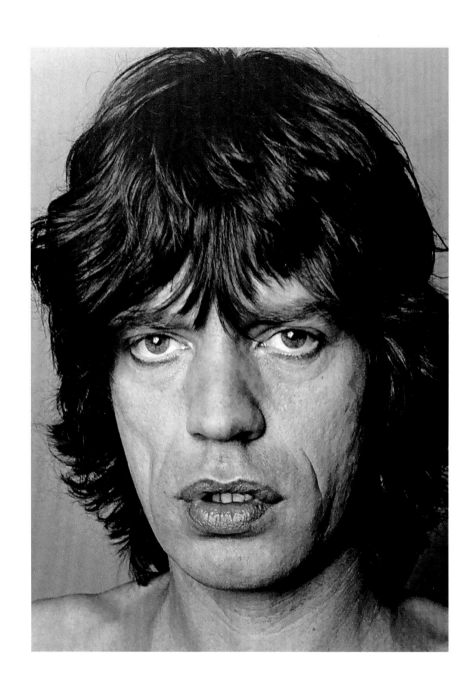

Mick Jagger

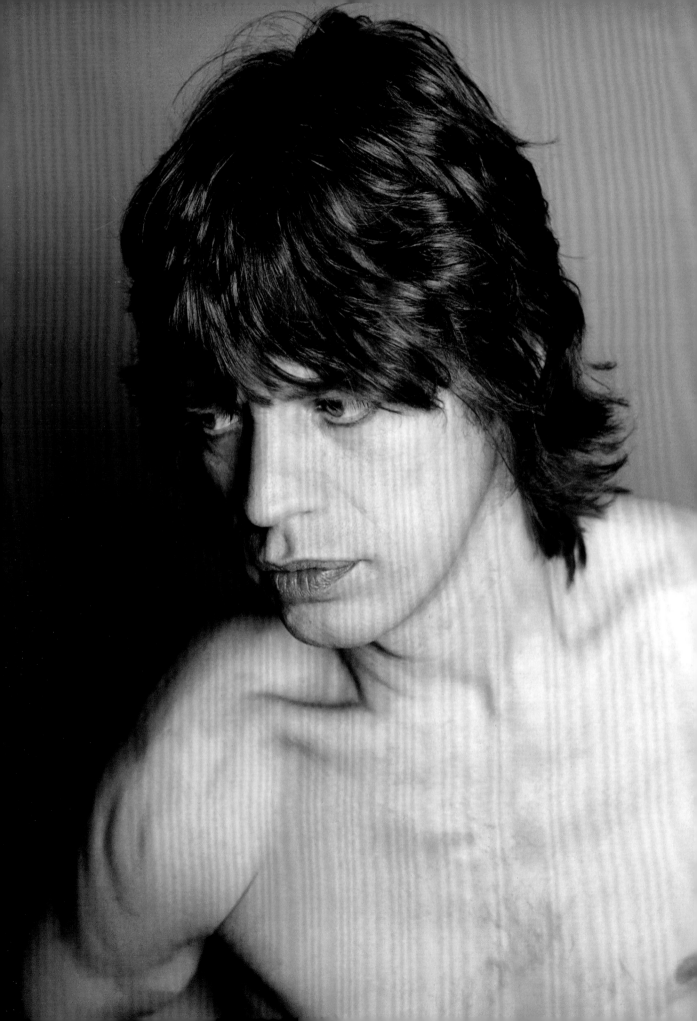

# WILLIAM BURROUGHS, ANDY WARHOL, AND MICK JAGGER
## A NIGHTMARE OF MISCOMMUNICATION

*The two developments since World War II were the use of the atom bomb at Hiroshima and rock music. The whole cultural revolution would never have been possible without rock music, which translated it into mass media.*
—From unpublished conversation between William Burroughs, Chris Stein, and Debbie Harry, New York, 1980

I HAD ALMOST FINISHED my book *With William Burroughs: A Report from the Bunker* (1981) when the opportunity arose to tape a conversation between Bill Burroughs and Keith Richards. I had interviewed Keith for *High Times* in 1977, and we had spoken of Bill in some detail. From my point of view, no meeting could have better completed my book. However, I had a deadline of March 1980, and as it approached the opportunity was slipping out of my hands. Then, writer David Dalton asked Bill to contribute to his book celebrating the Stones' twentieth anniversary, and I suggested Bill tape an interview—if not with Keith, then with Mick. This far-fetched idea was made possible by Marcia's connection with Liz Derringer. Liz asked Mick if he would accept an invitation to dinner at the Bunker, and in a surprisingly short time, he did.

On March 1, 1980, I recorded a conversation between Liz, Mick, Jerry Hall, Marcia, Bill Burroughs, and Andy Warhol. Unfortunately, at the time I was broke. So was Bill, and on the night of the dinner, I found myself walking over to the Bunker with a shopping bag containing a few pieces of pâté, a small, cold string bean salad, a loaf of French bread, and two bottles of cheap red wine for seven people. Mick was bringing Liz and his girlfriend Jerry Hall. Bill had suggested we invite Andy Warhol, and Marcia was coming to photograph the event.

Everything went well until Mick arrived. Instead of greeting Bill as an old acquaintance from the '60s in London, he acted suspiciously, asking us what this was all about. Bill couldn't remember which publication we were interviewing Mick for. My brain must have made an appointment with my ass behind my back, because when Bill asked me, I shot back, "Well listen, man, you told me about it!" (David Dalton had also spoken to me about it.) There then arose a moment of frozen silence in which Mick might have left at any moment. The scene was perfectly captured by Marcia's lens in her *Three Kings of the Counterculture* portrait.

Several things of note happened during the evening. First, Bill attempted to conduct the interview he thought the Stones, according to Dalton, had requested from him. He had obviously given it some thought, because his repeated line of conversation followed an attempt to elicit from Mick a response to one question: "I'm talking about the Stones as heroes of the [cultural] revolution, deserving citation, you understand. [Timothy Leary has said the revolution] is over and we have won. Then who are "we," and what have we won, exactly?" Well played, you might think, for an opening gambit—but Jagger trivialized and deflected it. Andy attempted to save the day by saying Bill was studying Mick because he wanted to play him in the film *The Mick Jagger Story* and "he's working on the part!" This was classic Warhol humor, and it worked, to an extent, although part of the problem all night was that Bill didn't really get Andy's humor on this occasion—nor did Andy and Mick get his. Then they talked about people who'd used their names: Andy said the star of his film *Heat*, Andrea Feldman, called herself Mrs. Andy Warhol before she jumped out of the window and committed suicide. Bill asked who Julian Burroughs was. "He was a guy who was running away from being in the army who said he was your son," Andy laughed. "And we starred him in a

Andy Warhol and
William Burroughs

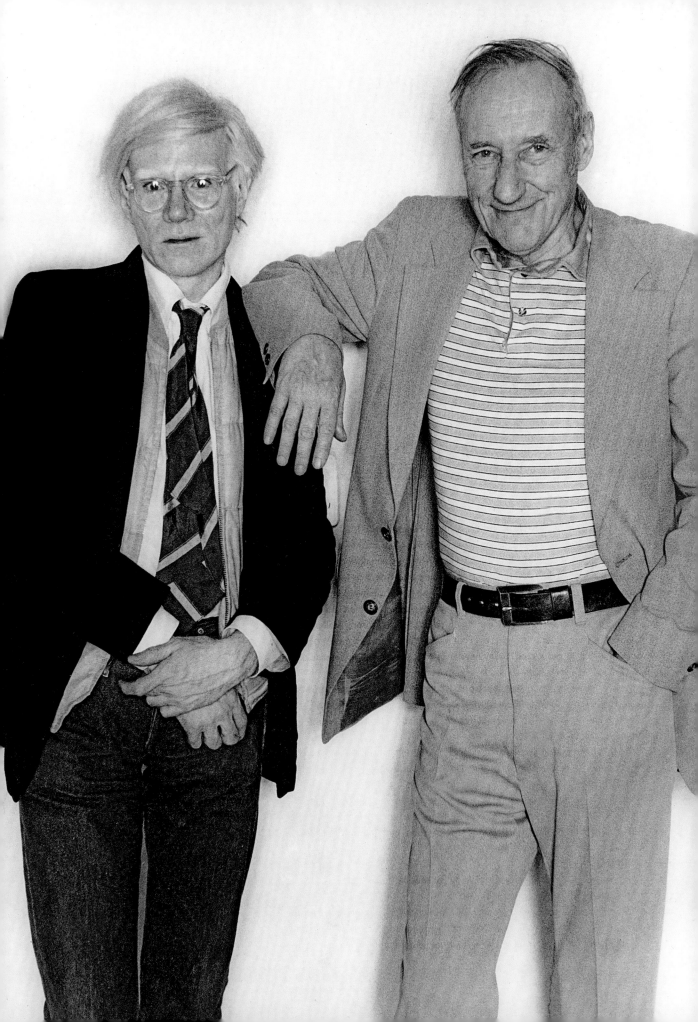

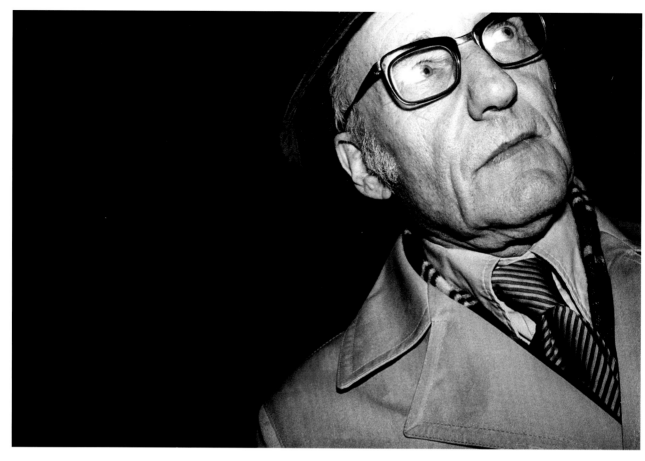

William Burroughs (ABOVE)
Mick Jagger, William Burroughs,
and Andy Warhol (FOLLOWING PAGES)

movie called *Naked Restaurant* [an obvious play on *Naked Lunch*]." Then Bill told
a convoluted story—about how his first wife found her employer, the playwright Ernst
Toller, hanging from the back of his bathroom door, dead—which nobody, including
myself, understood. That was the straw that broke the camel's back as far as Bill was
concerned; after trying once more to draw Mick into some meaningful exchange
about the counterculture and failing, his tone changed distinctly. When I mentioned
that people would be leaving the planet during our lifetimes and Jerry Hall said, "I
think lots of people would like to go," Bill shot back, "Yes, I'd love to go. I'd go *this
second*. Anything to get out of this nightmare of miscommunication!"—a line that
nobody, including myself, appeared to hear at that time.

I made the observation that the biggest cultural influence by Bill on Mick
appeared to be sartorial (because they were dressed almost identically). This
amused Jerry, who turned the conversation on again, bless her heart, and we started
talking about clothes.

"Andy has that special undervest," said Mick. "What's that thing you've got on?"

"What the hell is that thing?" Bill joined in. "I didn't even get a look at it."

"It's a bullet-proof jacket," said Andy.

"Yeah, it really is," Bill exclaimed. "Oh well, God knows you need one, Andy!"

Everyone started screaming in agreement. Then, after another sudden and stiff
silence, I burst out, "So Mick, did you ever shoot anyone, or did anyone ever try to
shoot you?"

"No," Mick replied.

I continued. "Bill shot someone, and Andy got shot, let's see . . . "

Mick inquired, "Who did you shoot, Bill?"

There was a pause. Everyone knew Bill had accidentally shot and killed his
wife in 1951. Burroughs's eyes pinned Jagger. "It's a long story," he said. "It's a bad
story. But I haven't shot anyone right lately. I assure you of that, Mick. I been on my

good behavior." After that it was *still* difficult to find anything to talk about, but the conversation about guns stumbled on, leading to this exchange:

BILL BURROUGHS: This fucking jerk mayor that we got now, he wants to pass some law about mandatory jail sentence for possession of firearms.

ANDY WARHOL: Well, more cops were killed . . .

BILL: Well, so what? You think the guys that killed a cop are gonna be deterred by an extra year in jail they might possibly get for a firearm? Holy God, what kind of thinking is this?

Earlier, when I'd blurted out my skepticism about the existence of a cultural revolution ("What cultural revolution?"), Bill responded, "Holy shit, man, what do you think we've been doing all these years?"

In August 1981, Jagger gave a press conference in Philadelphia to kick off the Stones U.S. tour supporting the album *Tattoo You*, and its monster number one single, "Start Me Up." According to Greil Marcus (with tongue in cheek?) in his book *In the Fascist Bathroom: Punk in Pop Music, 1977–1992*, the conference was recorded by the Los Angeles FM radio station KMET. Among the things Jagger reportedly said that day was the following:

> All right, *Some Girls* was good, *Emotional Rescue* was bad, this one's good, I agree—though this one's nowhere nearly as good as *Some Girls*. But don't forget—between *Exile on Main Street*, which was a great album, and *Some Girls*, we came up with four bad albums, and a couple of those were terrible. Consumer Protection Agency investigations, class action suits, the whole bit. But anyway, everybody will have forgotten about this one in six months. Sure, it sounds "pretty good" and it's even got a "rockin' side" and a "dreamy side," just like those golden oldies-but-goodies LPs, but I defy anyone to find a single song on—what's it called again? Oh yeah, *Tattoo You*, thanks—with a, as Sartre would have said, raison d'être. L'enfer, c'est les autres, you know. We could have done these songs or we could have not done them. Who'd know the difference? What people want is product. To assert that a tune carefully constructed out of half-forgotten Rolling Stones hits for the sole purpose of assuaging the listener with a sense of familiarity disguised as high-tech contemporaneity could possibly be compared in terms of emotional impact or social metaphor to a record on the level of Elmore James's "Done Somebody Wrong" is merely to reify the sort of false consciousness that may well make revolution in our time impossible.

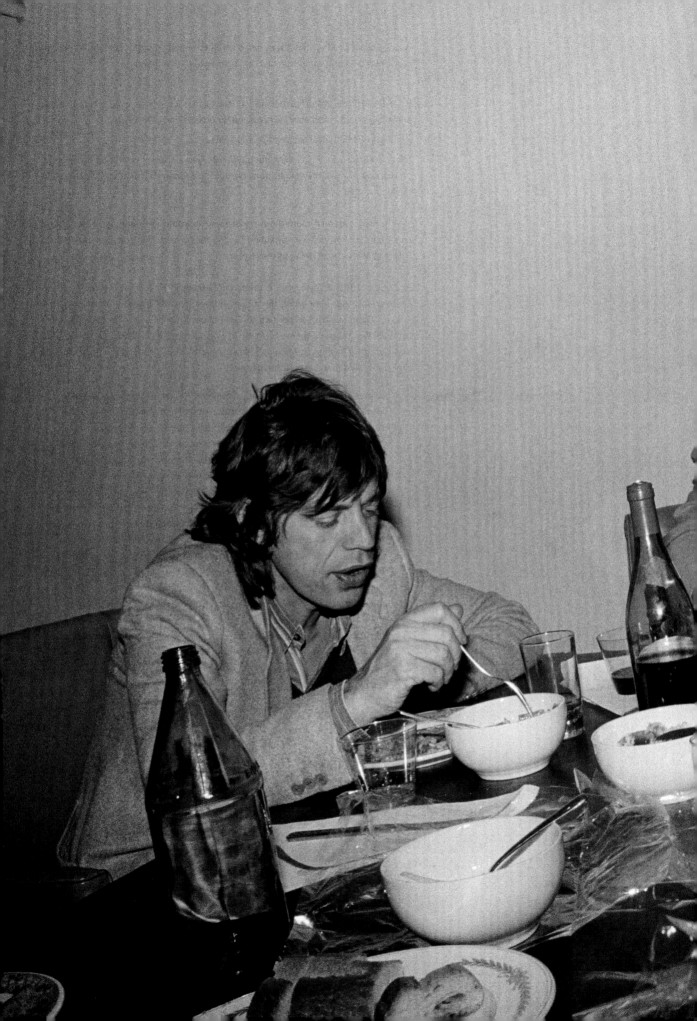

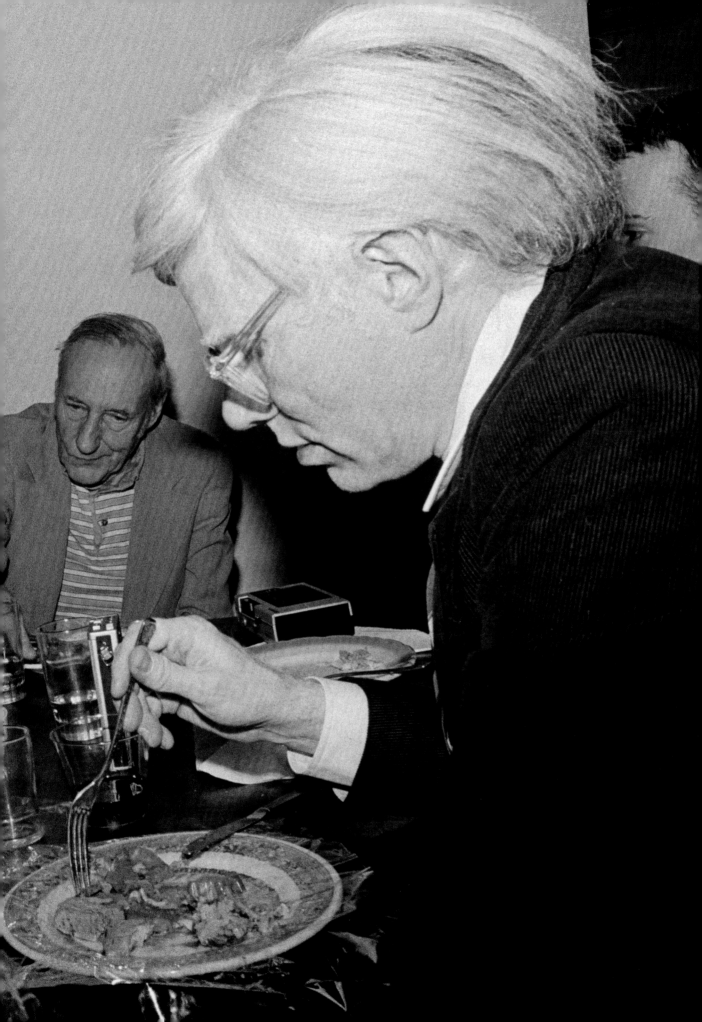

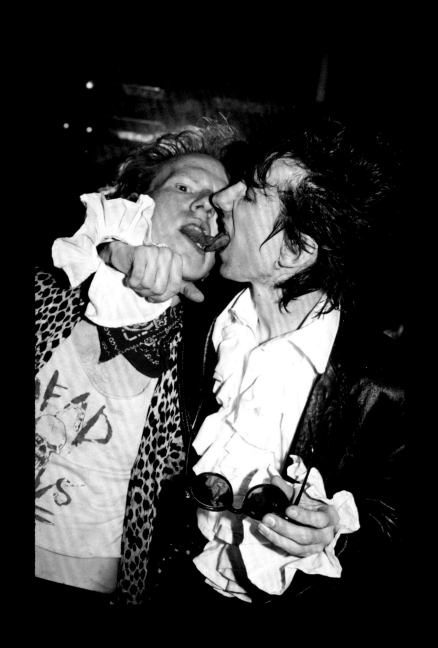

# PUNK ROCKERS
# AND MUSIC REBELS

"One cultural influence
[on punk] that's been forgotten
is 1970s minimalism. There was
a concerted effort by bands
like Suicide, the Ramones,
and Talking Heads to follow
the aesthetic that 'less is more'
and to strip music down to its core.
Blow it up and start all over again!"

—*PUNK* EDITOR AND
MASTER CARTOONIST
JOHN HOLMSTROM

Cheetah Chrome and Stiv Bators

"The complete masculinity allied with complete tenderness and vulnerability of the British rock groups of the '60s made it possible for all the young guys who went into punk to engage in emotionally creative relationships with their "brothers" that might otherwise have been interrupted by macho posturing and violence."

—ALLEN GINSBERG, *DELIBERATE PROSE: SELECTED ESSAYS 1952–1995*

THIS CHAPTER IS A GOOD EXAMPLE of how Marcia wove the photographs in *Punks, Poets & Provocateurs* together. The elder musicians—Chuck Berry, James Brown, Peter Tosh, Gil Scott-Heron, Dr. John, and Philip Glass—are the rock, soul, reggae, voodoo, and all-important minimalist sources of punk. The rockabilly of Robert Gordon and Smutty Smiff of the Rockats bridges the past and present, a theme that recurs throughout the book. Other threads can be discovered by comparing visual similarities in the portraits.

Marcia's double-panel portrait of Alan Vega and Martin Rev of Suicide belongs in a museum. Her vertical shot of David Byrne is the best reflection of the twisted author of "Psycho Killer" I have seen. Chuck Berry responded so well to Marcia's lens that after the session, with a twinkle in his handsome eyes, the "Johnny B. Goode" author invited her to visit him at his very own Berry Park in Wentzville, Missouri. Marcia's image of Bob Quine reminds me of her portrait of Gregory Corso. Both wear the sunglasses and hold the cigarettes that were customary for the Bad Boy.

Marcia's work is all about finding the beauty in the wreckage. Look at her odalisque of Joey Ramone. Joey was a highly strung, sensitive instrument. He had just completed recording *End of the Century* with Phil Spector and starring in *Rock 'n' Roll High School*. And he was in love. Marcia's portrait of the Ramones' vocalist lying on the pavement with his bony knees poking through the holes in his jeans was composed at the intersection of Bowery and East Second Street, one block north of CBGB, in the fall of 1979. (In 2003, this block was officially renamed Joey Ramone Place.) Marcia's portrait of John Lurie illustrates John's point: "We were so sure of ourselves, we never doubted anything." She also finds in these rather intimidating perfectionists the qualities of warmth and beauty that illuminated the New York scene.

The deeper Marcia submerged herself in the Bad Boys' world, the more the act of creating the photographs became a reflection of her life. Consider her portraits of John Lydon (aka Johnny Rotten), then the frontman of Public Image Ltd (PiL), which had just released *The Flowers of Romance*. One night, Marcia and John made an evening of gallivanting around New York. Their first stop was the luxurious apartment of a famous drug dealer. The pair ended up rapping in Marcia's loft, overlooking the Hudson River. As Lydon left in the early morning Marcia handed him her copy of Charles Bukowski's *Erections, Ejaculations, Exhibitions, and General Tales of Ordinary Madness*. The following night, PiL played what would become known in rock history as the "Ritz riot." Marcia was welcomed backstage, where she took a radiant portrait of Lydon at his peak. After the show, he was almost in tears.

A week later when she arrived at the Robert Gordon photo session, Gordon inquired, "Hey baby, what's your name?" To which Marcia responded, *"MY NAME IS NOT BABY."*

The punk-rocker texts begin with Max Blagg's classic interview with Iggy Pop. In it, Max gets Iggy—reborn yet again, via a Berlin collaboration with Bowie, who has just produced Pop's record *The Idiot*—to explain what being a rock star is all about. There were few higher authorities in New York punk than Iggy.

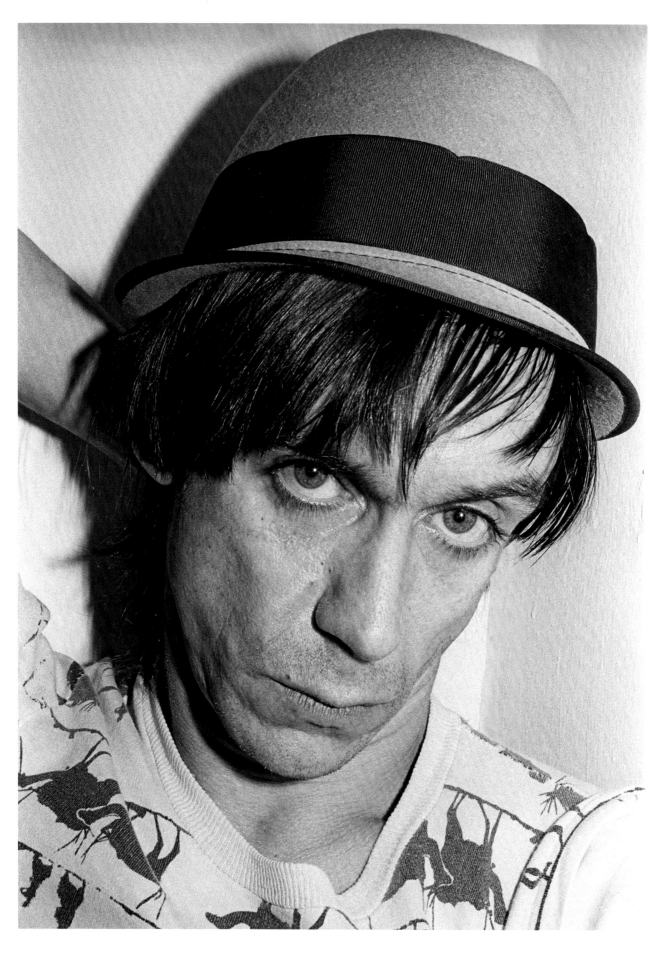

# IGGY POP
## LOSERS LEAVE TOWN

BY MAX BLAGG

**(ON THE OCCASION OF THE IGGY POP CONCERT
AT THE PALLADIUM IN NEW YORK, OCTOBER 6, 1977)**
Frwom *Traveler's Digest*, March 1978

AFTER A BRIEF INTRODUCTION by an early hero of American television, Soupy Sales (his two sons, Hunt and Tony, play bass and drums in the band), Iggy Pop runs front center: demonic smile, sweatshirt, ragged Levi's, kneepads, and two-toned Capezios. He takes off into "Lust for Life"—the entire audience is on its feet. Iggy Pop is on his knees, pumping, listing to starboard, upside, downside, inside the spotlight, giving us "something called love / oh love love love / Well that's like hypnotizing chickens." "Sixteen" comes next, and the shirt is *off*, exposing the rippling musculature of the Midwest farm boy gone stone crazy—curved, shiny, sexual locomotion—and he *knows*, he's teaching, we're reaching, bumping, grinding, some slutty suction building . . . but then after a couple more songs and some fast flashing headgear fashions, he starts to pull back, like he doesn't want to do it to us after all . . . power fading like a faulty connection. And though it comes back in flashes, brief moments of dazzle—like when he crawls into a bank of amps as if he's trying to reactivate himself and his audience—it stays on the blink till the end, right through to the last chord of a stylized encore, leaving us all wound up and no fuse to blow. The brief remarks that punctuate the songs seem, to say the least, disdainful: "Thanks for nothing, you fuckheads," "Didja leave ya brains at home?" and so on. But you know he's not really being a snot-nosed "rock star"; the Ig is just talking to himself.

The previous evening, through various vague connections, I found myself uptown bound at short notice to meet the Ig and maybe do some kind of interview with him. After around 1 a.m., I am introduced to a bespectacled guy in plaid work shirt and no underwear; Iggy Pop (aka James Osterberg), registered rock 'n' roll legend, looks more like a pre-med student than a crazy-head rock 'n' roller.

POP: Once you get across the bridge, out of Manhattan, you begin to relax a little. Because in Manhattan I know every five minutes I'm liable to meet someone who wants to do me harm.

BLAGG: Do you spend much time here?

POP: I do spend a lot of time here, most of it in social research—bold encounters . . . engaging strangers in conversation, or in the minutes, hours days of their lives. But I find my interest peters out very quickly, because most people here have an angle, and I don't. Most people finally give up and go home, it's like "losers leave town," and that's much more brutal than in, say, Berlin. In Berlin a guy can live in the same apartment for forty years, there isn't the same pressure—whereas in New York, I've seen, in the last ten years, from '67 to now, I've seen 25 or 35 of you come and go . . . 25 or 35 guys with the same sweatshirt, same haircut, same boots, I've seen multiples of you come and go.

BLAGG: Well, might as well switch off and fuck off—

POP: No, because you've probably seen multiples of me come and go too—I'm thirty and I've seen multiples of all of you . . . (To the girl next to him) Yes even you, although, as a woman, you charm me just enough to glaze over my objective view . . . It's only interesting in that the city we are all in now, it's the nature of this city to attract the most unusual specimens, from other localities, and stamp them out in multiples. Like me, I'm a kid from Detroit, right? And as I get older, I become unusually different, and I finally come to New York and BAM! My face is stamped out 35,000 times. Because I came here to make a record album, takes four days, they take a picture of me, and then it's reproduced 35, 40 thousand times and sent

"*If rock and roll had an Eartha Kitt it would be Iggy Pop. Mr. Pop is the greatest rock performer of them all.*"

—GLENN O'BRIEN

out to the boondocks, all over the world. And where was it actually made? In New York. And how many other people came here at the same time as me, hoping to be made into multiples, and failed? For every one of me, a thousand failed. They failed because their problem was, although they were more beautiful than me, they weren't as ready for the market as I was. . . . That's why I wouldn't live here, you know? That's why this city is full of beautiful, gorgeous people who haven't got A CHANCE in the world, because they're only suited to the look of this city. But they haven't got the Product. . . .

BLAGG: So you regard yourself as a product?

POP: I am a total product, 100% a product, and totally dependent on Manhattan because that's where I'm validated . . . I come here and I say, well I look as good as you maybe, but I have this magic difference—I know how to BE the product . . . 'Cos a guy like me, comes from the Midwest, and they look at my shoulders, they look at my significance . . . they look at my guts . . . and they say, "Aha, here's a guy who could mean something in Cleveland, that we could never mean, no matter how many kerchiefs we dress up in."

BLAGG: But how do you get that ability to mean something in Cleveland?

POP: By first of all staying away from this place (Manhattan), and once I had got that ability, I could slide up to it sideways—

BLAGG: But you wanted to come, then—

POP: No I didn't, 'cos I never lived here (and I never will). But I talk to it straight, like I am to you now, (that's why I'm pleased to be talking to you like this tonight)—it's not strictly for my own benefit—Tonight I'm being very honest . . . When I first came here it imme-diately became obvious to me that there were many men and women who were more aesthetically beautiful, and valid, than me.

BLAGG: Was that by your own judgment?

POP: By my own judgment, yeah, and I took that judgment on the chin, 'cos you know I always wanted to be the prettiest thing in the whole scheme of things . . . so I took it on the chin and I said, 'These people, they lack one thing, and that is the ability to touch—to touch Cleveland, Paris, wherever it is, and so I will torture them, because I have the ability—because let's face it, that's something you would desire, the contact to various places in the world, not necessarily as a pop star (or whatever). . . . The only reason I do this right now is because it helps me. . . . You dress up, I dress down. I look at you and I see a guy who in his heart wants and needs exactly what I want and need . . . but you don't have the access that I have, so it hurts you. I look at myself: I have a bit more of the want and need, and a bit more of the access—So it hurts me even more, but I surpass you, and my hope is that by surpassing you, you will follow me, follow my path and get your own want and need. Because down here (points to gut area) and down there we're the same, and the difference is that I can do it right now, and you can't. Because I believe that by following me, you will surpass me, and you will become something even better than me, you will go beyond me . . .

BLAGG: So how do you get the Access?

POP: Very simply. By realizing the facts—it's quite obvious right now—look at us all . . . who is the least attractive in this room? Me . . . (general disagreement from everyone else in the room). YES, because I try Very Hard to be the lowest—

BLAGG: Why?

POP: Why? Because it pushes you, because it messes you up, because it confused you, and I like for you to be confused, and I want you to push me, to force me into a con-frontation where you're better than I am—if you can do that to me, then I can grow, if you can't then I'm left alone, then I'm left all alone . . .

Iggy Pop

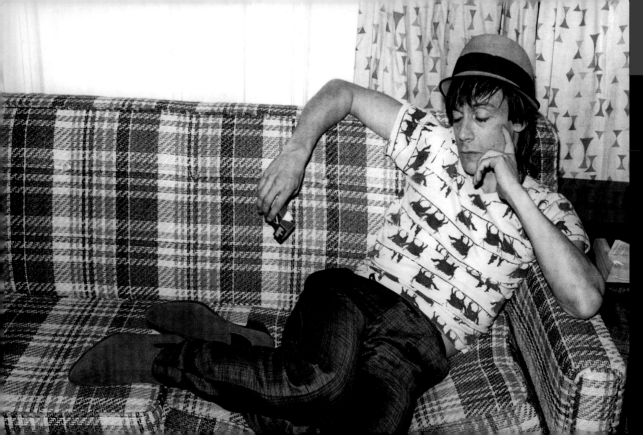

# BRIAN ENO

## NEW YORK, THE MOST BEAUTIFUL CITY ON EARTH

BY BRIAN ENO

From *No Wave: Post-Punk. Underground. New York. 1976-1980*

WHEN I ARRIVED IN NEW YORK in 1978, theoretically for a week, it was the end of April and it was the most beautiful weather and I thought, "God, this is the most beautiful city on earth." Which is something that can happen to you in New York on a nice day. And I ended up running into Steve Mass, who would soon open the Mudd Club. I met him though Diego Cortez. And Steve said to me, "I have a sublet here you can have if you want to stay a bit longer." Because I had been saying, "It's so nice here—I wish I could stay longer." So I sublet his upper floor on West Eighth Street and Fifth Avenue. It was a lovely place. I really enjoyed it. It was sort of loftlike, but it was an apartment. I thought, "Hmm. Well, I'll stay a little longer."

It was during this period that I met all those no wave people. I first met Arto Lindsay. I became friends with Arto, and have remained friends with him ever since.

At this point, the Kitchen was a venue, and Rhys Chatham was director there, and I saw the Theoretical Girls. And I thought, "Wow, this is very unusual." Coming from England, we had punk, of course, but it wasn't anywhere near as sort of self-consciously artistic. What I saw in New York clearly connected itself with a fine arts tradition, I thought, rather than with a punk music tradition. I remember just sort of hanging out and visiting various people. It was all happening very quickly. It was kind of a tumult. There was a lot going on. I very much had the sense that this wasn't going to last very long. It just seemed to me like one of those flames that burns very brightly for a short time and then goes out. And I thought, "It would be great if someone recorded this." I wanted, for historical reasons, to document this moment in time when this amazing scene erupted.

I was interested in it as an art historian. One of the things that really struck me was how brief some of these scenes were. I was particularly interested in early-twentieth-century art, and I studied the ferment that was going around in Europe in 1913. There was this whole scene of people suddenly noticing what Russians were doing and Russians noticing what the French were doing. And it lasted for a very, very short time, but paintings last, so we know what happened then. But music doesn't, unless it's recorded. This is how I sold the idea to record *No New York* to Chris Blackwell, who was to put up the money: I said, This is a piece of history, and I don't expect it's going to make a lot of money now. But I think it will end up being an important document. I also said it would cost nothing to record. Diego, Arto, and Anya Phillips were all important in creating connections for me with those bands and sort of letting them know I wasn't a . . . some of them were very suspicious of me, in the sense that I was an Englishman coming in to rip off their music and steal their ideas. Especially, of course, James Chance. I remember we had this big meeting at Steve Mass's sublet, and all the members of the four bands came. One of the points of controversy was my whole thing that it should be a collection—that we weren't going to do a separate album for each band.

In regards to the album cover, I had complete say over that. I wanted to put pictures of everyone, from all the bands, on there. And, of course: "Oh God—a photo session with all those people! What a nightmare!" Then I suddenly had this idea. In Europe, we had all this stuff with Baader-Meinhof and the Red Brigades. Every time you would go to a railway station or an airport, you'd see these posters that had several identical-sized black-and-white photos of people who were terrorists or people the police were looking for. What was very interesting about these photos was that they were very different in quality from each other. Some were obviously cut from newspapers; they had different textures to them. And I thought, "Oh, that's a good idea." So I just said to everybody, "Just give me any photograph of yourself that you have." And that's what it was. And then for the front cover, I went with the photographer Marcia Resnick and all her gear and a few of the musicians to the World Trade Center, and whilst in there I took that picture using her camera.

Brian Eno

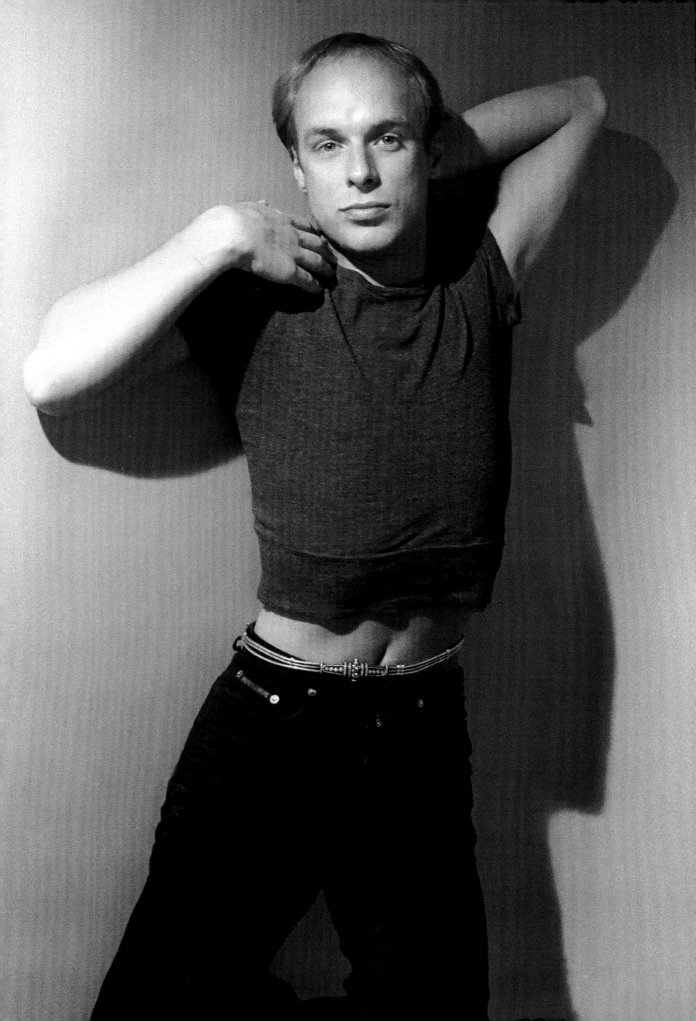

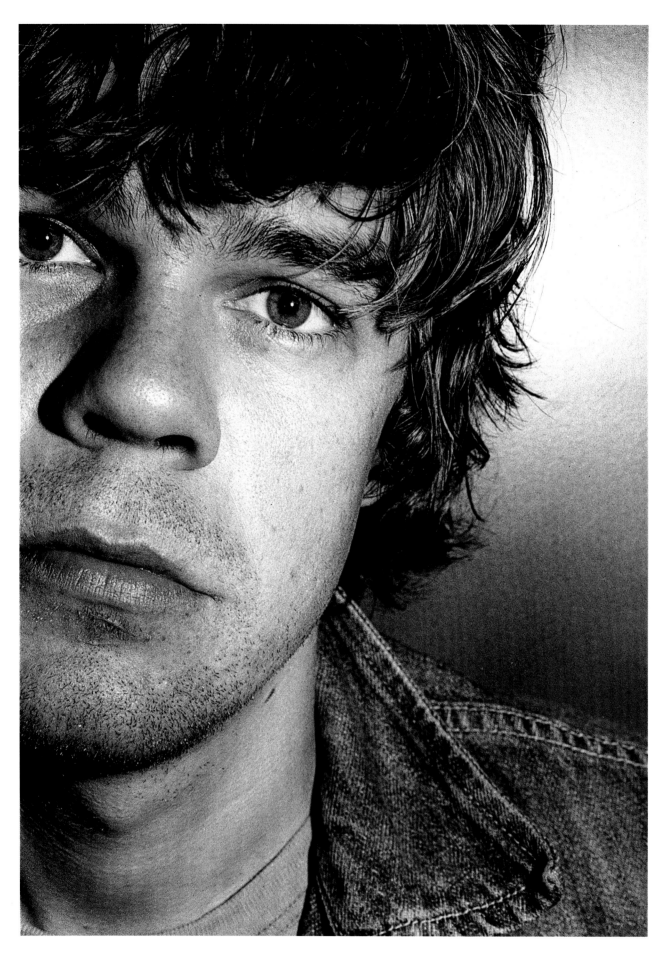

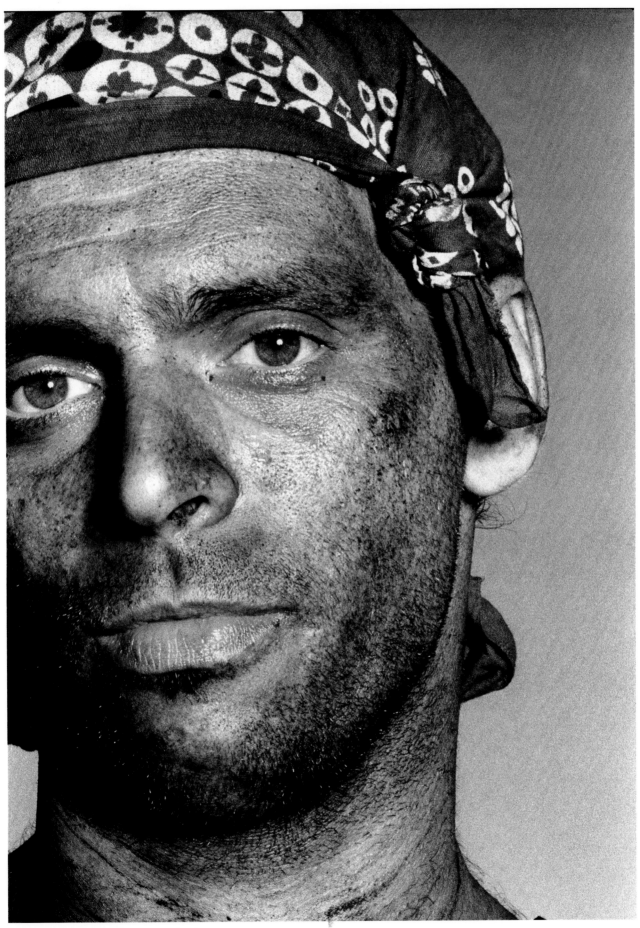

David Johansen (OPPOSITE), Wayne Kramer (ABOVE)

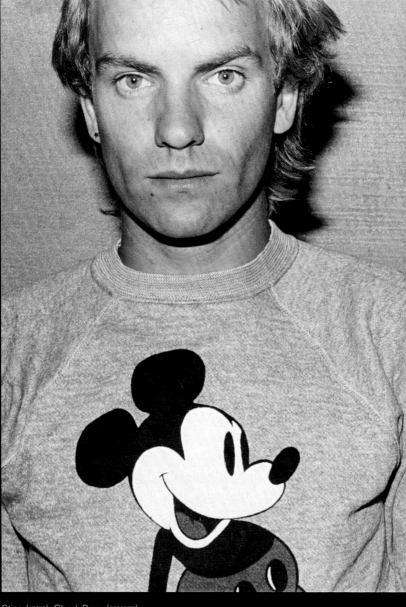

Sting (ABOVE), Chuck Berry (OPPOSITE)

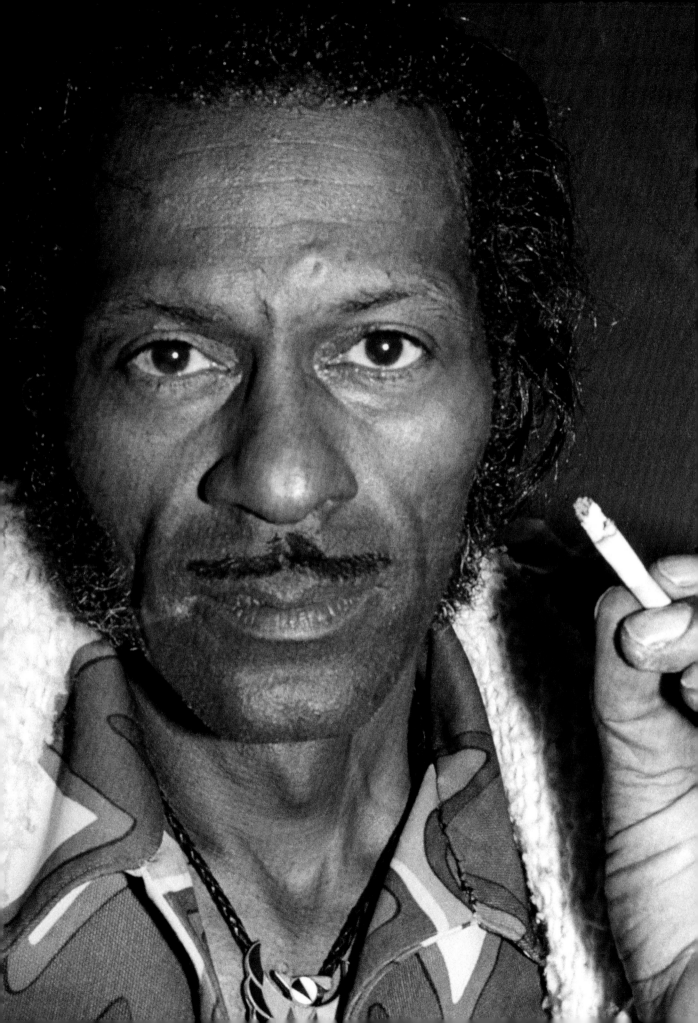

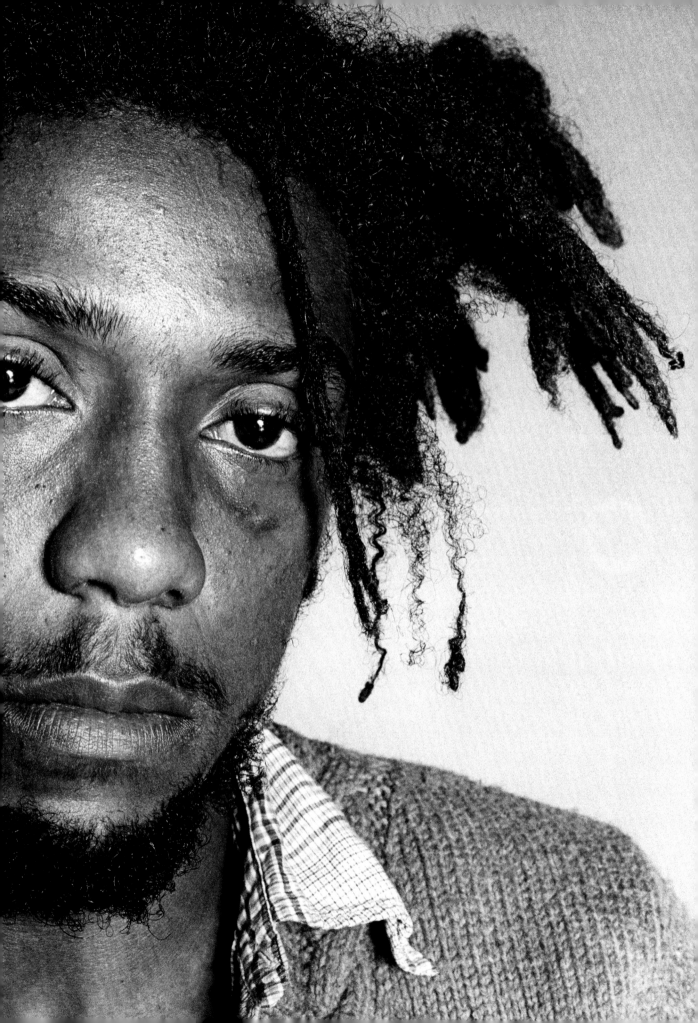

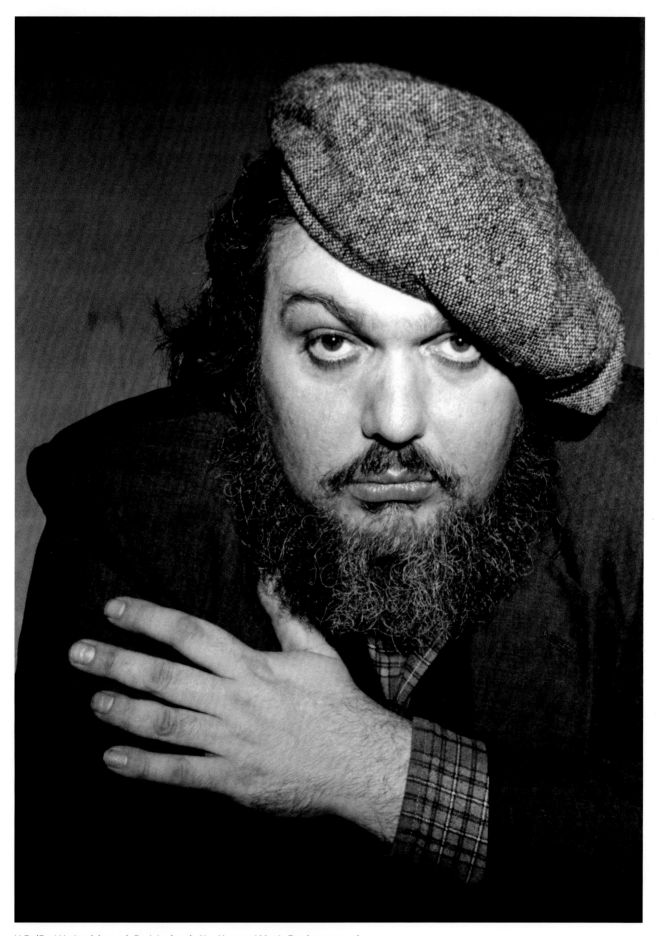

H.R. (Paul Hudson) (OPPOSITE), Dr. John (ABOVE), Alan Vega and Martin Rev (FOLLOWING PAGES)

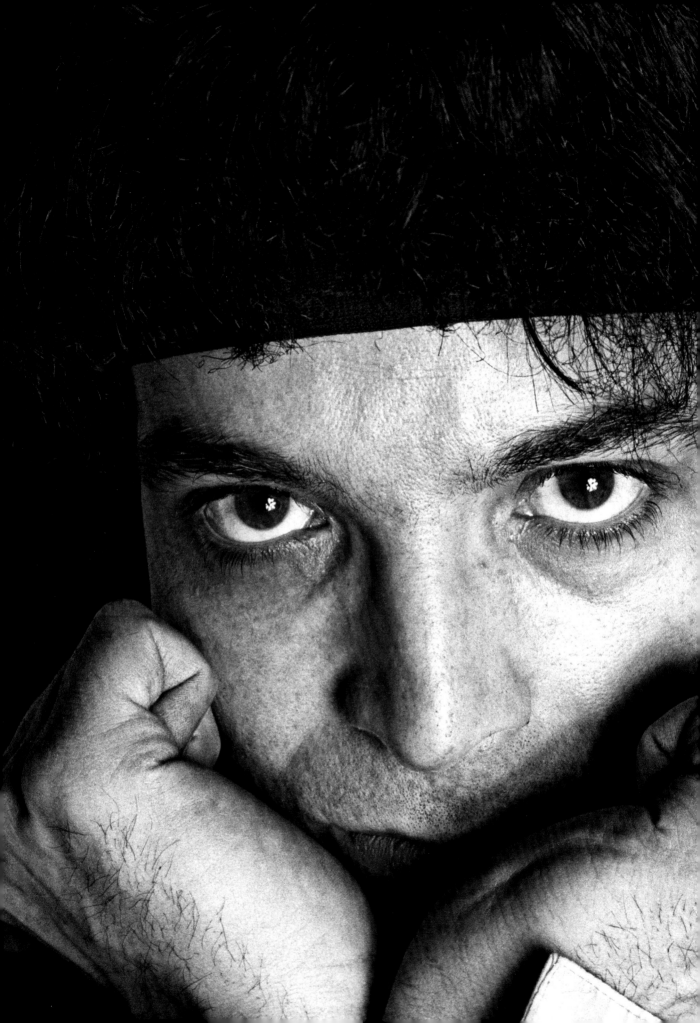

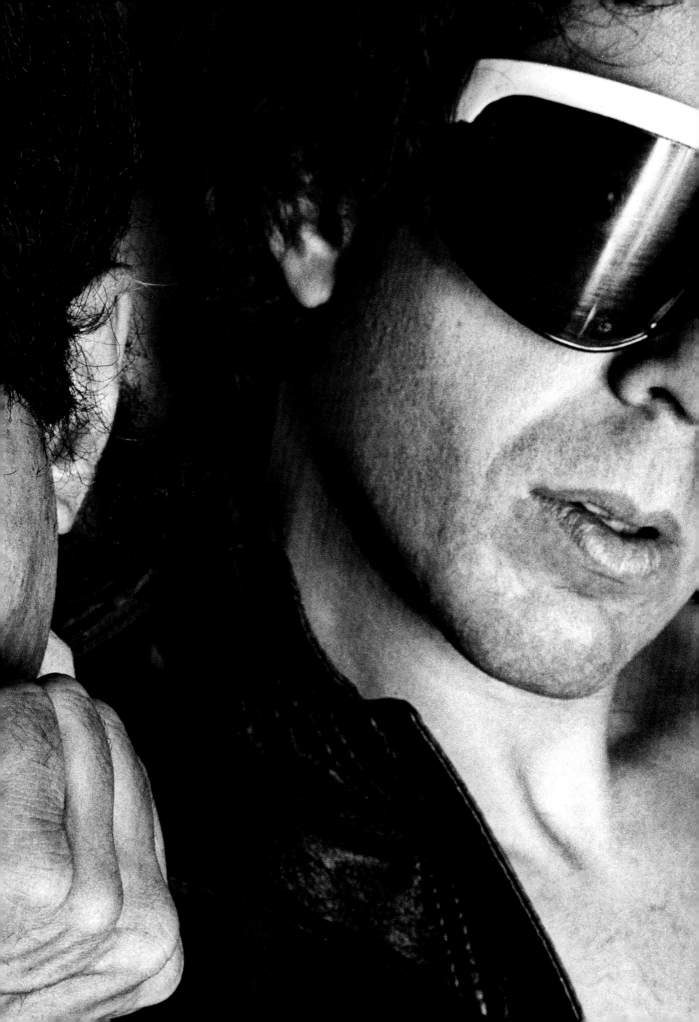

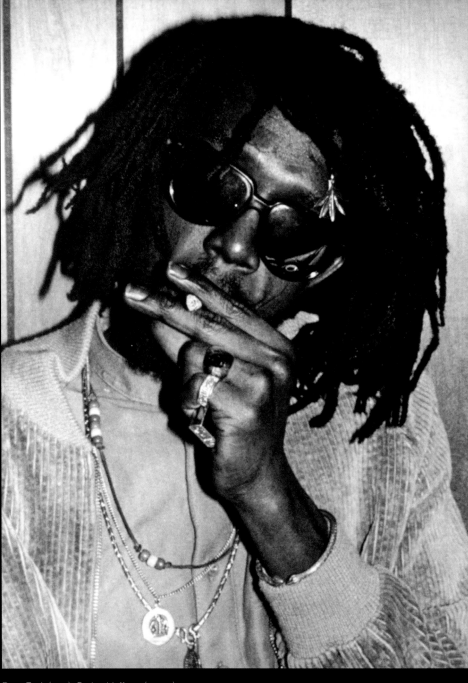

Peter Tosh (ABOVE), Garland Jeffreys (OPPOSITE)

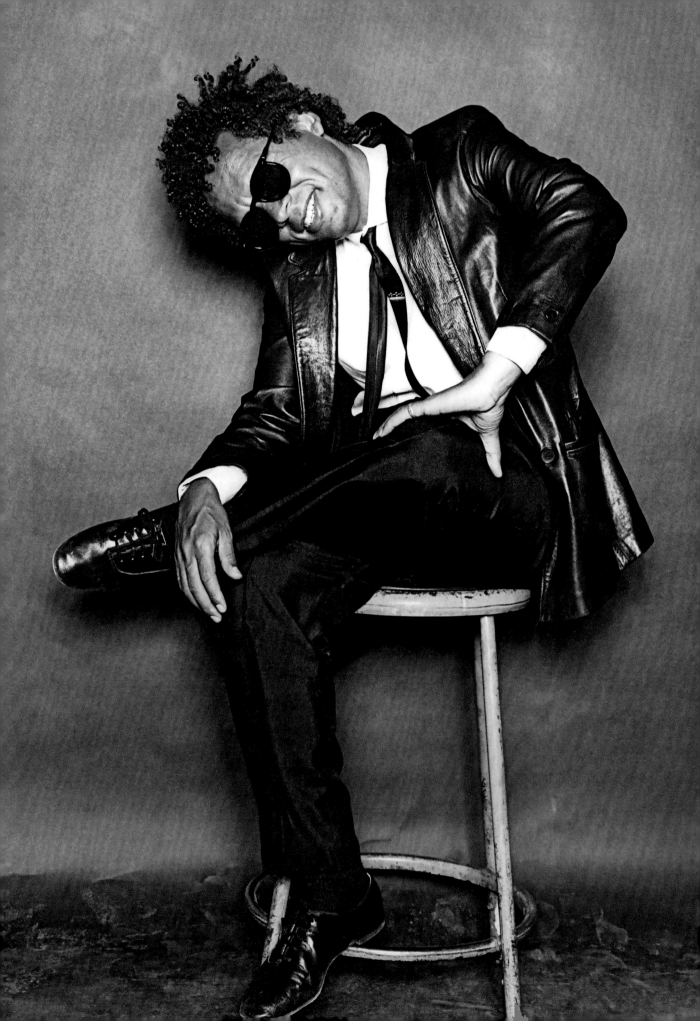

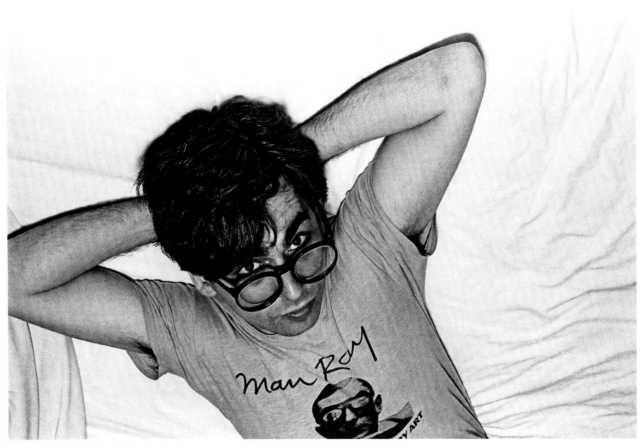

Chris Stein (ABOVE), Walter Steding (OPPOSITE)

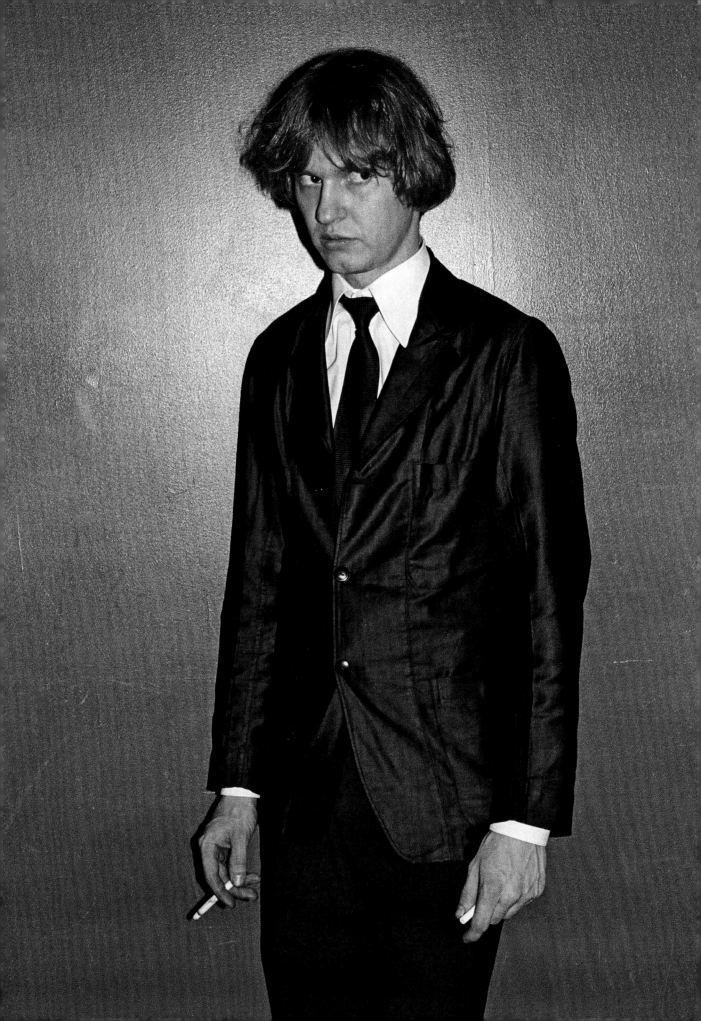

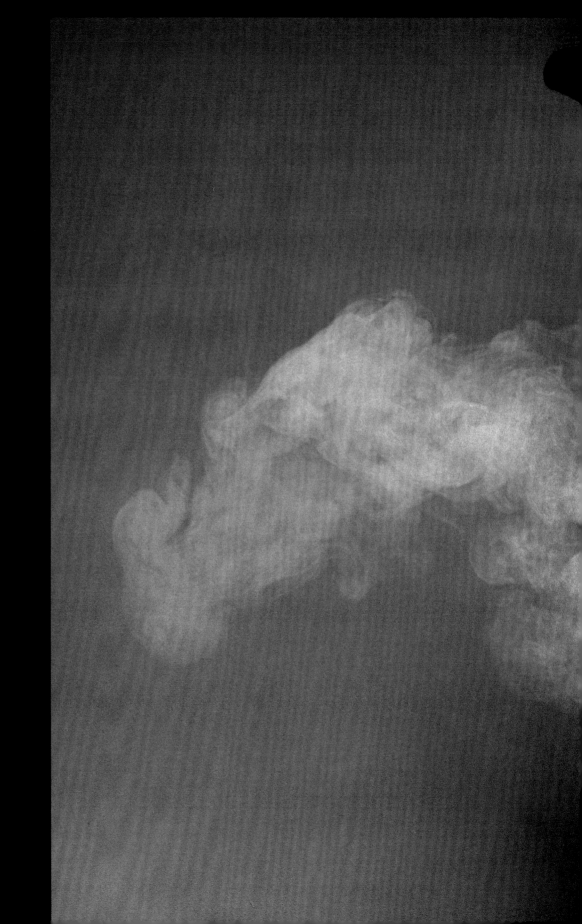

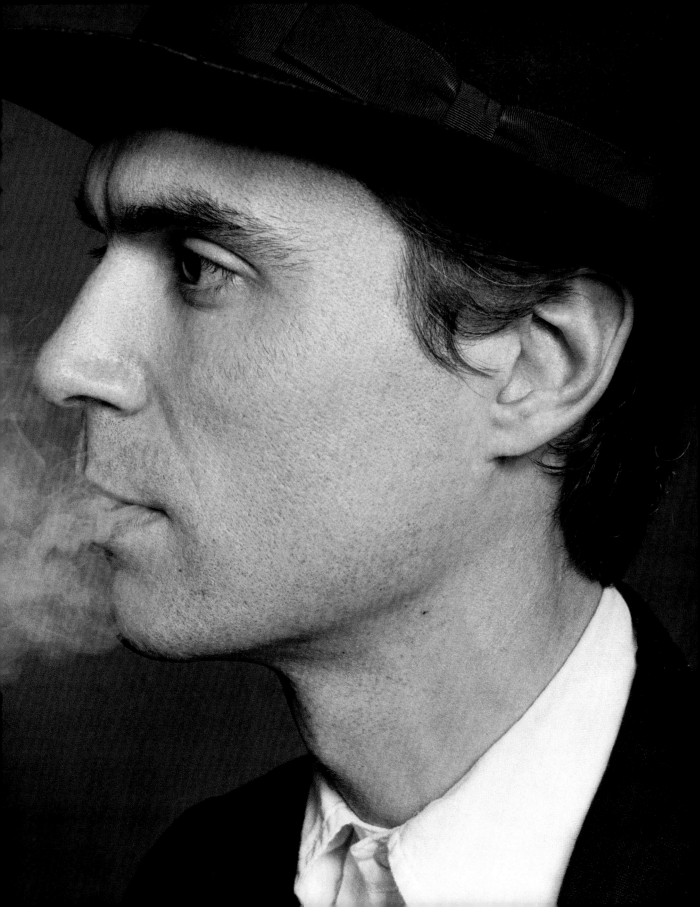

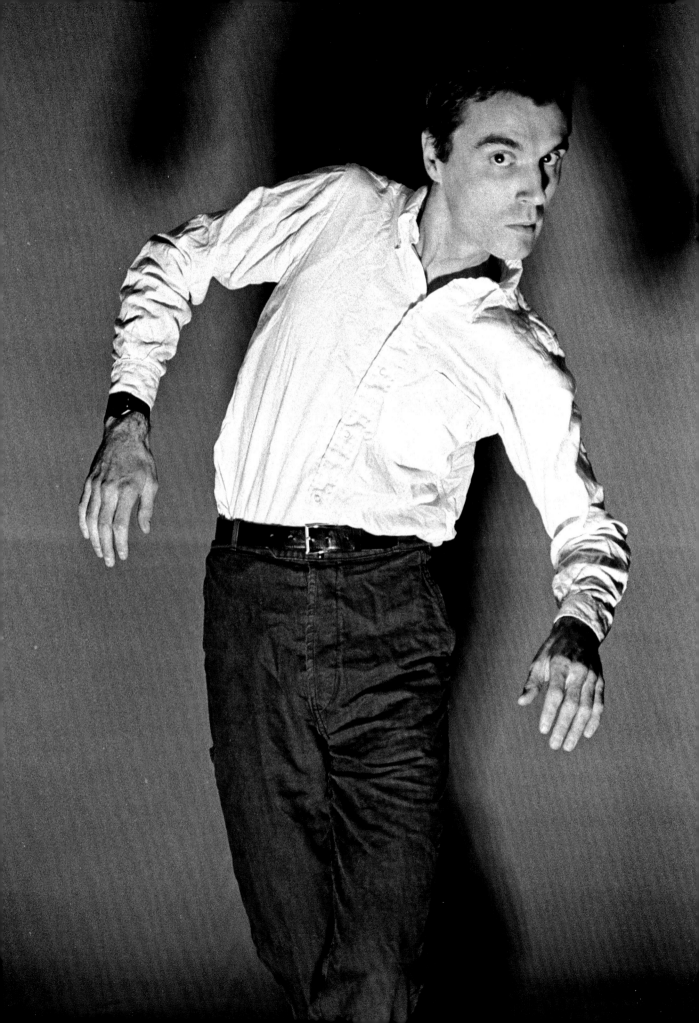

# DAVID BYRNE

IN 1977, David Byrne met Brian Eno during a Talking Heads–Ramones tour of the United Kingdom, where David was later described in *Mojo* as "a mad-eyed frontman who looked like Gregory Peck's undernourished younger bother and sang as if enduring a manic episode." Between 1978 and 1982, Eno produced three classic Talking Heads albums and both men did some of their best work, culminating in the Byrne-Eno collaboration *My Life in the Bush of Ghosts*. They both approached songwriting as a journey of discovery, with similarly playful spirits.

Many of Marcia's men have their roots in writing. David Byrne is a good example. He once came to a party at my apartment on Perry Street and agreed to contribute a list of predictions, titled "In the Future," to my roommate Jeff Goldberg's in-house magazine, *Traveler's Digest*. Out of forty-six predictions at the end of 1977, these stand out vividly today:

In the future half of us will be "mentally ill."

In the future water will be expensive.

In the future everyone's house will be like a little fortress.

In the future there will be mini-wars going on everywhere.

In the future people will constantly be having plastic surgery,

altering their features many times during a lifetime.

In the future there will be many mass suicides.

In the future there will be starving people everywhere.

In the future the crippled, retarded, and helpless will be killed.

In the future there will be so much going on that no one will be

able to keep track of it.

More recently, David has taken to writing books. I recommend his latest, *How Music Works*. It includes an intriguing chapter called "How to Make a Scene," in which David uses the punk scene that inspired Marcia to pursue *Punks, Poets, & Provocateurs* to show his readers what you need to make your own scene today. His key points are:

–There must be a venue of the right size in the right place, like CBGB.
–The artists must be able to perform their own material.
–Performers must get in free on their off nights and have free drinks.
–There must be a shared sense of alienation from the current scene.
–Rents must be low.
–Bands must be paid fairly.
–No social gap between musicians and audiences.
–Do girls like it?

"The mere existence of CBGB facilitated the creation of the bands," he wrote. "Some of the most innovative and viscerally moving theater in America at that time was not being made in proper theaters, but taking place on the stage of this grotty club on the Bowery." He states, "If I were to diagram the art/music connections, I might say that the Ramones and Blondie were Pop-art bands, while Talking Heads were minimalist or conceptual art with an R&B beat. Suicide was minimalism with rockabilly elements. And Patti Smith and Television were romantic expressionists, with a sometimes slightly surrealist slant."

Elsewhere in the book, he writes, "A certain romanticism about the cultural history of the area did linger in our minds. . . . William Burroughs lived nearby, as did Allen Ginsberg . . . they, and their attitudes toward life and art, were a part of a funky mystique that gave the squalor a kind of glamour in our eyes."

David Byrne

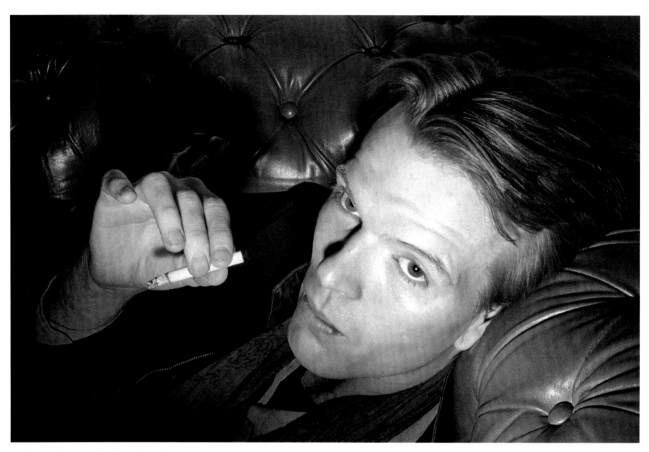

Jim Carroll (ABOVE), Philip Glass (OPPOSITE)

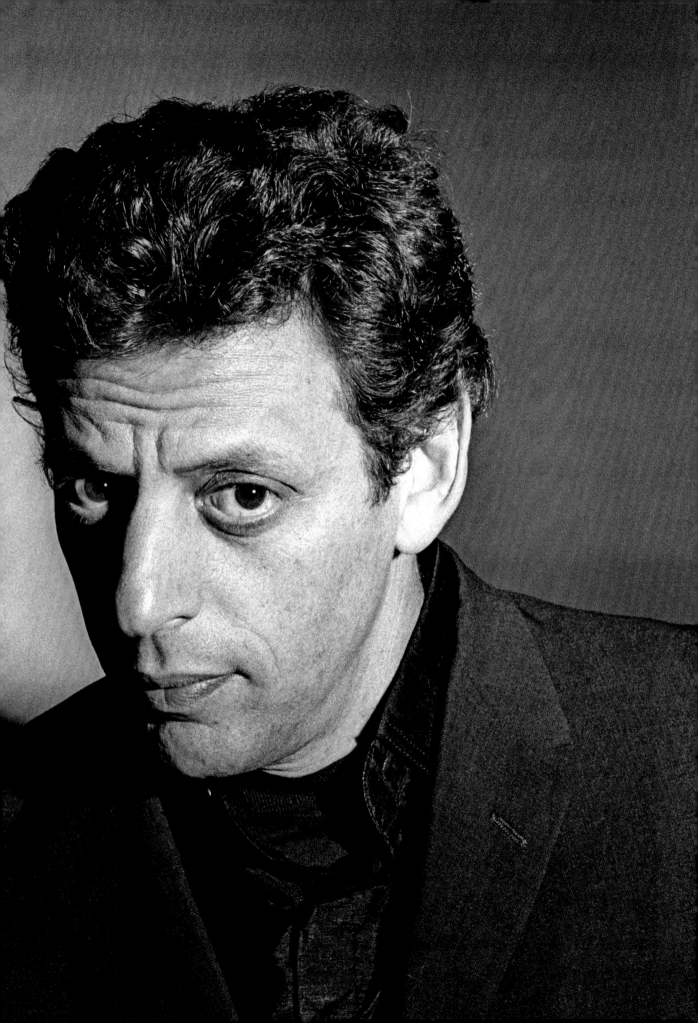

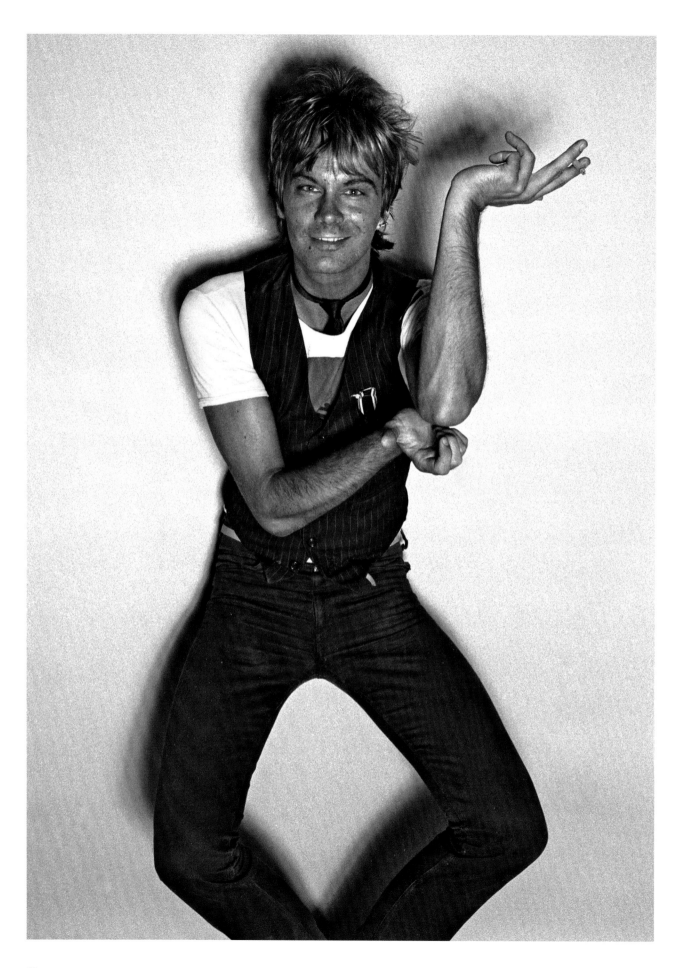

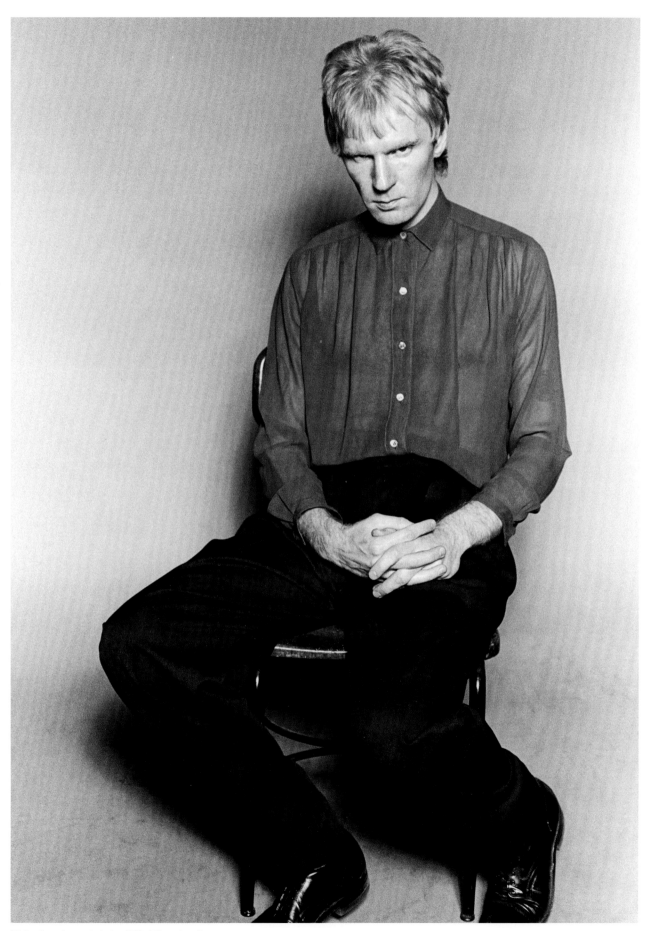

Walter Lure (OPPOSITE), Arthur (Killer) Kane (ABOVE)

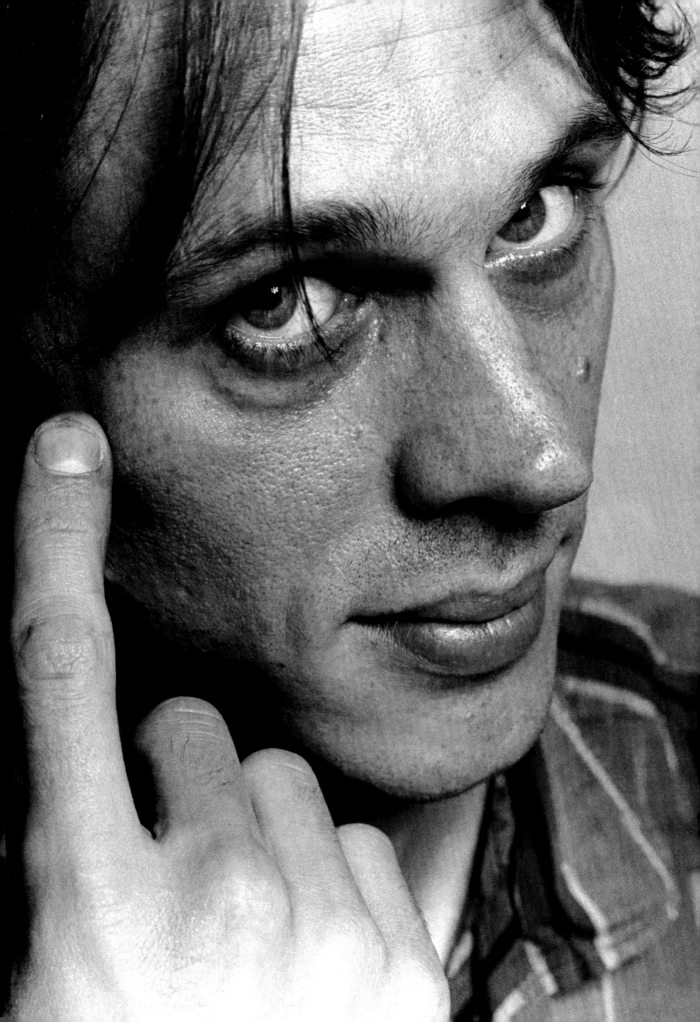

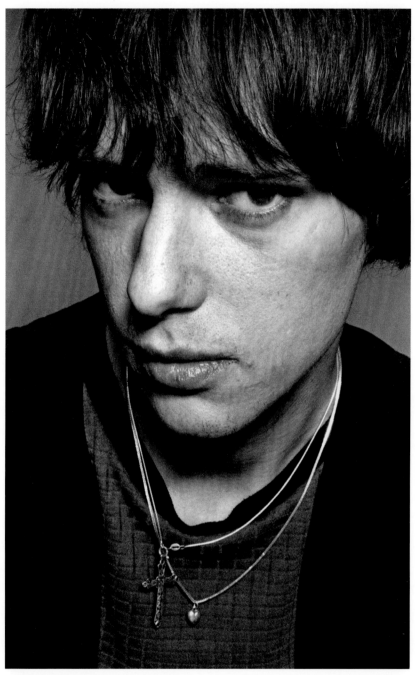

Tom Verlaine (OPPOSITE), Richard Lloyd (ABOVE)

# RICHARD HELL
## DINNER WITH SUSAN SONTAG

From *The Poetry Project Newsletter*, Winter 1992

*History is a form of sentimentality. Like the content of television shows. Television is abstract. It's a joke. History is a joke. Television and history are the center of nothing. They are auras, like hair, available for styling twenty-four hours a day.*
–*The Voidoid*, 1973

RICHARD HELL is one of the founding fathers of punk rock. Like several New York punk stars, he had his roots in the St. Mark's Poetry Project on Manhattan's Lower East Side. In 1974 he formed Television with longtime friend Tom Verlaine. In 1975 he left Television and formed the Heartbreakers with Johnny Thunders. By 1977 he was fronting his own band, the Voidoids, with the brilliant guitar player Bob Quine. Their album *Blank Generation* quickly became a punk classic.

I had known Richard since 1972. One of his favorite writers was Susan Sontag. In February 1978, I gave a dinner party for Richard and Susan in my apartment and tape-recorded the conversation for Andy Warhol's *Interview*. Susan had almost finished her book *Illness as Metaphor*. Richard was in the midst of starring in the film *Blank Generation*.

According to Hell in his memoir, *I Dreamed I Was a Very Clean Tramp*:

> I'd long admired Sontag, as did most halfway literate people. She was about twenty years older than me and had been a trendsetter among New York intellectuals all that time. She set the standard for aesthetic and moral values, and for subtlety of perception, in her essays on literature and film (and dance and photography, and a few other art mediums). She affirmed an "erotics" of art rather than an interpretation of it. Furthermore, she was beautiful physically and a gracious, charming person. . . .
> The dinner was just the three of us, in February, at Bockris's apartment on Perry Street in the West Village. It was a magical few hours, tucked cozily murmuring and laughing, in that little apartment . . .

RICHARD HELL: The way I feel is that the generation I belong to has more in common among its members than any other generation that ever existed because of television and public school systems. What I'm relying on is that if I go as far as I can *being* myself that it will arouse something in all those people, but the problem is that you then become *merchandise*. . . . You realize that as a commodity, who also has all the same intentions and attributes of somebody who's working in high art, the way to protect yourself is to regard celebrityhood as being your real art form. It's just your personality that's the commodity and not your work. That's the only way to stop being packaged by the merchandisers. They then become your tool rather than you becoming theirs.

SUSAN SONTAG: Most people who are involved in so-called high arts, if they have any degree of success, would describe very similar things. One way of being a celebrity is to make yourself totally inaccessible and never manifest yourself and never do anything and be as pure as the driven snow. Your purity will become a product, and it can be sold, and it can make your reputation. But do you think, Richard, that rock has really changed people? I know it has changed me, but then my whole being is interested in being changed by what I experience, I'm open to change.

RICHARD: Oh yeah, incredibly. By marijuana legalization, by Jimmy Carter getting elected, by hair lengths. The fact that on the radio every day during the '60s there was this information coming across that affected what happened to the world . . .

Richard Hell

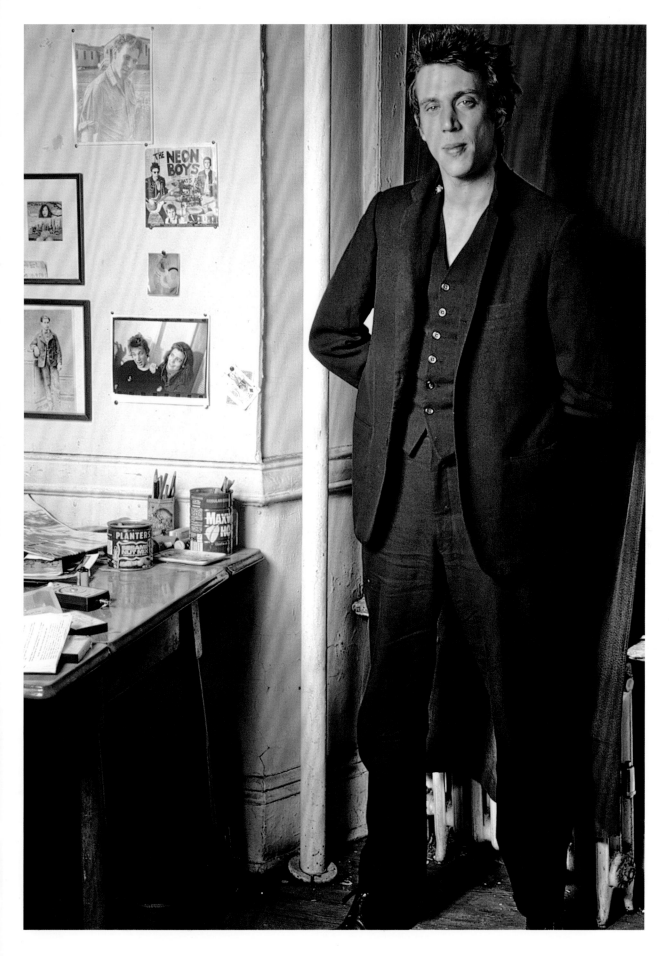

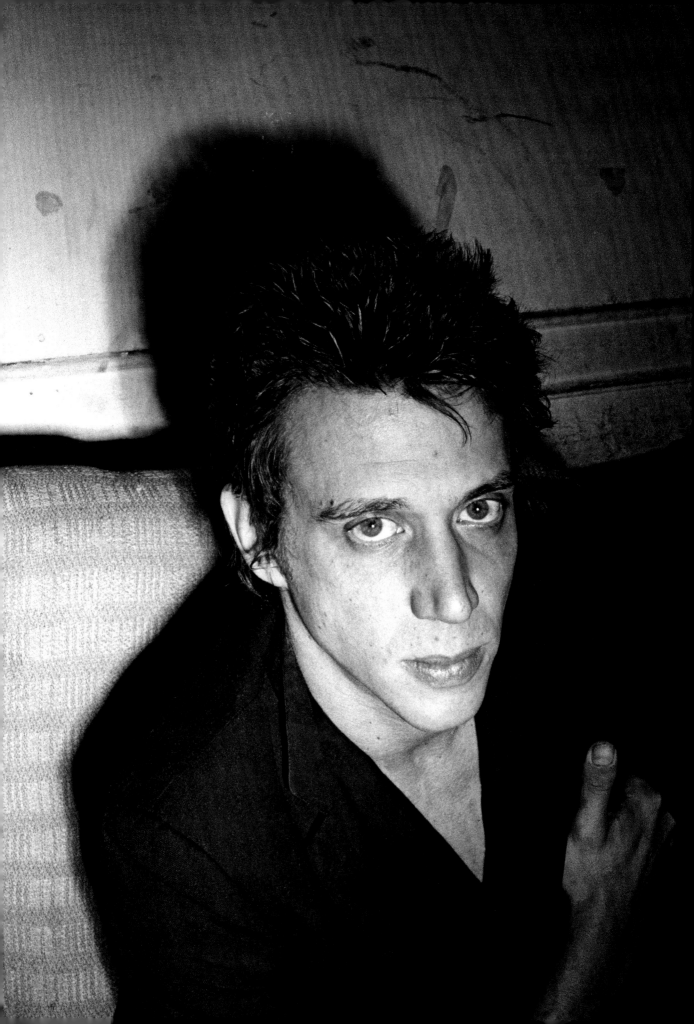

SUSAN: . . . But then what happened in the '60s was really interesting. People started buying records and listening to records the way they were buying and reading books. You'd play a record and listen to a record by yourself and then talk about it. That did not exist before the '60s.

RICHARD: There was an extraordinary number of teenagers in the '60s. There became this thing where suddenly there was this specific period of life—teens. There was acknowledged a period between being a child and being grown-up and this became power. . . . It's a very subtle consciousness, being a teenager.

SUSAN: Which can last to approximately thirty-five.

RICHARD: It's the most attractive consciousness to speak with. It's the most sensitive because it hasn't solidified yet.

SUSAN: It hasn't completely sold out. Essentially what's happening is that everybody's got ten more years, that's my idea. In other words, for a woman to be in her early forties now is just like being in her early thirties a generation ago. It used to be when you were over thirty you were old, you were out of it, finished. Now people start to have that anxiety at forty, and even at forty they manage to stave it off and go on. Also it's terrific how people have a much longer time in their lives to be young and they look better.

RICHARD: . . . The way I feel, I want to encourage in my songs and stuff, that feeling of being an adolescent throughout your whole life, of rejecting the whole idea of having a self, a personality.

VICTOR: Are you writing songs during this period while you're making movies?

RICHARD: I just wrote one last night: "The Kid with the Replaceable Head." No, I haven't actually written any since the album came out, until last night, because I've been working on this movie. What I usually do, really, as a policy is to do it at the absolute last minute. I figure you know more at the last minute than you did at the next-to-last minute.

SUSAN: I always put everything off until the last minute too. . . .

RICHARD: . . . Are you still interested in making movies?

SUSAN: Yeah, I'd love to make movies, but I had a very discouraging experience with distribution. I had a very good experience making them. I'm not enough of a businesswoman to know how to organize distribution. The problem is there aren't any theaters [for independent films] anymore. That's something you're going to discover with this movie you're in, Richard, and I hope it goes well. That's the most heartbreaking part of it. You have this thing, and then maybe it goes to some festivals, okay, and gets some reviews, and where is it? It ends up in some colleges.

RICHARD: That's my base fear.

SUSAN: . . . A lot of theaters have been taken over by sex films. There just aren't the theaters where [independent films] can be shown. I mean, even Fassbinder—how many people have actually seen a Fassbinder movie? . . .

VICTOR: . . . Do you think people are still fascinated by space, or has that fascination been killed?

SUSAN: I'm amazed by how unfascinated they are. In 1969 when people went to the moon it was amazing how unimpressed people were.

RICHARD: . . . The only kind of travel which is available now in space is not available to anyone but these astronauts, so it's really boring. Who cares about it if you can't go and the only thing is to watch it? My biggest ambition is to get out into space as soon as possible. . . . I've got this fantasy which says when I get to be forty they won't just be choosing astronauts to go. That's why I want to establish my reputation as a poet—so I can convince people in Congress that you gotta have a guy who can explain what it's like to be there . . .

Richard Hell

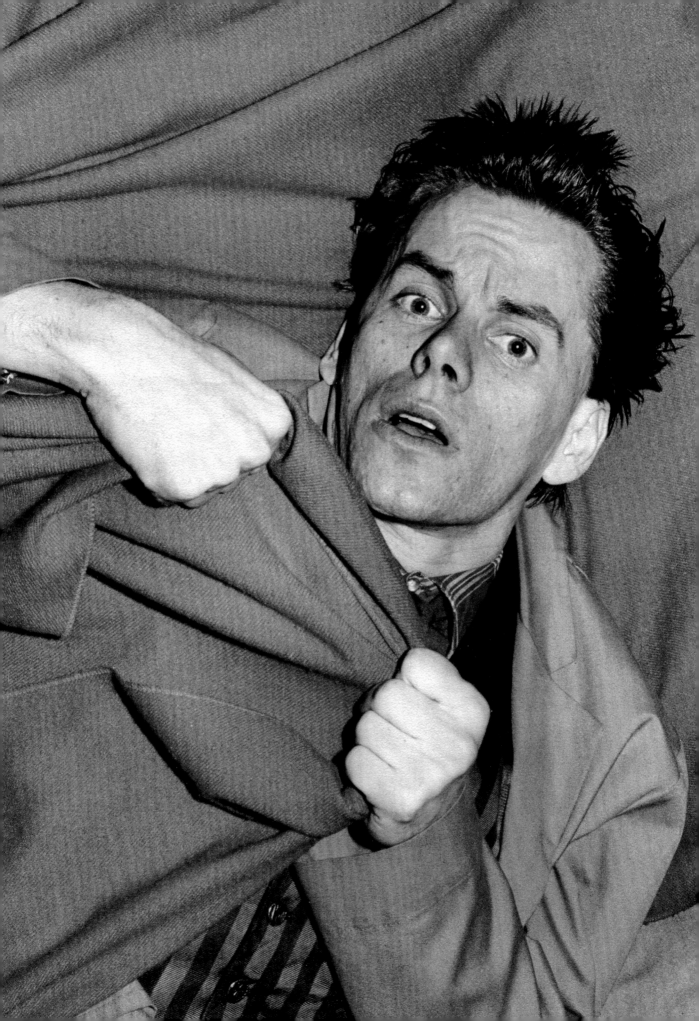

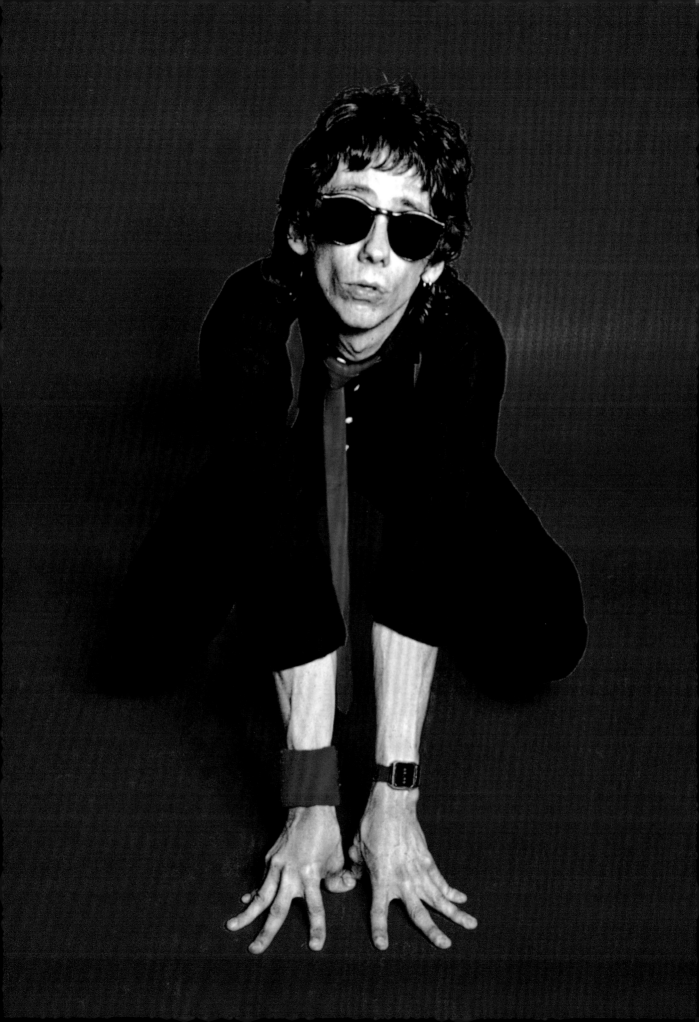

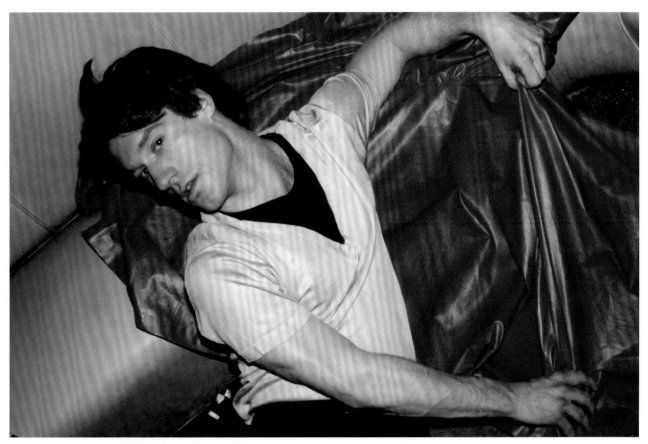

Stiv Bators (OPPOSITE), Lance Loud (ABOVE)

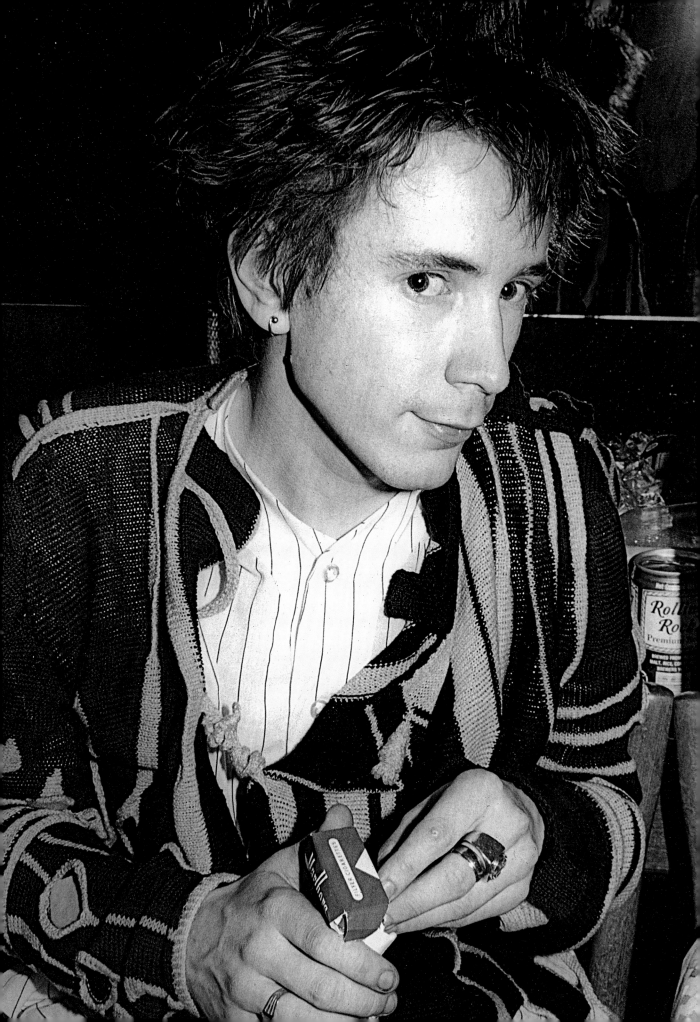

# JOHN LYDON
## ANGER IS ENERGY

*"Chaos was my philosophy."*
–John Lydon

JOHNNY ROTTEN (LATER KNOWN AS JOHN LYDON)—frontman of the Sex Pistols, the most dangerous band in the world, dubbed public enemy number one by the press—was a huge figure. Greil Marcus, in his legendary secret history of the twentieth century, *Lipstick Traces*, quotes the Who's Pete Townshend discussing the band:

> When you listen to the Sex Pistols, to "Anarchy in the U.K." and "Bodies" and tracks like that . . . what immediately strikes you is that this is actually happening. This is a bloke, with a brain on his shoulders, who is actually saying something he sincerely believes is happening in the world, saying it with real venom, and real passion. It touches you, and it scares you—it makes you feel uncomfortable. It's like somebody saying, "The Germans are coming! And there's no way we're gonna stop 'em!"

Marcia's 1981 photograph of John Lydon, taken backstage with his wife, Nora, at the Ritz in New York, pins him at a creative height. His second group, Public Image Ltd (PiL), had just released *The Flowers of Romance*. In *Rolling Stone*, Mikal Gilmore described the record as "the most brutal frightening music Lydon has ever lent his voice to."

Few stars of his magnitude have been able to turn their backs on their original bands and within the same year reach even greater artistic heights. John Lennon comes to mind with his solo albums between 1970 and 1974. In 1978, the year Lydon disbanded the Pistols, he introduced Public Image Ltd with punk veterans Jah Wobble and Keith Levene, then recorded with them over the next four years, 1978–1981.

"The Sex Pistols was a legacy," Lydon said in a 2003 interview with the fan site Fodderstompf. "It was a serious problem to have to deal with at the time about what I would do next. I didn't want to do anything like the Sex Pistols, and Public Image just came around really very naturally from just hanging around with Wobble and Keith. It just fell together. . . . We never really discussed much before we went in, we just chucked it all at once on the table, and worked it out that way. But that nervous energy and doubt and fear of your own capabilities is what makes it."

Over a career that now spans forty years, John Lydon has also become a good nonfiction writer. His first autobiography, *Rotten: No Irish, No Blacks, No Dogs* (1994), with its encomium to "enjoy or die," was damn good; a later volume, *Anger Is an Energy: My Life Uncensored* (2014), is even better. Like many great artists, Lydon suffered a severe childhood illness, at age seven, that opened up his road. John Harris wrote in the *Guardian* that the book's "fundamental spark" came from "the sense of raw working-class art, and someone driven to create by the furies to which the title alludes."

His association with punk is another line of continuity: although he transcended it, Lydon *is* punk. He always does the best he can, and he doesn't fuck around. An artist of great integrity, Lydon is, as he told Fodderstompf, "utterly fearless, 'cause I really *feel* what I'm doing. If you're not offering what you are to the world, then I don't want to know," he continued in the 2003 interview. "I'm not singing, I'm not a singer, I'm telling you how I feel, there's a difference. . . . I cry for humanity, I really do."

His current advice, shared in an interview with Channel 4 News' Jon Snow, is "Really, bloody learn to love each other properly."

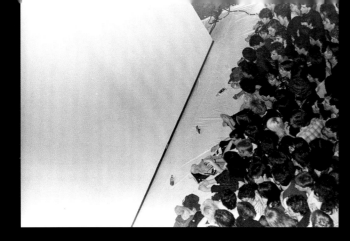

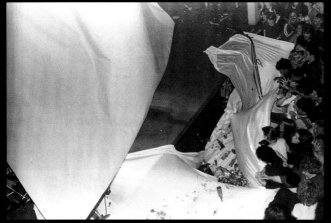

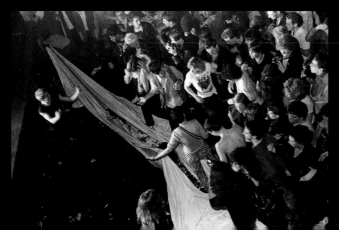

"When PiL played the Ritz in NYC on May 15, 1981, the audience had to wait outside in the rain for over an hour. Their expectations of seeing a spectacular show were crushed when they couldn't actually see their heroes, but saw only their silhouettes. Enraged, they lost it and began to assault the stage, throwing beer cans and chairs at the screen, while fighting amongst themselves. It was a great experiment in confrontation, but was also tragic. PiL was booed off the stage. After leaving the club, I began to understand how ingenious they were. People were complaining about being ripped off, but they couldn't stop talking about it."

—MARCIA RESNICK

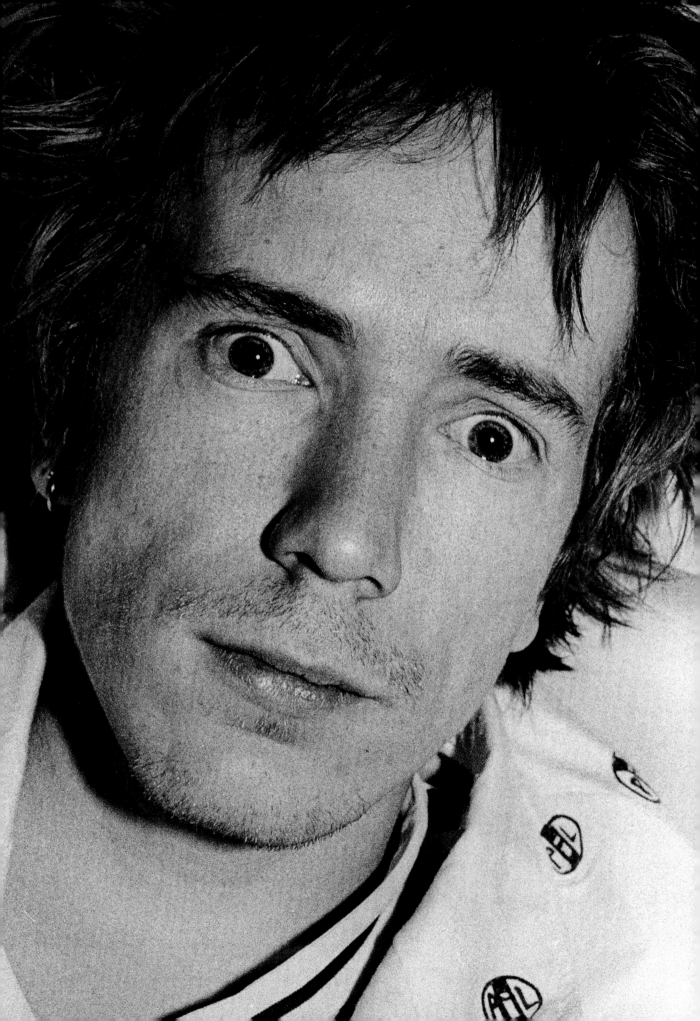

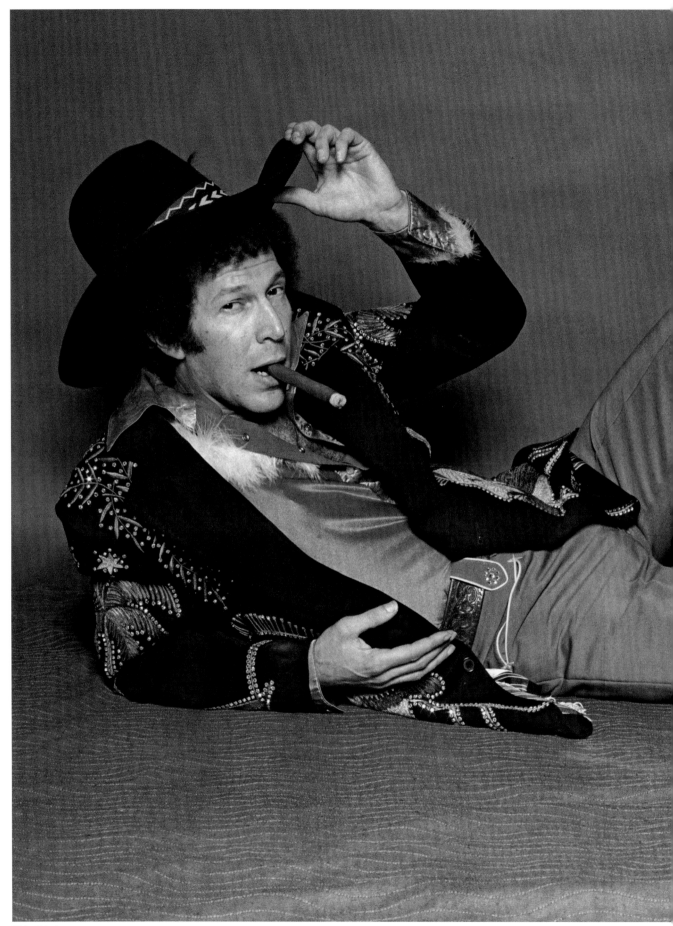

Kinky Friedman

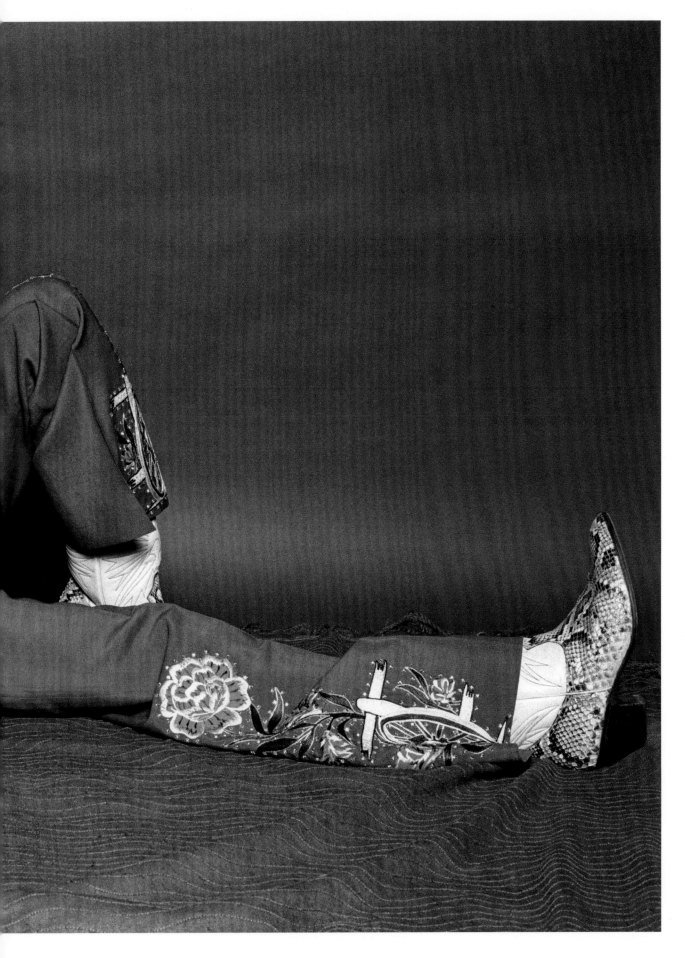

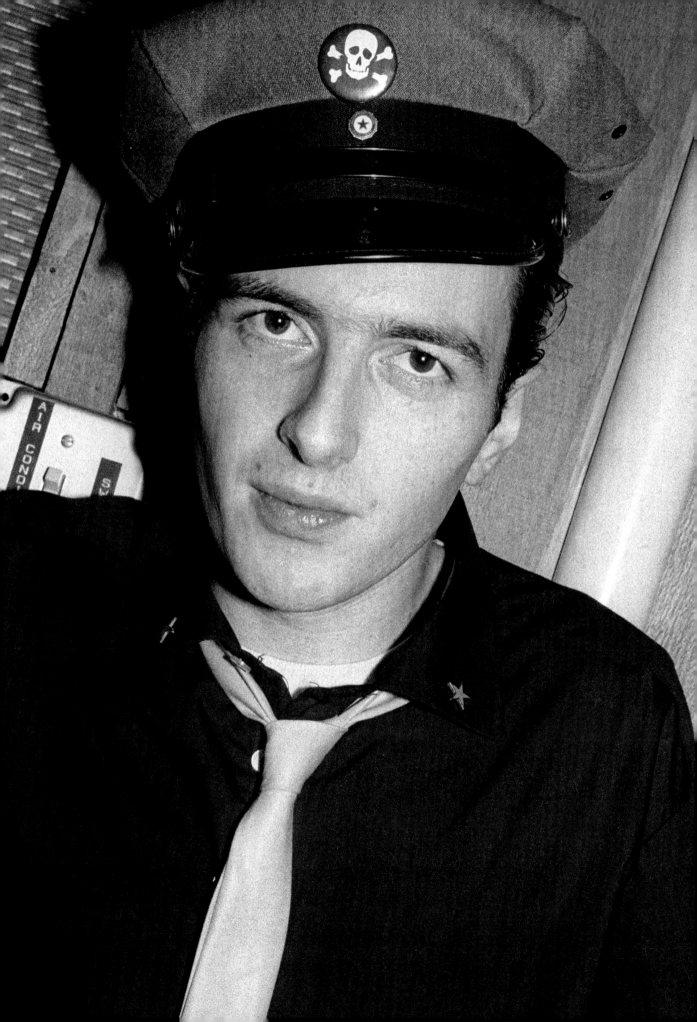

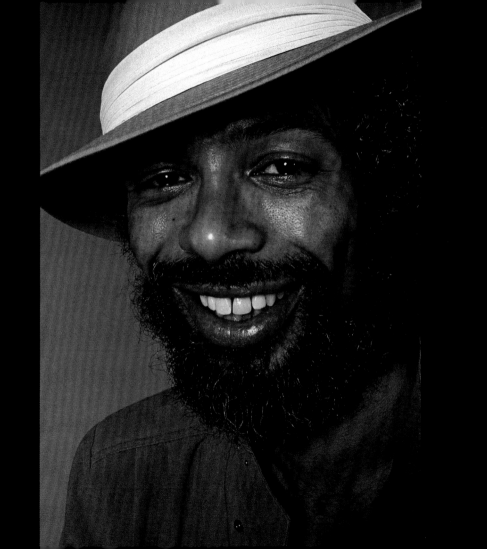

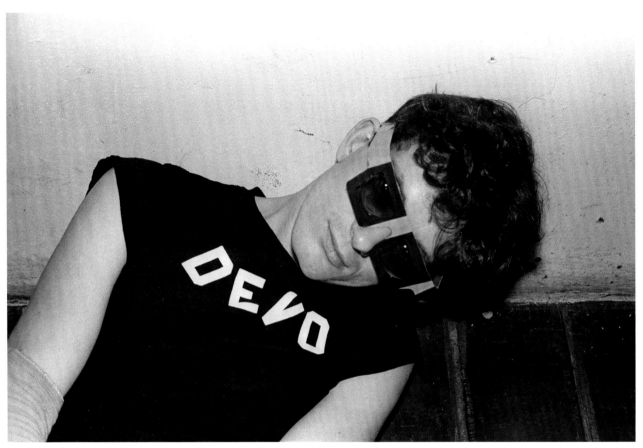

Mark Mothersbaugh (ABOVE), Jello Biafra (OPPOSITE)

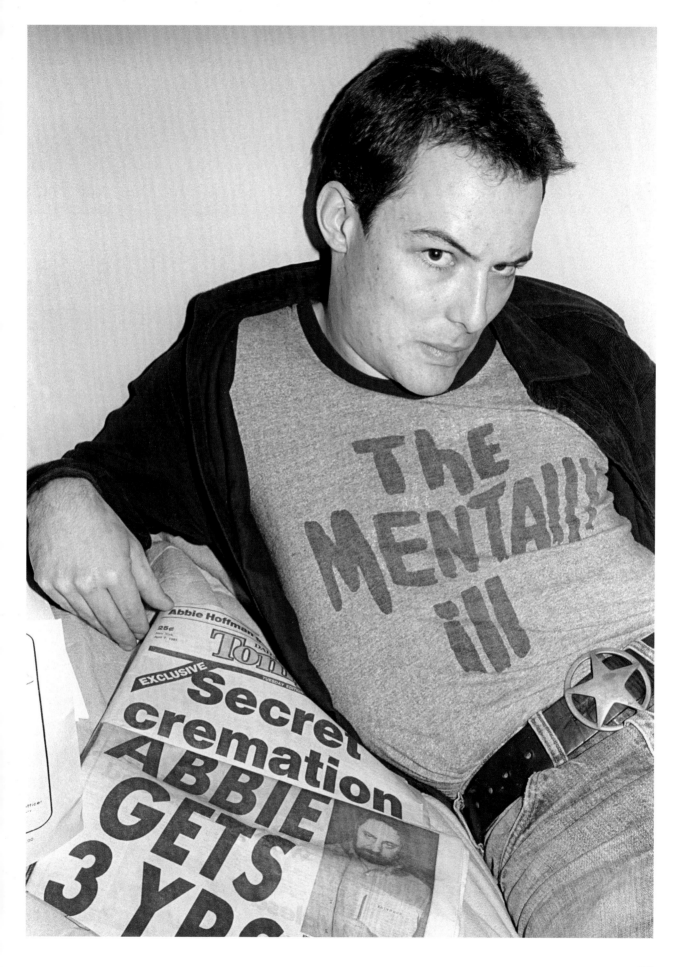

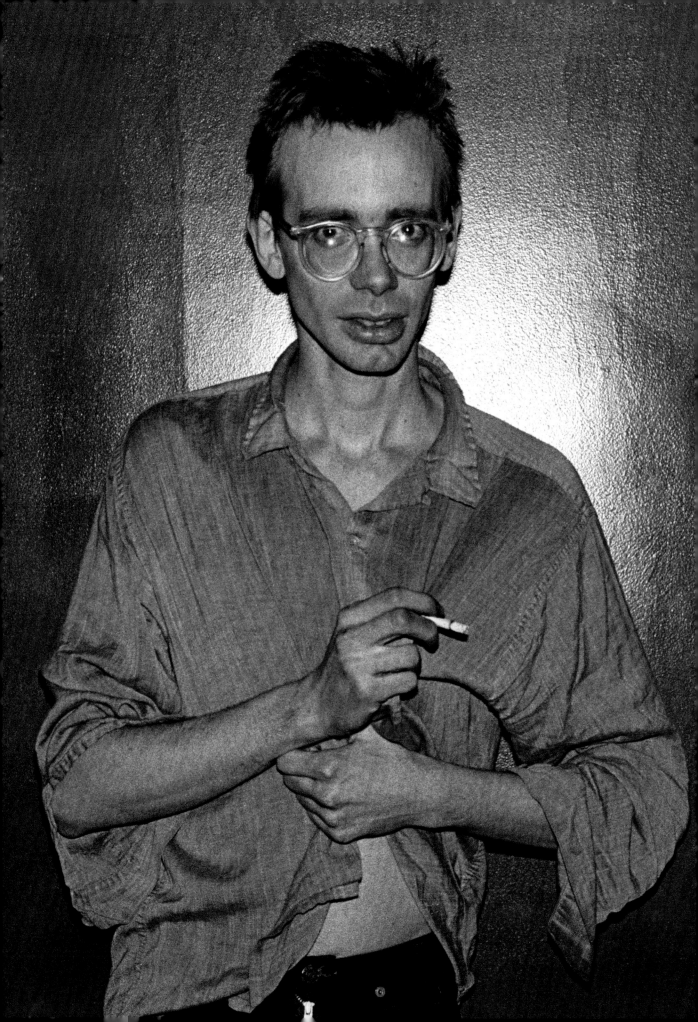

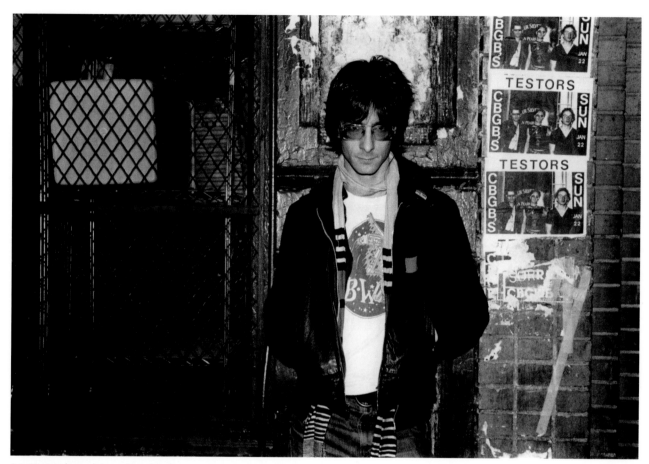

Arto Lindsay (OPPOSITE), Lenny Kaye (ABOVE)

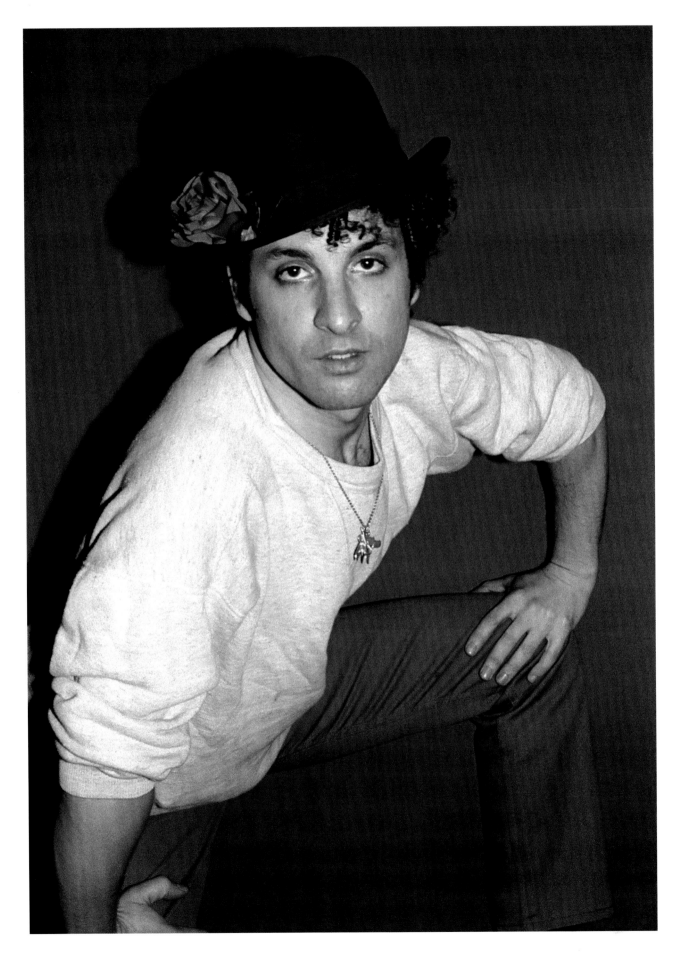

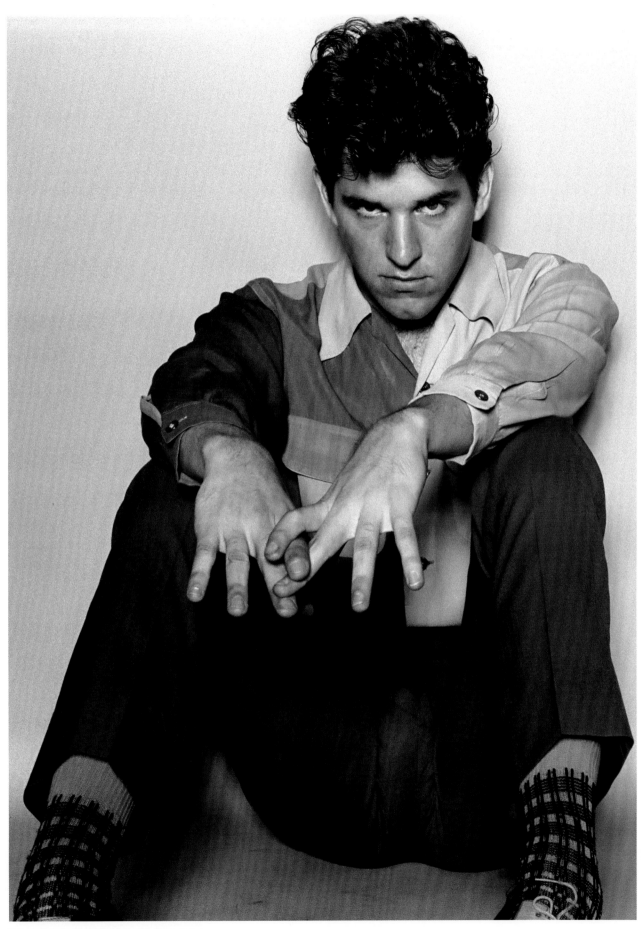

Sylvain Sylvain (OPPOSITE), Kristian Hoffman (ABOVE)

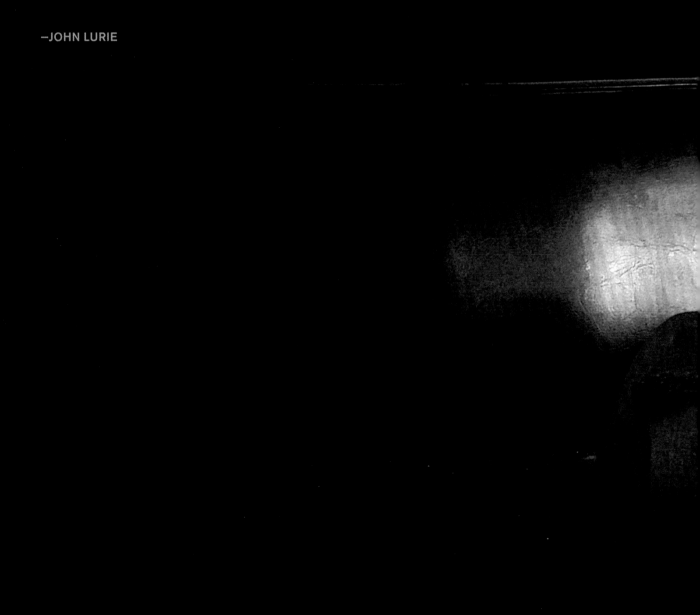

*"We were so sure of ourselves, we never doubted anything. We were powerful, smart, energetic, confident, egocentric and astonishingly naïve. Nothing outside of our fourteen block radius mattered."*

—JOHN LURIE

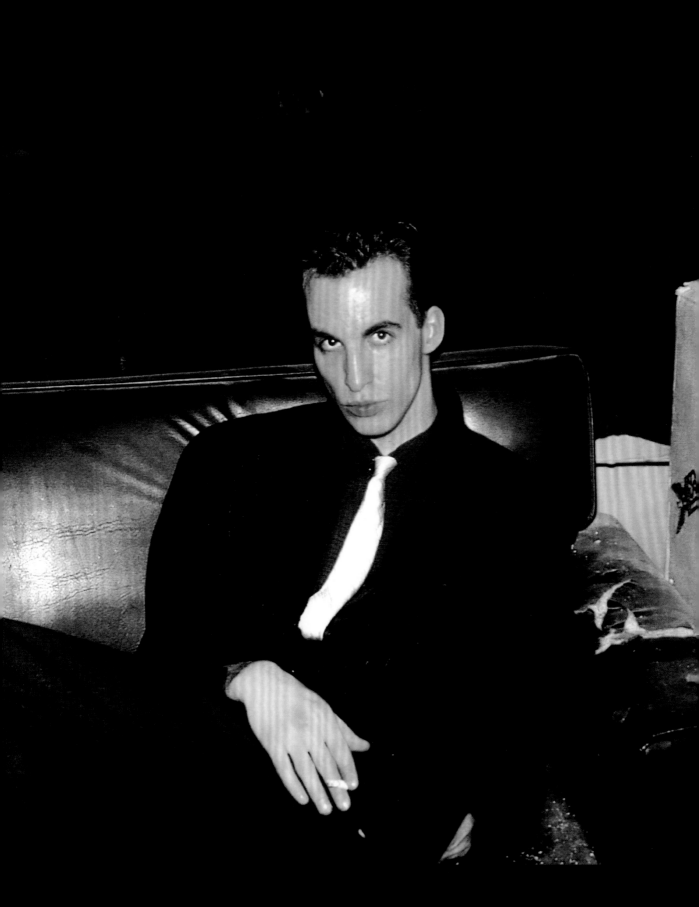

John Lurie

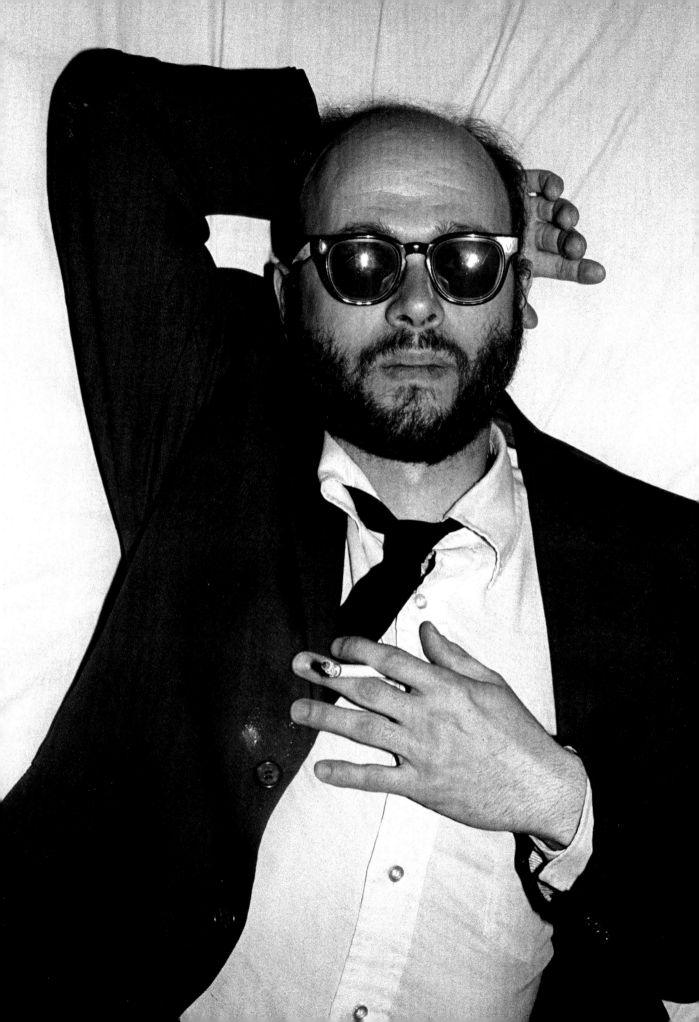

# ROBERT QUINE
## THE MAN IN THE BLUE MASK
From *Transformer: The Complete Lou Reed Story*

BOB QUINE was a unique figure in punk. Apart from being a brilliant musician, he was also one of the finest people I met during the time Marcia was taking these photographs. Like his closest friend, Lester Bangs, Bob Quine was an eccentric who hid a highly sensitive personality and a deep intelligence behind a series of masks. Of all the men who died in this book, Quine, who committed suicide in 2004 following the sudden death of his wife, had the most tragic passing. Marcia had a long, deep friendship with Quine; more than anyone, she tried to take care of him during his last days, despite the fact that her own boyfriend had committed suicide only weeks earlier.

Robert Quine, born in 1942, was from Akron, Ohio, where the DJ who gave rock and roll its name, Alan Freed, got his start. Though he had gone to law school and become a member of the Missouri bar, Quine had never practiced. Instead, in the early '70s he moved to New York to pursue his love affair with the guitar. A staunch Velvet Underground fan who had tape-recorded the band's San Francisco performances in 1969, Quine developed a slashing, tense style. "Lou Reed became such a big influence on my playing," he recounted. "He was a true innovator on the guitar who was never appreciated at the time. I completely absorbed his style. I've always liked those basic, simple rock-and-roll changes."

In the mid-'70s, Quine worked with Richard Hell, with whom he formed the Voidoids and recorded the groundbreaking album *Blank Generation*. Quine's spare, impeccably timed sonic assaults were in the vanguard of punk music.

"Around October 1977 we were playing at CBGB," Quine recalled. "I didn't know Lou Reed was there, but he was at the front table. We had done a pretty good set. I was walking by the table and he grabbed me and said, 'Man, you're a fucking great guitar player.'" Reed sat Quine down at the table and proceeded to lay into the band, snarling, "That is not a band you're playing with. I hope you know that. Music is about domination and power. You should fucking just dominate these people. They're not musicians. You should go over to the other guitar player and put him out of his misery." As somebody passed the table, Quine looked away for a second, suddenly Lou said, in a very low, serious voice, "When I'm talking to you, listen, goddamn it! When I'm talking to you, you look me in the eye, goddamn it, or I'll fucking smash you in the face—and I'm serious. I'm deadly serious."

Four years later, Quine got an opportunity to play with his hero. In October 1981, Lou went into RCA's studio in New York with his new band: Bob Quine on guitar, Fernando Saunders on bass, and Doane Perry on drums. Everybody knew the songs, but nothing was too structured. Quine remembered how liberating Lou's approach was: "We went into that studio with no rehearsals. I had a basic sound down on 'Waves of Fear.' I said, 'I think I can do this here,' and he was just surprised and happy. He pretty much liked everything I did. So I was free to come up with whatever I came up with."

Bob, who harbored a near-pathological fear of mediocrity, brought all the preventive emotion he could muster to the sessions: "I had my share of fear and anxiety," he remembered. "I always bring that to the studio almost deliberately; you play better, and it's a great relief and happiness when it works. That's the only way I can put it. But I would work myself up into a state of fear every day for the next session, because when really great stuff happens, you don't know exactly where it's coming from and you don't have a lot of control over it, so how can it happen again? Every night I'd come home, my girlfriend would see me freaking out, and I'd frantically trying to figure something out. 'Oh, no, this is fucked! I can't come up with anything decent on this song; I'm screwed!' And then it would just happen again."

Robert Quine

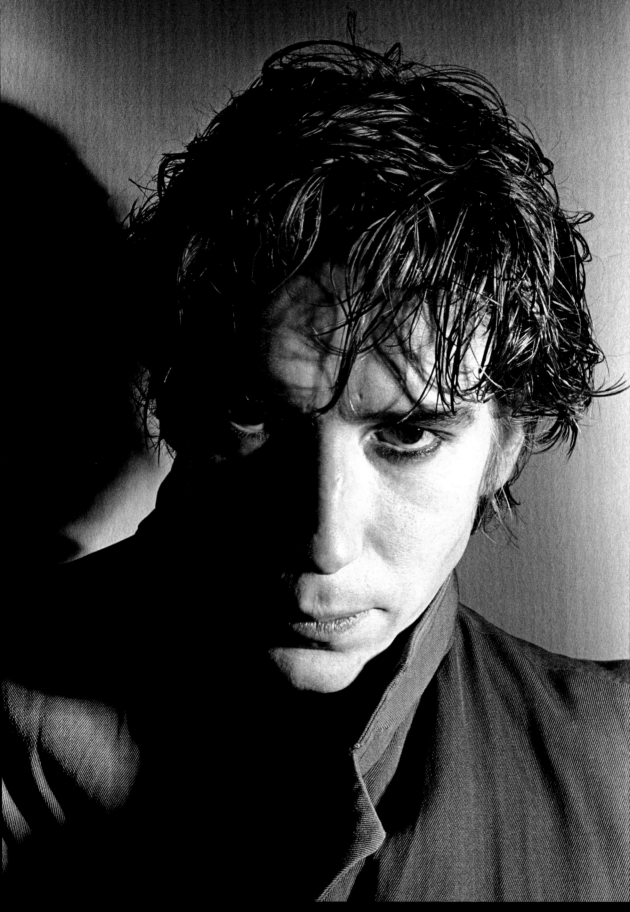

Richard Butler (ABOVE), Robert Gordon (OPPOSITE)

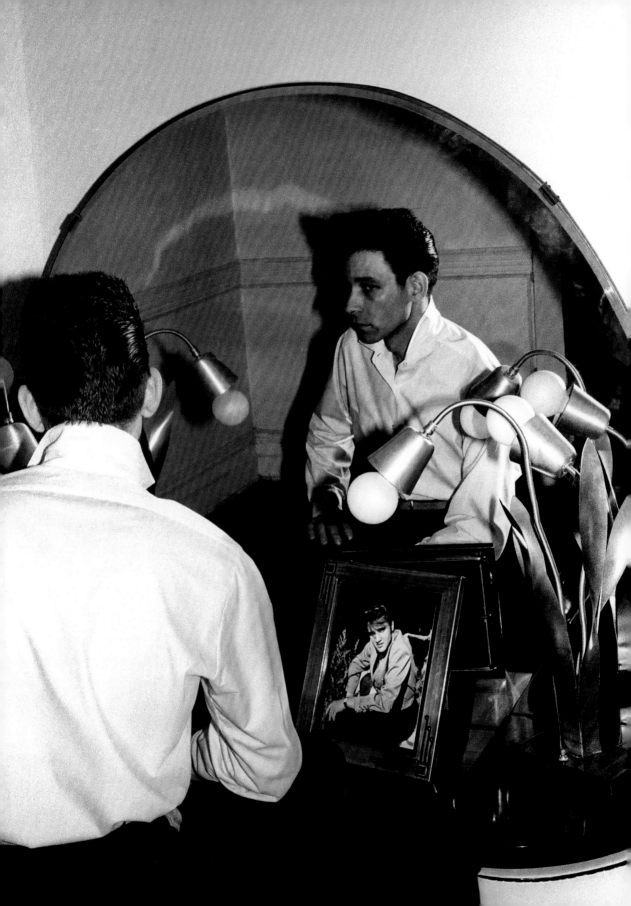

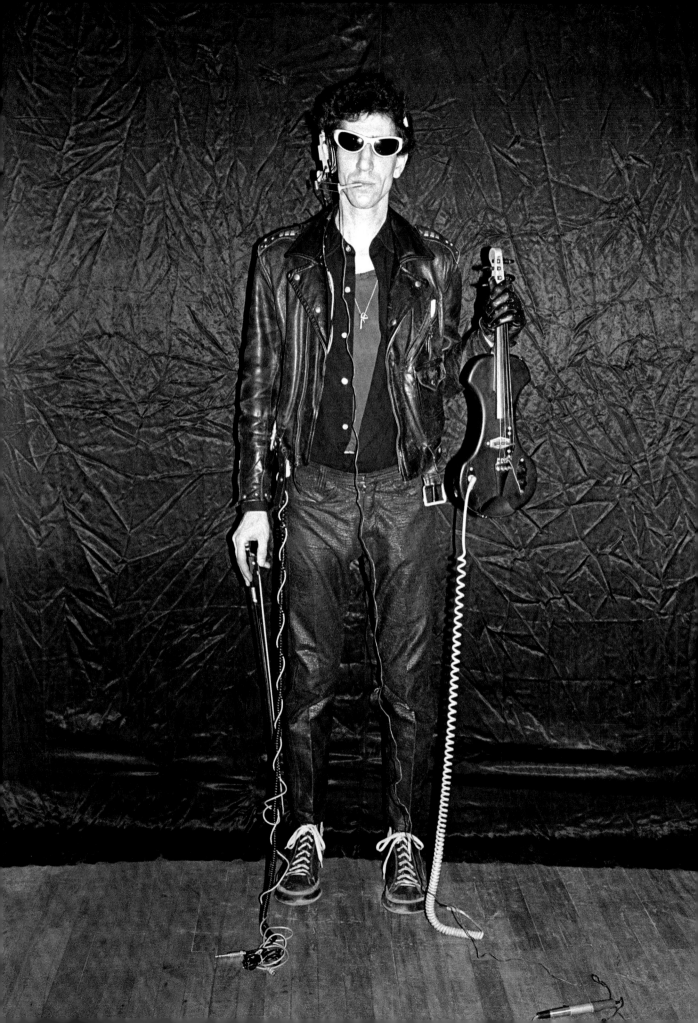

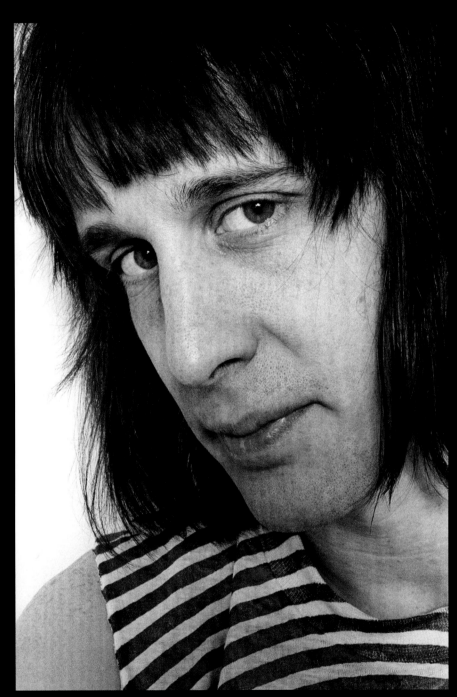

Boris (Policeband) (OPPOSITE), Todd Rundgren (ABOVE)

# JAMES CHANCE

*He still sings like a nervous, neurasthenic James Brown, plays manic squeals,*
*honks and moans on his alto saxophone, and shamelessly parodies both*
*James Brown's show business routines and his own reputation.*
–Robert Palmer, *New York Times*

## AARGH!

BY ROY TRAKIN

From *New York Rocker*, February 1979

ROY: Is the saxophone the only instrument you play?

JAMES: No, but I don't really wanna talk about that.

ROY: How long have you been playing?

JAMES: What interest is that to anybody? Why would anyone care how long I've played the saxophone?

ROY: I guess to get an idea of where you've been and where you're going. Do you not want to talk about your past?

JAMES: Not only that . . . I'm not interested in having a perspective on things.

ROY: Why do you insist on performing different types of music under different names? Why not emphasize your eclecticism, rather than deny it?

JAMES: Well, that's pretty boring.

ROY: Why did you change your name?

JAMES: To make it more commercial. Because I don't like my original one.

ROY: Do you believe in flexibility regarding the musicians you collaborate with, or do you favor sticking with one group through thick and thin?

JAMES: I hate all that sentimental crap. Every person in my band is totally for themselves.

ROY: Does that mean you allow each of the individual members to explore his or her own particular obsessions?

JAMES: I'm pretty dictatorial. I do what I think is right.

ROY: Was your entry into the music world through jazz?

JAMES: I'd rather we not discuss it.

ROY: What are your feelings about the *No New York* album? Are you satisfied with the results?

JAMES: Take it or leave it. They should buy it. I'm not giving them a free peek.

ROY: How did you feel about sharing the LP with the three other groups [Teenage Jesus and the Jerks, DNA, and Mars]? Do you feel akin to those groups or not?

JAMES: No! I feel akin to Teenage Jesus, but not the other two . . . wait, I don't feel akin to Teenage Jesus either.

ROY: What was your experience with Eno in the studio? Did you relate well to one another?

JAMES: I do not relate to people!!

ROY: Are you disappointed with the way it sounds?

JAMES: "Disappointed" is not a word I would use.

ROY: What is it about sentimentality, about viewing the past, that you abhor?

JAMES: It's liberal crap. I just don't want to hear about it. Why should I clog myself up with that garbage? I mean, I try not to sit around pondering. I try not to think.

ROY: Does that make you a man of action, then?

JAMES: No. I'm a man of reaction.

ROY: Haven't you discovered a community of peers with similar interests in the new wave?

JAMES: No!

ROY: You don't consider yourself part of any movement?

JAMES: Aargh! No! I despise movements! I'd never be part of a movement!

James Chance

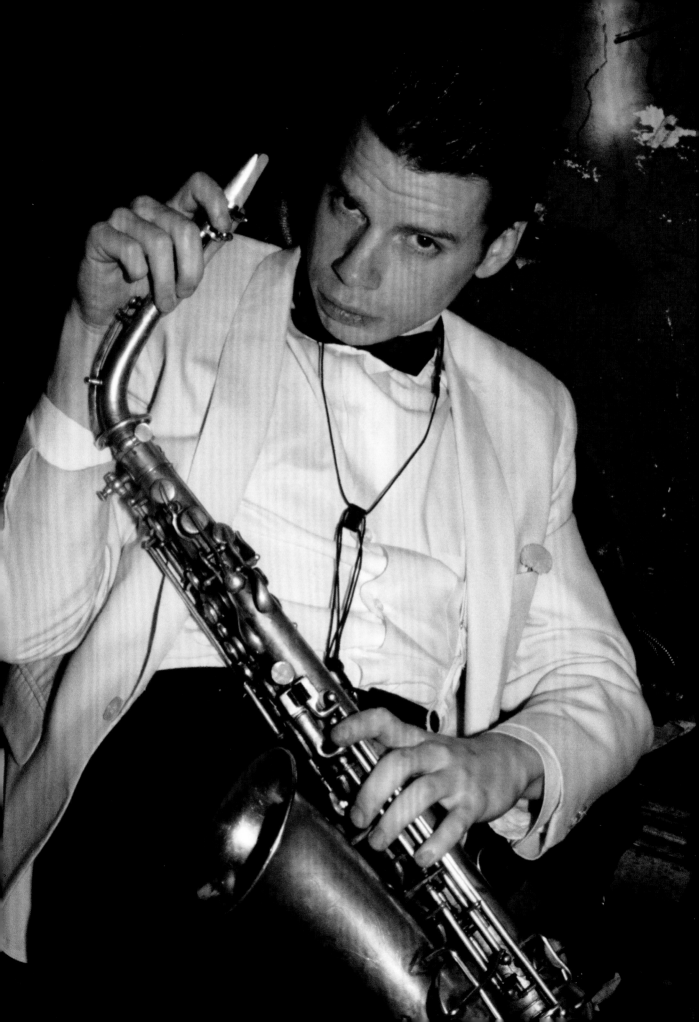

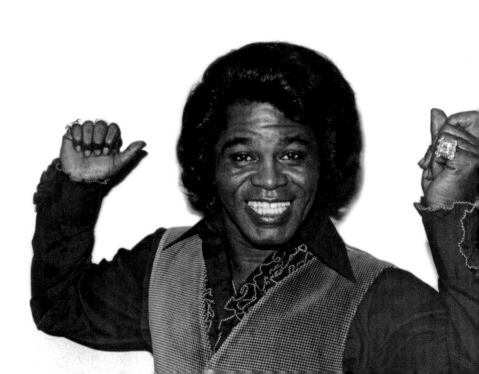

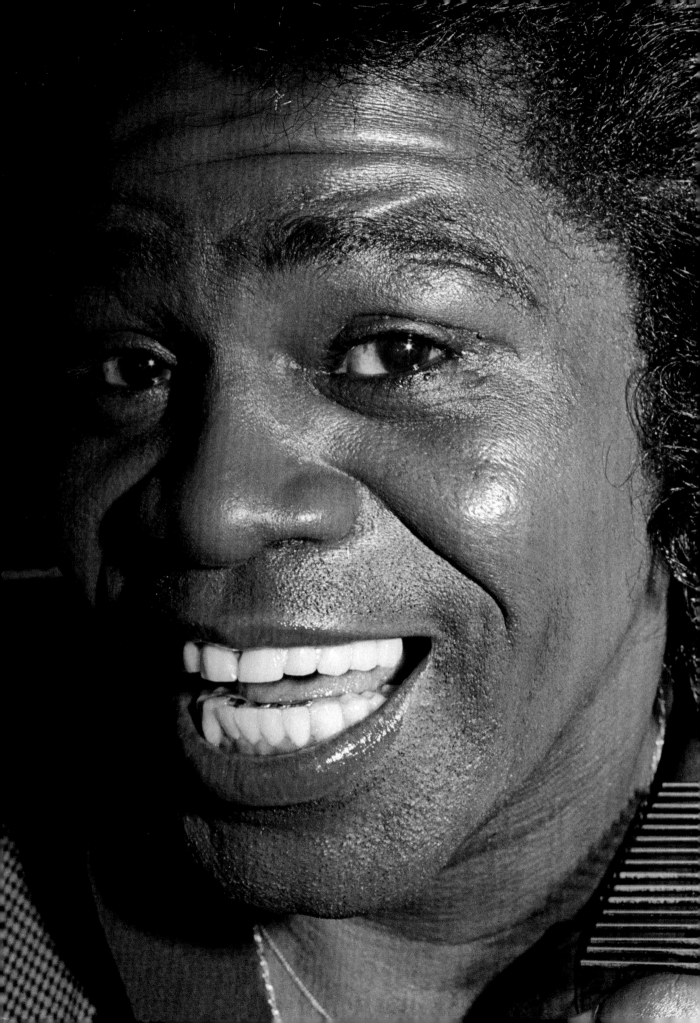

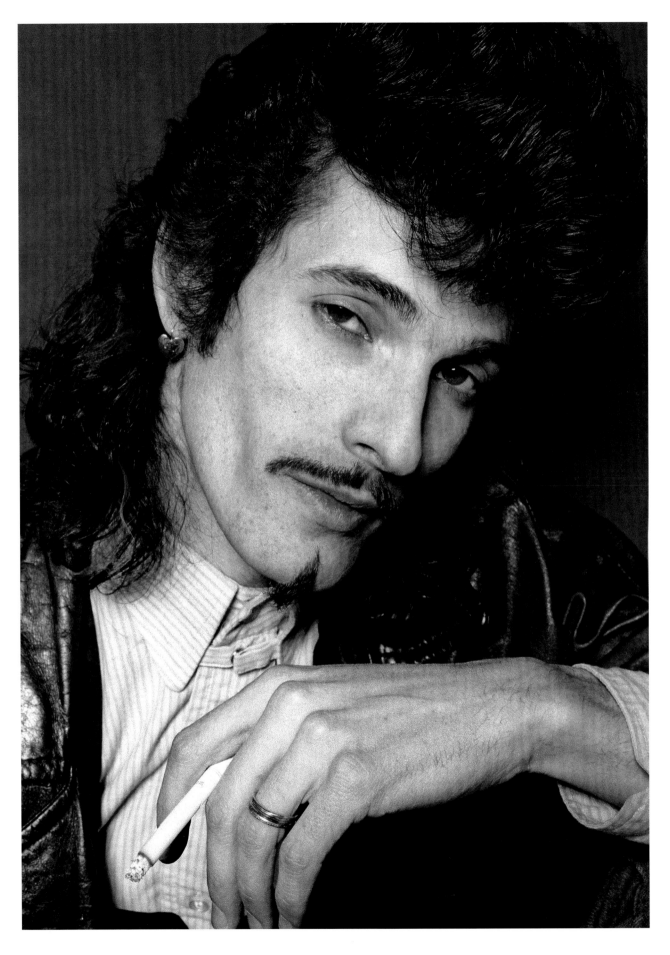

Willy DeVille

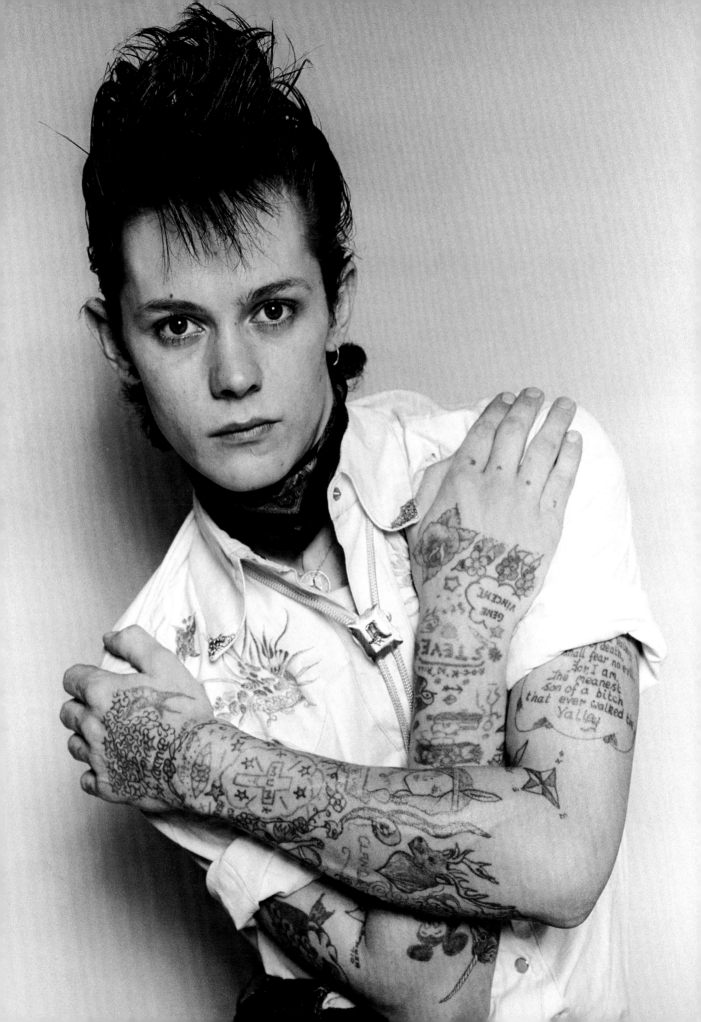

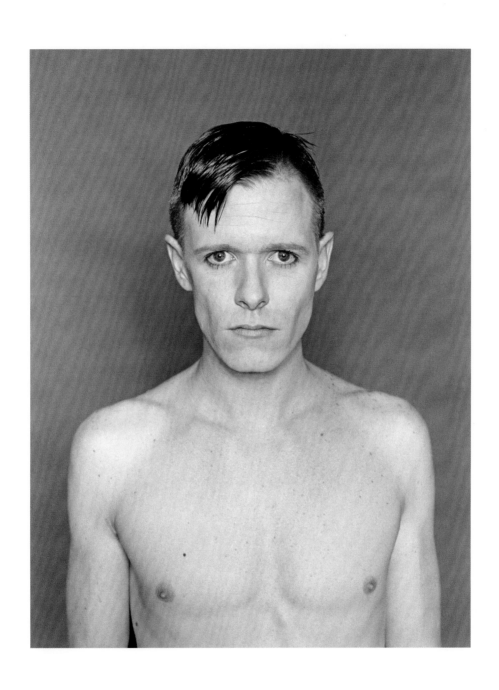

Smutty Smiff (OPPOSITE), Michael Gira (ABOVE)

# KLAUS NOMI

## WILL THEY KNOW ME?

BY KRISTIAN HOFFMAN

KLAUS NOMI appeared on the NYC scene suddenly, leaping from his spectacular debut at the *New Wave Vaudeville* show (where the astounded audience had to be told repeatedly that the voice was truly live) to spearhead a futurist movement of militantly fashionable avant-misfits—before any new romantic notions occurred to Spandau Ballet, and after Bowie had abandoned the future as an archaic concept.

Klaus was a face—elfin and painted as a Kabuki robot. He was a style—a medieval interpretation of the twenty-first century via 1929 Berlin. He was a voice—almost inhuman in range, from operatic soprano to Prussian general. He was a master performer—a master of theatrical gesture. Above all, he was a visionary. He said the future was based on the need of the artist, deciding how to live and living that way every minute. Klaus, the man from the future, lived that way in the present, and held out his hand, saying, "Come with me. You can do it too."

His vision was naïve, quaint, almost foolish, but forceful in its purity and innocence. Even at his most wildly ridiculous ("Lightning Strikes") or quaveringly sublime (Purcell's "Death"), there was an acknowledgment of impending apocalypse that lent his work conviction. For Klaus, apocalypse was a metaphor for purification, and as the oddball optimist surrounded by cynical detachment and resignation, he dared to believe in a better world.

Klaus rose quickly, independent of the critical machine. He was never "cool," and was resented by some who thought Fame should have hipper tastes. He gained a following in New York and used it as a springboard to even greater success in Europe. He dearly loved New York, felt it was his true home and was distressed that he couldn't work more. He requested that his remains stay here, despite family ties in Germany.

He did not end life at the end of his career, but in the middle of it. His biggest accomplishments were ahead of him. He was on the verge of Canadian and American deals, and was full of ideas and plans, positive and humorous. He was tortured by impossible and endless management complications, and a disease whose myth exploded through thoughtless babble and media saturation, until the only sensible solution was to move far away.

His was always a message of great instinctive hope.

I was introduced to Klaus as most were in my small, fortunate group of East Village friends: when he sprang, as fully formed as Athena from the head of Zeus, onto the scuffed stage of the grubby Polish music hall known as Irving Plaza, singing "Samson and Delilah" in a clear plastic raincoat that belonged to Howie Pyro's mother. We were—and are—transfixed by this alien angel. A voice like no other, ethereal and wondrous—and a vision that took the ridiculous and made it achingly, ravishingly sublime.

I was the musical director for that *New Wave Vaudeville* show, and thought my theme song for emcee David McDermott carried a certain "amusement" factor: "There's no wave like the new wave, and the new wave is the no wave, so I say yes yes to the new new no no wave."

Klaus's aspirations were altogether more grandiose, and I was lucky that he dangled that glittering plastic coattail for me to grab: from the moment (the very next day) that Anya Phillips suggested I form a band for Klaus, and the moment Klaus replied with a Teutonic chipmunk "Yes!" I was swept away on a soaring flight of fancy and success and wonder and pain and disappointment and tragedy no one could have foreseen.

I might say that in the years since, I have become aware of what a gift it was to collaborate with him—but that would not be strictly true: even as a young, foolish

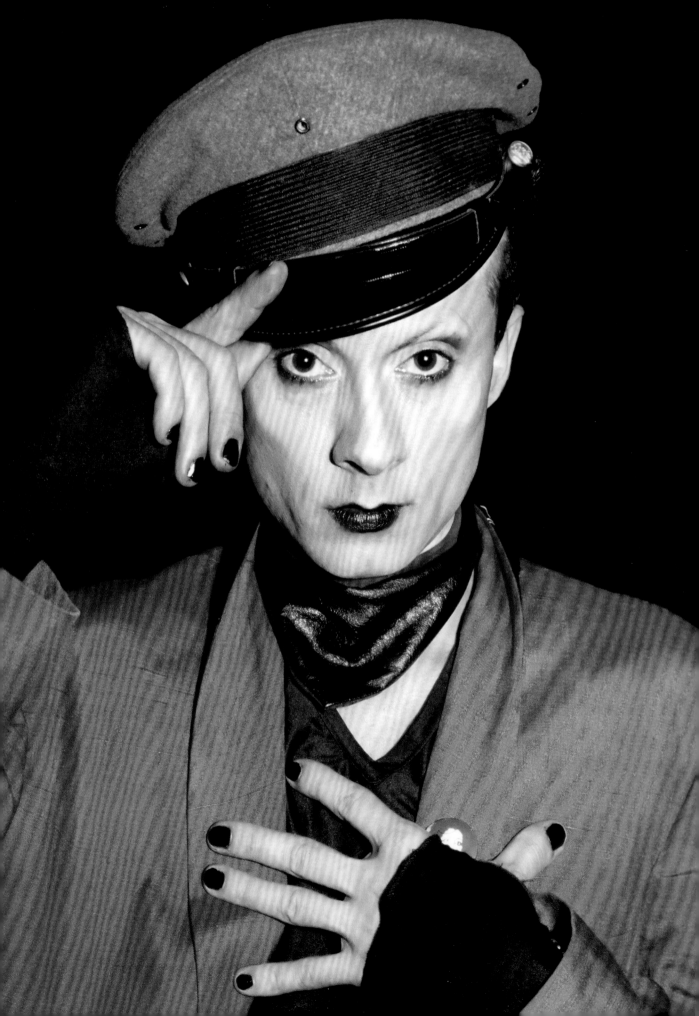

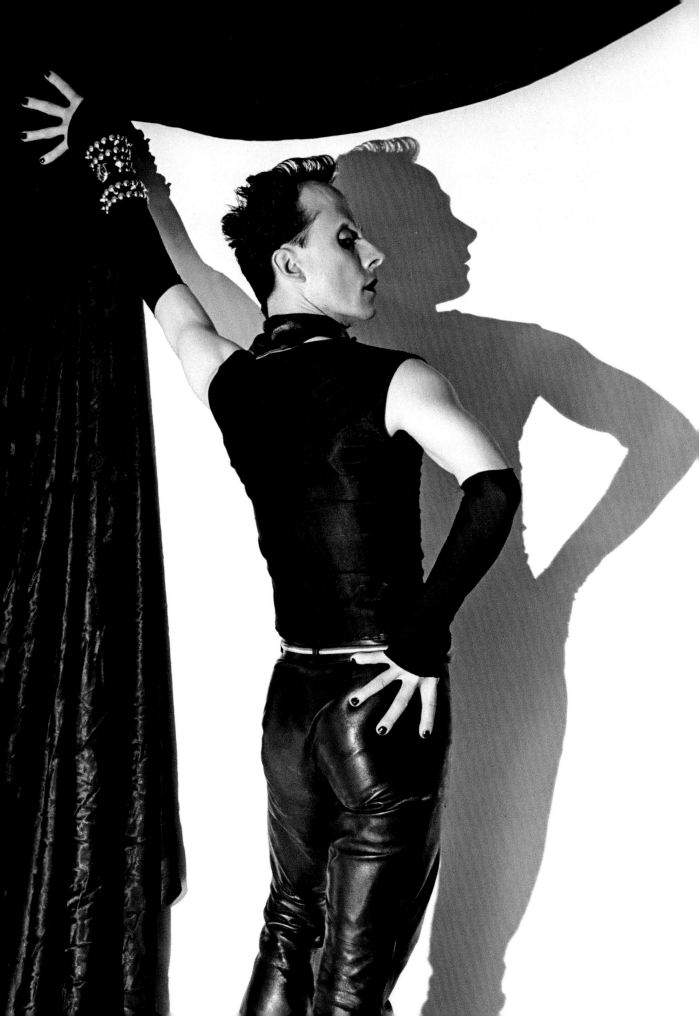

man, I knew that fate had handed me a miraculous opportunity that was likely to be without equal, and I grasped it with my unschooled hands, and for a few brief moments that act of being an artist was a revolution of beauty. I am a very lucky man!

When I wrote his obit at the urging of James Marshall all those years ago, I had no inkling of the odd immortality Klaus's legacy would achieve—one that taunts the perceived "stars" of any given era. That cults everywhere should embrace Klaus's eccentric, outlandish, contrarian will to a novel beauty lets us continue immersion therapy in the part of Klaus that is utterly divine: his unlikely, unearthly voice joined with his bizarrely succinct and deliciously charismatic self-mythologizing.

People often claim AIDS as part of Klaus's story. I say it is not. It is the instrument that arbitrarily felled him before his time, and he faced it with grace and even humor. But it does not speak to his vision or legacy. The only part that AIDS played in Klaus's life is that we were all robbed of the gorgeous music he would yet have made, which is unfathomably troubling. His greatest moments had yet to come.

Klaus's story does include a subplot morality play of sorts: He was dominated by a management team so maniacal that they named the price Klaus must pay, as an artist, to be seen, and, as a singer, to be heard: they dangled the mesmerizing prize of a record contract to him, lectured him about scarcity until something in Klaus began to believe it, and told the guileless pastry chef from the tiny East Village apartment, "You must abandon all whom you know here: there is no other way. Without us you will be utterly silenced."

That Klaus was convinced of this, even for a moment, is the small tragedy of his life.

But ultimately, this is all moot. Klaus's accomplishments in the face of those depraved corporate machinations are magnificent, immortal. And, obviously, had Klaus survived, he would have taken these fleeting lessons and everything would have changed—he would have restored his community and made even greater works of astonishing beauty.

But still—through all of Klaus's fantastic and sometimes maddening foibles, through his tragic demise, through all the bruises and batterings I personally was handed because of my proximity to the machine that held him somehow hostage, through all the wonder and joy I experienced being a part of the creative whirlwind that sprang up around him (and, because of him, around me) from the moment of that astounding *New Wave Vaudeville* debut—Klaus's message always held true: "I use the vessel I was given, one that may alienate others from me, and I exaggerate it, embrace it, and become the creation I was meant to be. Then I am whole, when I find the beauty in my own strangeness. Then the strangeness *becomes* the beauty. I *am* my art. You can be too. I see myself as universal, not of any one nation—we are all living on the earth. People are always waiting for the future to come. The future is *now*. The future has begun. Revel in it—we are all in the future, now. I am *now* wave. Come now and take my hand."

Klaus Nomi

# JOEY RAMONE
## A LITERARY FRIENDSHIP

*Living on the Bowery's very exciting, people are getting stabbed and murdered all the time. It's very exciting, lots of atmosphere. Tomorrow we're playing the First World Festival in Toronto with Ted Nugent and Aerosmith, a whole day affair for a hundred thousand people. Gotta get up and fly at 5:30 a.m.*

From the diary of Joey Ramone

IF JAMES CHANCE was the poster boy for no wave, Joey Ramone was the poster boy for punk rock. Joey was the coolest punk rocker I met in New York. *Punk* magazine editor John Holmstrom introduced me to him in classic punk fashion back in the fall of 1977. Joey was living with the painter and Ramones lighting designer Arturo Vega. It was just off the Bowery, a block above CBGB, on East Second Street. One night, after a gig, John and I came careening out of the club and took turns creaming Legs McNeil, who had recently attempted to sleep with my girlfriend when I was in Australia. After we left Legs lying in the street, I found myself following Holmstrom up the block and literally up the face of Arturo's building, via those metal screens that close across ground-floor windows at night to keep out robbers. Entering the loft through its second-story window, I charged the unsuspecting Ramone, but soon found myself getting the worst of the altercation. Joey pinned me to the floor, one bony knee plunked on each shoulder, demanding surrender. No sooner had I introduced myself than we became fast friends.

Joey was a wildly creative, intelligent guy. He loved nothing more than settling down in a comfortable place and spending the balance of the night solving the problems of the world. Since I was working hard to make it as a writer and was getting up at 6 a.m., we met much less than both of us would have liked. Consequently, even when he was on the road, Joey made a real effort to keep in touch, as one can see from these extracts from two letters.

"Hey ol boy whats the doop?" he wrote from Los Angeles, where the Ramones, in their single most productive period, were recording *End of the Century* with the great Phil Spector and filming *Rock 'n' Roll High School* with, among others, the ex–Warhol superstar Mary Woronov (of *Exploding Plastic Inevitable* and *Chelsea Girls*).

> What's doin. Hanging out swatting flies recordin the album it sound incredible really explosive! Can't wait for ya to hear it through it's only half done. Just saw a picture of Wayne County [which Joey thoughtfully included] with his new operation he looks more like Debbie Harry every time I see him. Saw Robert Gordon and [Chris] Spedding he's great—say hi to Jeff and everyone. See ya soon. Hi from everyone here. P.S. Los Tacos is the best Mexican dump in L.A. better than Lucy's. No gas. Aggressive flies. They repainted the Trop pool black and filled it with turquois green shitty water it looks like a lagoon Joey Ramone.

In another missive from the road, he wrote,

> Last nite I saw something on TV that really flipped me out. This was the first report ever let out in the whole US about cloneing. This guys putting out a book called Who Will Be the Next God. Anyway Upjohn the Quaalude Corp. & 20 other major drug corp. have gotten the rights from the Federal Gov. to synthetically create & clone & own!!! people & that until recently only frogs could be successfully cloned. But some scientist from New York has just successfully created a 14-month-old kid that's an exact replica clone of himself. That's fuckinamazin that's really weird. I mean when ya think about it. Anyway I thought you should. They said that this would come out nationally in June. Hanging out in N. Carolina. Don't understand what people do here since I haven't seen one

*"Rock and Roll teaches you how to live."*

**—JOEY RAMONE**

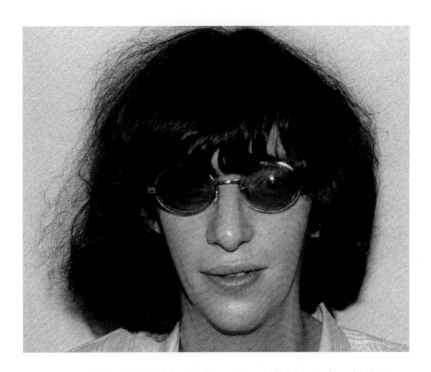

person outside of the hotel. Last night went to see High Anxiety. It sucked but was really great, I'm really into Cheap Trick. They're fucking incredible. Listen to their 1 & 2 albums. Legs story in new Hit Parader was fucking riot. Best thing he's done fantastic. See ya. Joey Ramone.

At one point I gave Joey a copy of Franz Kafka's *Metamorphosis*—the famous story about a man who wakes up one morning in his parents' home, where he lives as an adult with a job to go to, transformed into a six-foot-tall insect. There were some intriguing parallels between the great writer and the great singer. I also talked to Joey about my experiences with a succubus.

Perhaps appropriately, considering he wrote songs and I wrote celebrations of artists, our friendship turned into something of a literary one, and I found myself collaborating with Joey on an editorial he had been commissioned to write for *High Times* in 1978. This is the first of its eight pages:

I just saw the Who movie The Kids Are Alright. It's fucking fantastic. It doesn't come off as just another documentary, it's loaded with charm and character, excitement and the genius of the Who (if you love the Who as much as me). But for me it was more of a movie that reflects the current sad state of rock and roll. After seeing The Kids Are Alright, I felt really enraged.

The Who are the perfect example of what rock and roll stands for and was always meant to be. Whether it be '60s, '70s, '80s, or '90s the definition of rock and roll is: Daring. Exciting. Going out on a limb. Very visual, catchy, and melodic tunes. Not half-hour boring guitar solos or mindless songs about sex: She Left Me. Who the fuck cares!!! The kids of now are being deprived, cheated and brainwashed bad. It's not their fault, most of them just don't know better. Rock and roll is dying 'cause the media is trying to kill it as it's always been trying since the days of Elvis and Gene Vincent ('50s). They're spreading propaganda about how youth listening to this music have their minds poisoned and turn into habitual sex-crazed hardcore tri-sexual mindless pill-popping pot-smoking dropout mass murderers, which we all know is bullshit, but it's always worked successfully to promote the clean-up-the-image campaign. Remember Pat Boone and Doris Day—the soft-décor public image that parents will approve of. Rock and roll is for rebels and outcasts. Rock music was not meant for parents' pleasure.

Joey Ramone

139

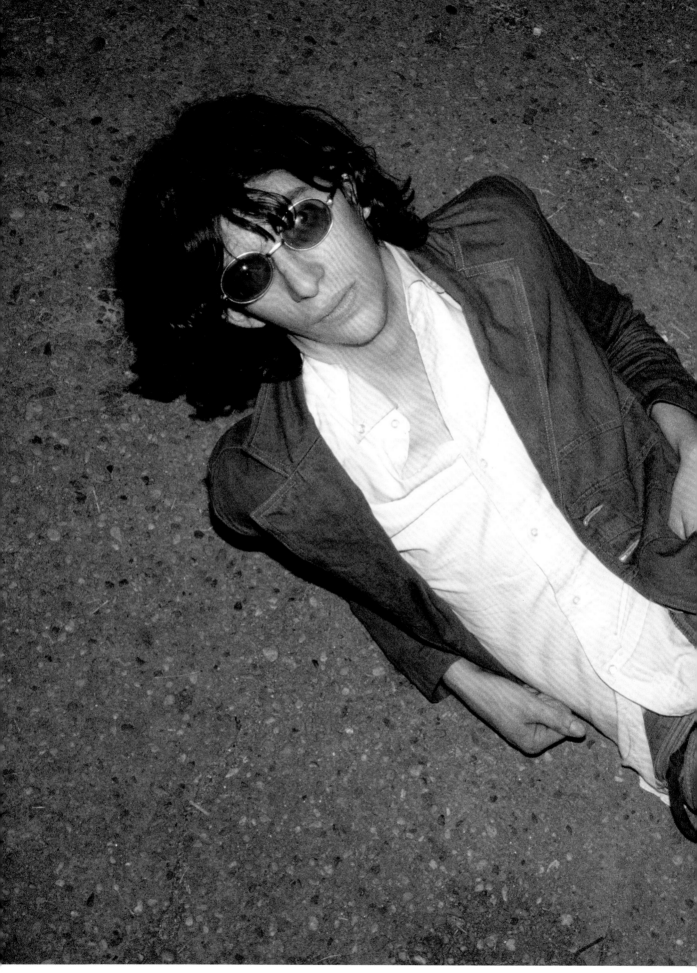

Joey Ramone

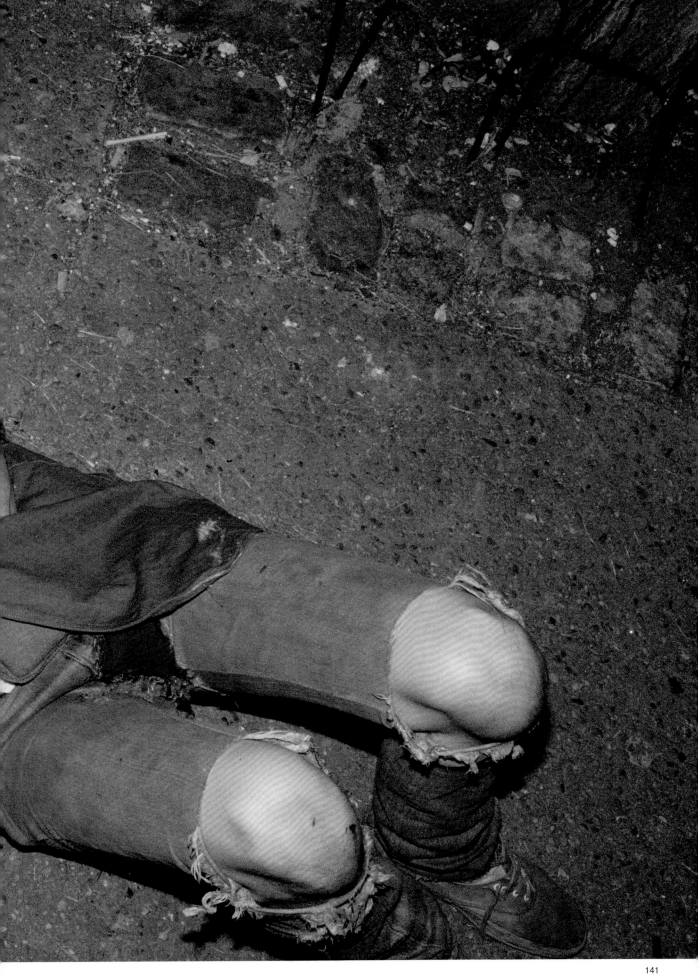

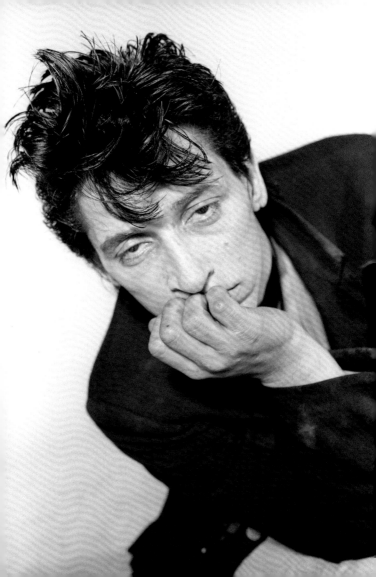

# A BAD BOY NAMED JOHN

## JOHNNY THUNDERS

" *Too fast to live . . .*
*too young to die.* "

—TATTOO WINDING AROUND A BLACK
CROSS ON JOHNNY THUNDERS' ARM

Johnny Thunders

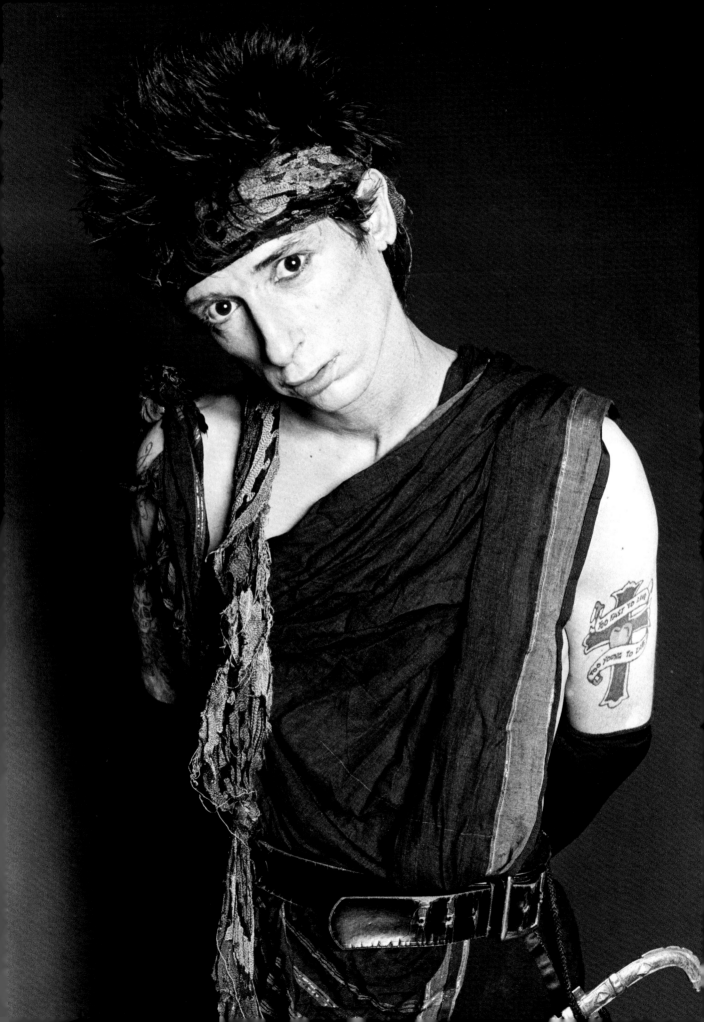

IF MARCIA HAD DREAMED UP a Bad Boy model, he could not have surpassed Johnny Thunders, who combined all the characteristics of the dark triad. The glamorously wasted ex–New York Doll, member of the Heartbreakers, singer-songwriter, and guitar hero had just recorded an album called *So Alone*, featuring "You Can't Put Your Arms Around a Memory." Thunders made a career out of defying death with music. That Johnny got so much adulation from punks for his heroin chic is the paradox of *Punks, Poets & Provocateurs*.

Marcia Resnick first met Johnny Thunders in the Gramercy Park Hotel, where she took the double-page portrait of him in the bathtub. Johnny was often homeless. When the cold New York nights made it impossible to survive on the streets, he would find somebody to take him in. In the winter of 1978 Johnny moved into Marcia's spacious Canal Street loft. The space overlooked the Hudson River through a series of twelve large windows. It was a fantasyland concocted out of her *Re-visions* persona, with its dark promise of adolescent sex, hard drugs, and rock 'n' roll. Cocaine and heroin turned the loft into a dreamy cocoon in which dress-up transformation became the name of the game. Soon Johnny and Marcia were appearing on the scene as the ultimate enfants terribles of punk.

This was a photo marriage resonant of Man Ray and Jean Cocteau. "He" was "her" model. Marcia had a large collection of thrift-shop-chic clothes. Her adventures with Johnny consisted of ransacking it to concoct costumes for him to wear in her pictures. In Marcia's Thunders series, Johnny emerges as a Chaplinesque clown— and at his most fragile, as a rock 'n' roll harlequin.

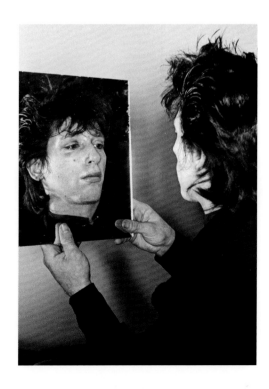

Johny Thunders (OPPOSITE, RIGHT, AND FOLLOWING PAGES)

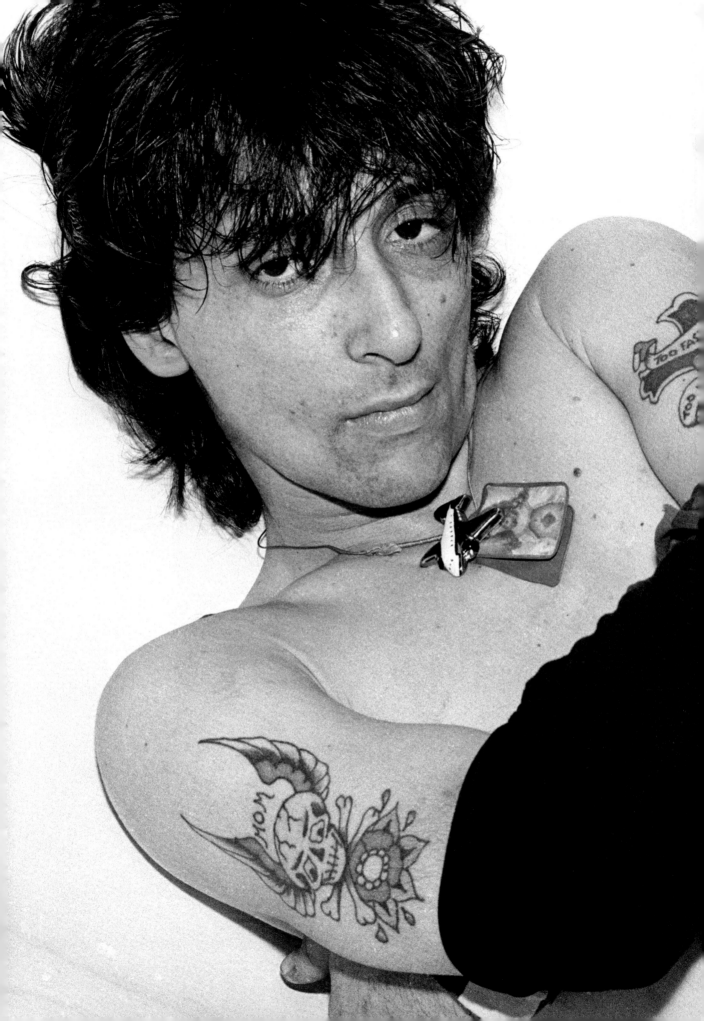

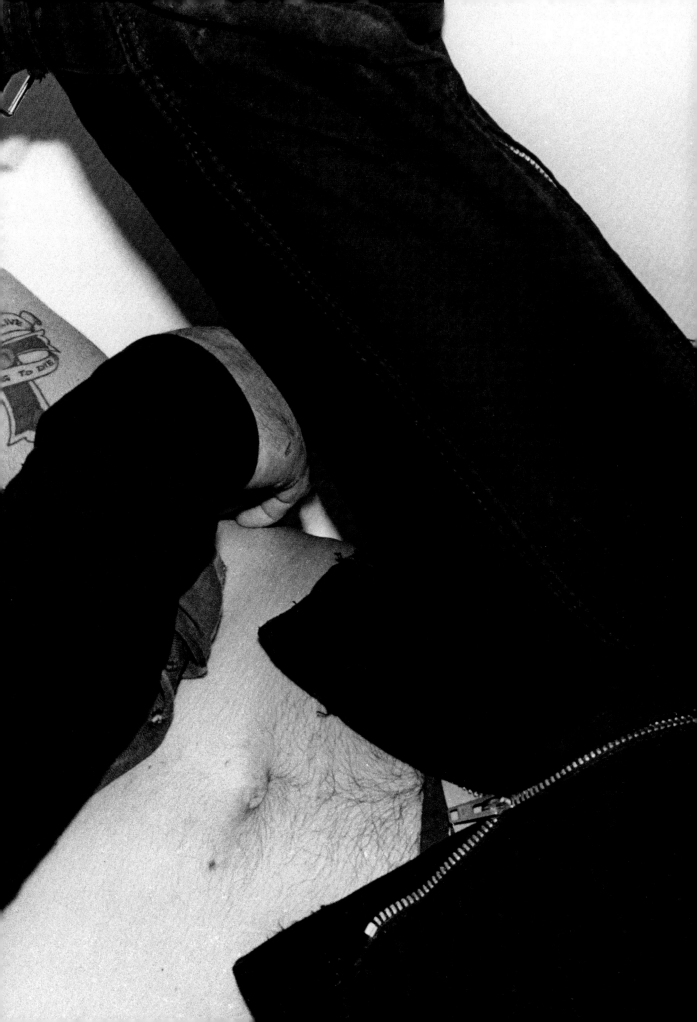

# JOHNNY THUNDERS AND THE ENDLESS PARTY

BY RICHARD HELL

From *Hot and Cold,*
*Johnny Thunders and the Endless Party*

JOHNNY'S PARTY IS OVER. Thinking about him this morning (May 9) in New York. It's another drizzly colorless day as it was for his funeral last week.

I hope when I die people don't go soft about me. It's stupid. Apart from his family and four or five lifelong friends, probably the people who'll miss Johnny most are those he exploited. The ones who were made to feel important because he spent time with them in order to get them to do things for him. Of course, he never even really had to try to get this kind of treatment: people fell over themselves to get next to him. They liked to be near him just to look at him, as you would a jungle carnivore. And a girl could not be wrong to have him at her side. That's how he made his living, like a lot of rock and roll performers. I don't think Johnny would want people to go soft about him.

Then again, he lit into journalists a lot for not treating him with enough respect. He even wrote a song ("I Tell the Truth Even When I'm Lying") replying to what he considered their unfair and insulting treatment of him. It included this "open letter to the music press: / I revoke your poetic license / you probably got on Forty-Second Street / same place you got your lover / same place your mother got your father." When he told me how much he liked Japan, it was mostly because the people are "real polite and kind. I tell you I did forty or fifty interviews and not one person asked me about drugs." That's what he attacked them for, asking him about drugs. While of course he himself exploited heroin's significance in the maintenance of his bad boy image. He included conspicuous syringes in publicity photos, and frequently mimed jamming needles into his forearm during his stage act.

I've found my try at writing this—including viewing videos of recent Thunders shows, reading old interviews, listening to tapes and records, talking to some of his closest old and new friends, and, especially, recalling in detail a lot of time I spent with Johnny myself—spooky and scary as well as sad (where's the good part?). Mainly because I find myself identifying with him, so that it becomes almost as if something I say about him I'm saying about myself. And that to feel something or evoke a feeling about him is to feel the same thing about myself. (Of course, that's what stars are good for.)

But the main qualities, the virtues, that set Johnny apart were that he didn't give a fuck and he dressed great.

Johnny, of course, was the rock and roll Dean Martin of heroin, at least in his last decade. I've known him since 1974, which I think was the last year before he had a real narcotics habit. I admired the Dolls; they inspired me. They were the first pure rock and roll group. "Pure" in that they knew and operated on the assumption that rock and roll is at least 50 percent (maybe 100 percent, maybe 200 percent) attitude. They were the first group that regarded themselves as stars rather than thinking of themselves as musicians, or writers, or vocalists. The Dolls were for New York groups sort of what the Sex Pistols were for British groups. They excited everybody by being flawless: in it for fun, never pretentious or pretending to be anything they weren't; they were ballsy, noisy, tough, funny, sharp, young, and real. Stupid and ill. They mocked the media, threw up on grown-ups, and kidded with the kids in a language of drugs and sex.

And I don't think there's really much of an argument to be made against the observation that Johnny peaked with the Dolls, when he was twenty or twenty-one. Even his most recent sets undeniably picked up whenever he played a Dolls tune. (He didn't do many of them, but you'd hear a "Lonely Planet Boy" or "Personality

## THEMES OF JOHNNY'S SONGS
—a million girls want him but he kicks them all in the face
—he's completely lonely (uh, see previous)
—the world is fucked up, don't bother me
—party time

## GUITAR STYLE
—the way it sounds sarcastic, the drawn-out bent off-notes
—piercing tone
—the sneering throwaway monster-chord fuck-you noises he tended to end songs with

Johnny Thunders

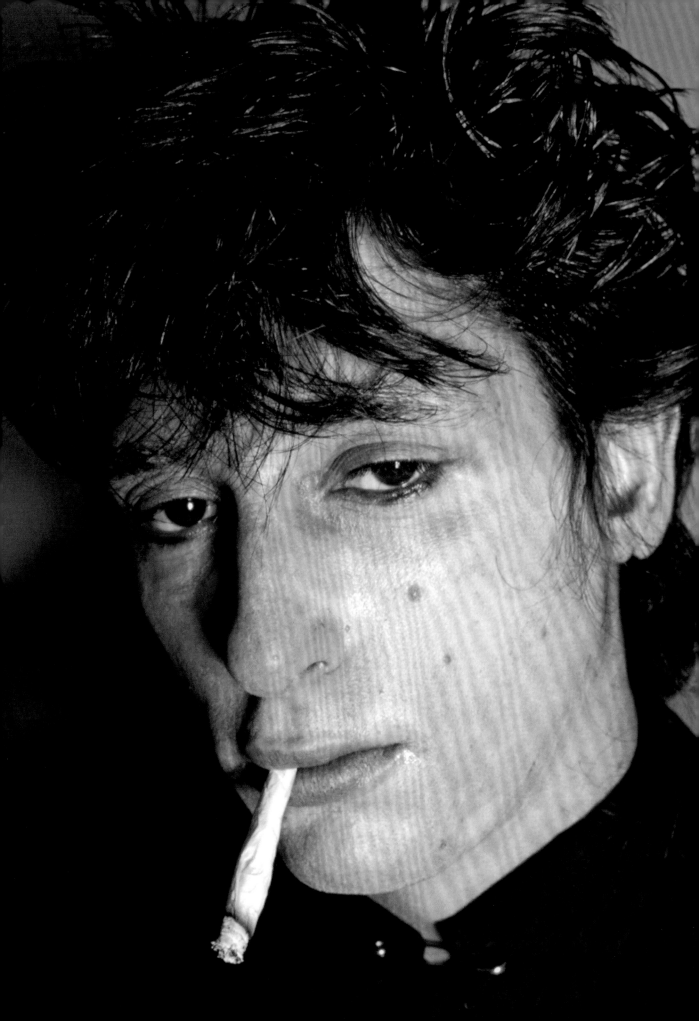

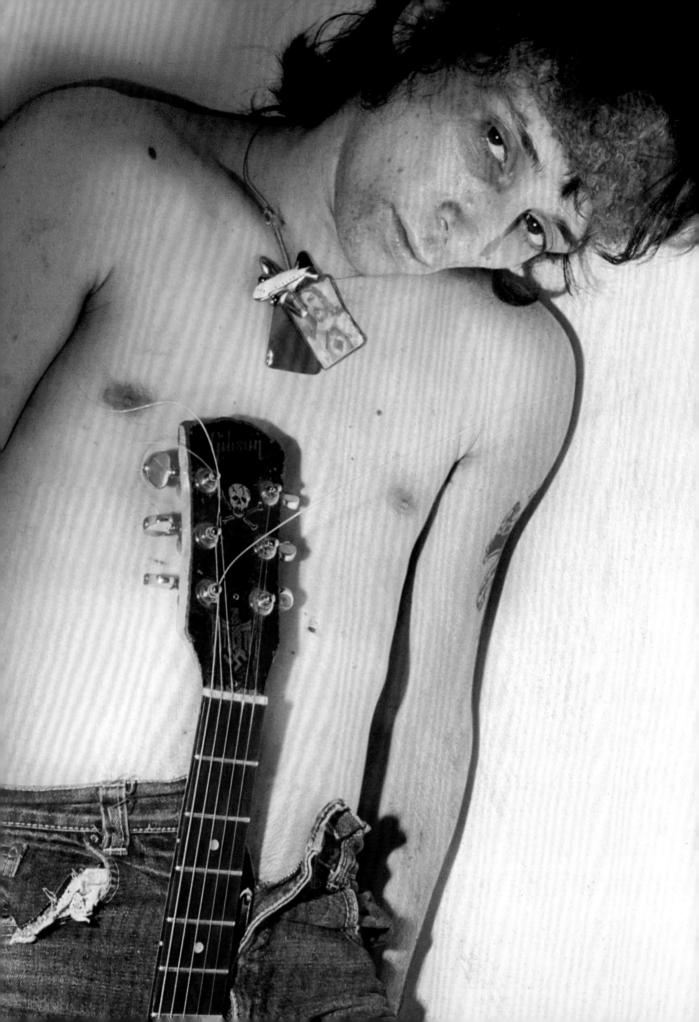

Crisis.") The next seventeen or eighteen years were just spent getting to know him a little better.

There was something perfect about Johnny. Though because he was a legendary archetype, you tended to think of him as predictable, as a type. You tended to condescend to him because you thought you had him nailed (and otherwise he might be a threat). But he always surprised me when I talked to him. The surprising thing was how smart he was. He was smart in the same way he dressed so perfectly. Smart the same way Elvis Presley was. You couldn't top him and he didn't delude himself.

(I remember the revelation it was to me when I realized I'd rather be smart in the way Elvis Presley was than in the way, say, Ludwig Wittgenstein was. The thing was, you could imagine you could be smart like Wittgenstein by just thinking hard enough, but Elvis just had it. It was almost spiritual. A kind of grace. A kind of innate ruling of the world. That's what you wanted and Johnny had it. And he knew it—to him, the highest compliment was to be "as good as Frank Sinatra and Elvis.")

He was perfect because he made no apologies. He was just graceful. He instinctively knew how to make do with what he had. (Though he made a lot of bad records.)

Rock and roll, of course, is about not growing up and settling down, defying those who have, and living for sex and other types of fun. That's who Johnny was. The New York version.

Johnny made his choice, or lived out his destiny, and he had a right to it. He always went to drugs to be able to face the day, and he always went to his guitar to be himself. (Though he spent most of his time watching TV.) There's no judging to be done. It's like Marlene Dietrich in *Touch of Evil* when she sums up Quinlan with "He was some kind of a man. What does it matter what you say about people?" I've got to admit it annoys me too to see cynical, exploitive, self-centered death drive get glamorized. I hated the Chet Baker documentary for that reason and Chet and Johnny have a lot in common. They were both junkies who always put themselves first and treated their talent as just another little windfall they could squeeze for all the narcotics and fancy clothes they might be able to drain from it. (Johnny: "I would never become righteous. Everybody's entitled to do what they want if they don't hurt me." It took Johnny to say "me.")

Johnny though was the kind of person you always forgave. He did everything with such impenetrable confidence, everything about him was so up-front, with his soulful murmur in your ear making you feel like a human insider, you could only say "Well, that's J.T. . . . " and write it off. (His most frequent companion of the last year telling me with real fondness how he'd always *bring* her something—some knickknack from his bedroom wrapped in a scarf—before he asked to borrow money.)

It was impossible to insult him to his face; he could hold his own with anyone. You wouldn't want to anyway; he was so sweet and soft-spoken (still conveying that you'd better not touch his hair).

One of the most widely felt reactions to Johnny's death has got to be that the conclusion has been foregone for so long now that there isn't any drama left. In other words, we've considered him dead since 1980. That's a nasty thing to say, and, even though I myself must admit it occurred to me, it isn't really true or fair. In fact, one of Johnny's distinctions was that he was always worth seeing. (For all the above reasons: he had that kernel of talent, he didn't give a fuck, and he dressed great.)

April 29. Johnny's funeral today. At the cemetery, as words are spoken over the coffin, and flowers dropped on it, out in the dreary day, finally tapping into the sadness. Like the sadness is a dimension that is always there but we have developed over the years such a way of avoiding. Sort of like the way in his last concerts, in the light, he looked scary, like an accusation or a reminder you'd rather not get.

## CLOTHES WORN DURING JAPANESE CONCERT THREE WEEKS BEFORE DEATH

–starts in knee-length blue Edwardian-type coat
–over tight matching red plaid pants and vest
–with formal white shirt with wing collar
–and old-fashioned dark flowing bowtie with white pin polka dots
–after a few songs, replaces blue overcoat with motorcycle jacket that appears to have a high school pennant sewn to the back
–and dons what looks like a fancy French sailor's cap with a red bow around it
–replaces cap with woven wreath of red roses

## THINGS HE SAID TO ME

–(all the time) "Fuck 'em if they can't take a joke."
–in London, 1978, comparing rock and roll to prizefighting (sleazy managers and promoters profiting from the self-destructive labors of street youth): "I'll retire if I lose my hair or grow it on my chest."
–"I get fucked up because I want to get fucked up."

Johnny Thunders

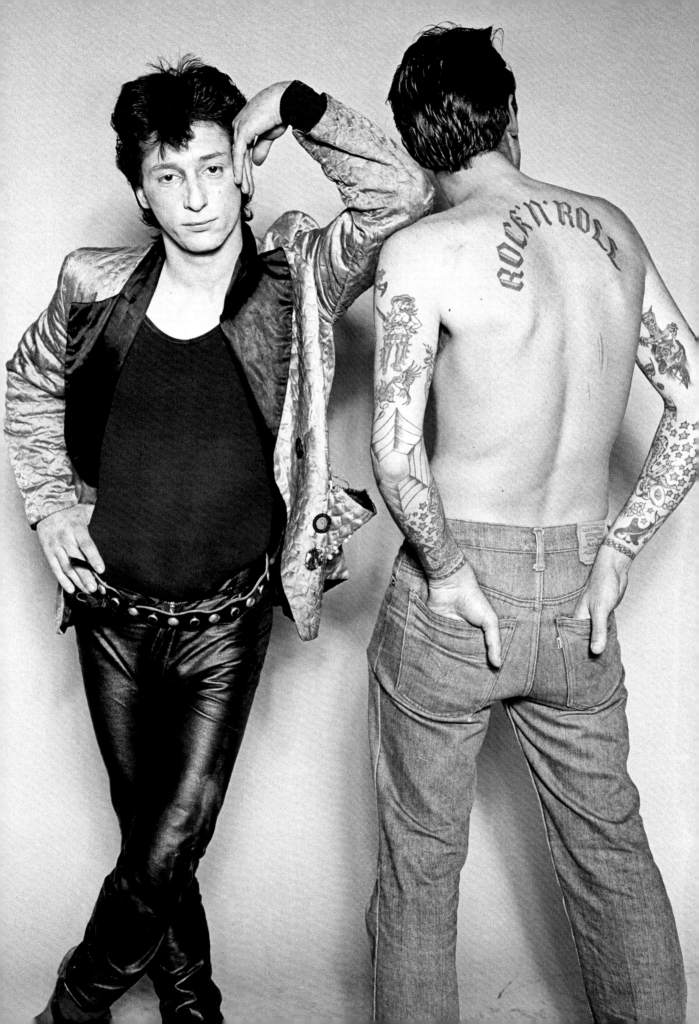

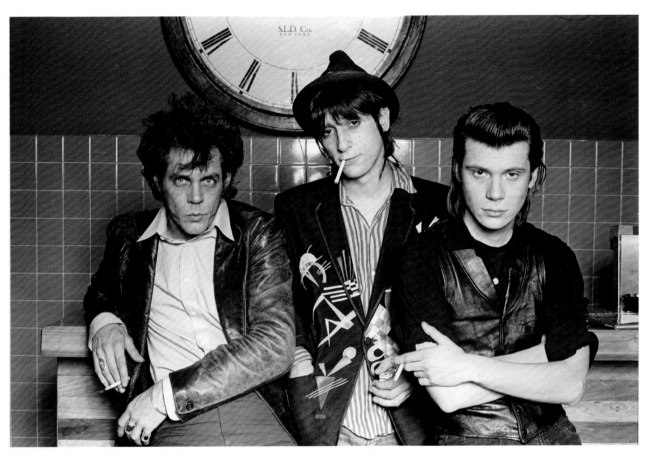

Steve Shevlin, Johnny Thunders, and Philippe Marcade (ABOVE)

Johnny Thunders and Teddy Boy (OPPOSITE)

Johnny Thunders (FOLLOWING PAGES)

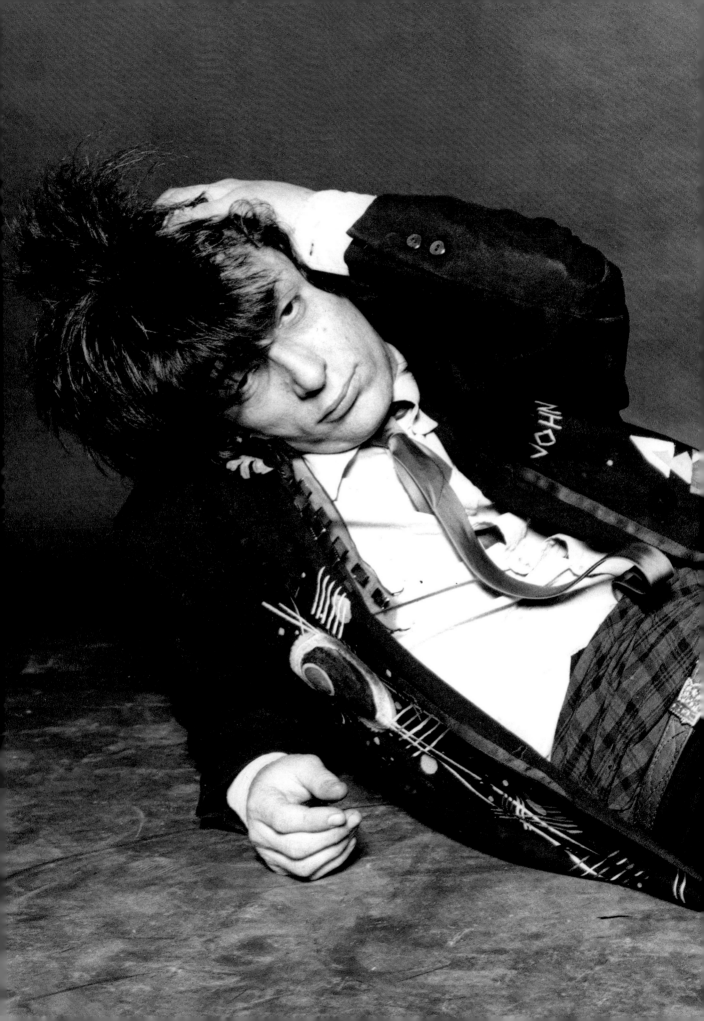

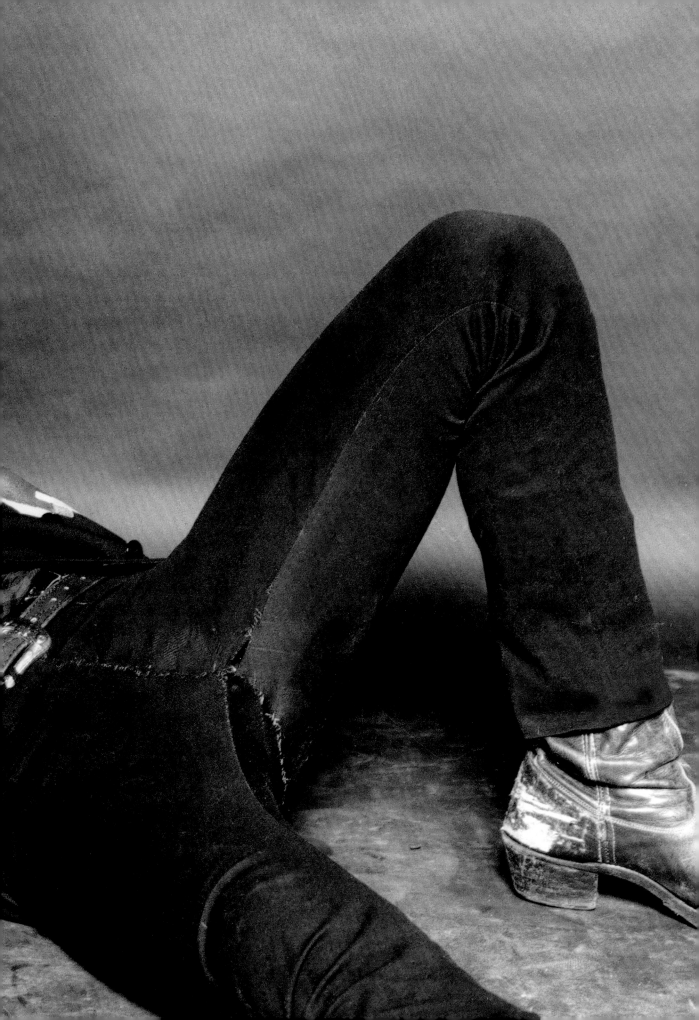

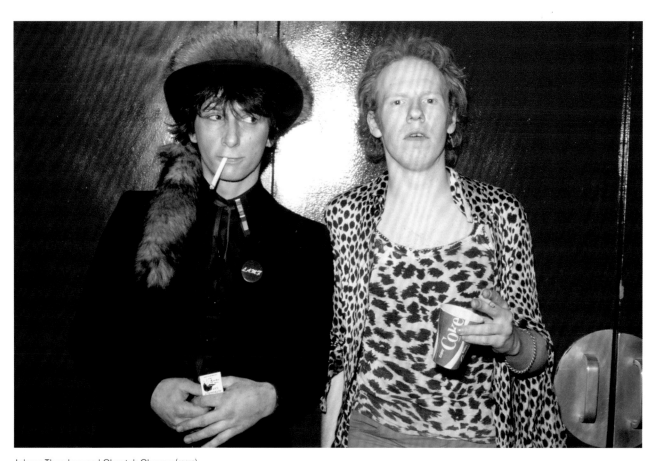

Johnny Thunders and Cheetah Chrome (ABOVE)

Johnny Thunders and Jerry Nolan (OPPOSITE)

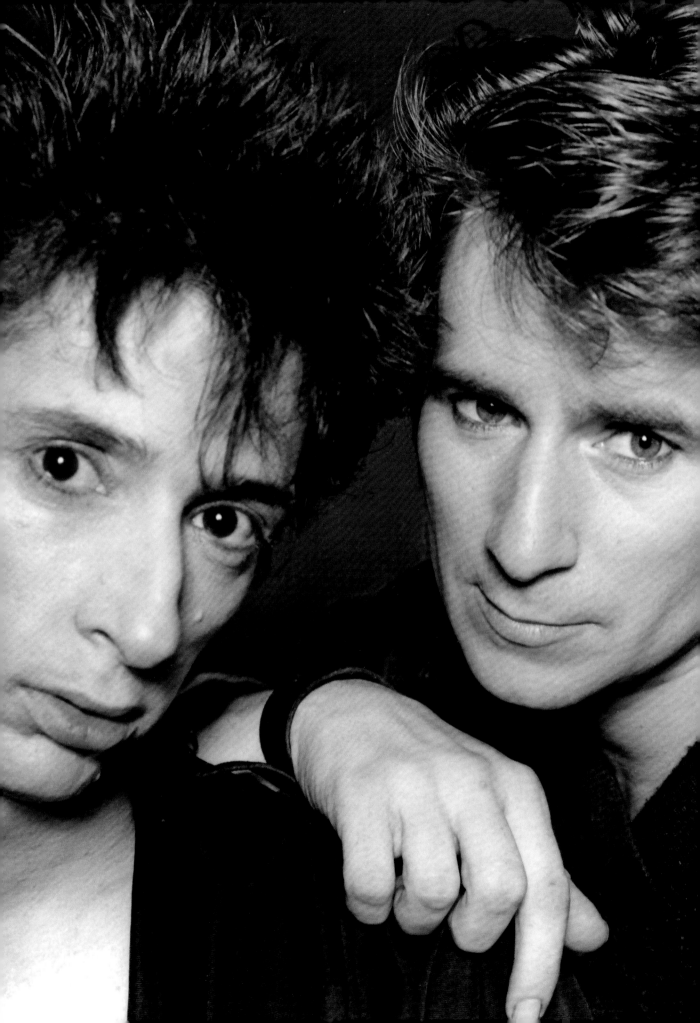

Johnny Thunders

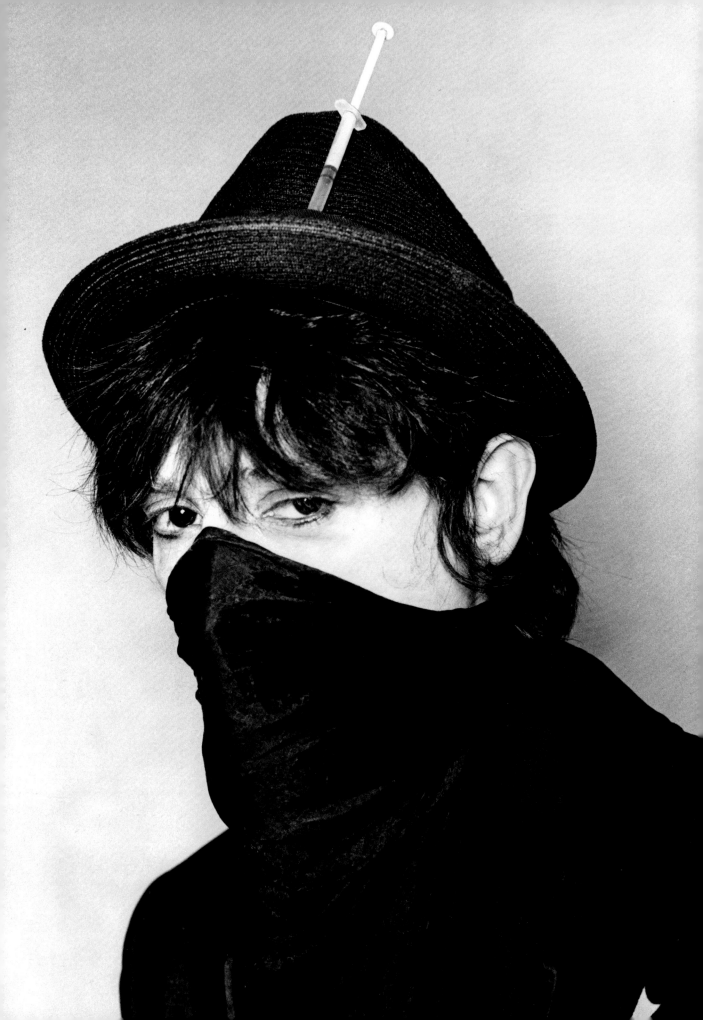

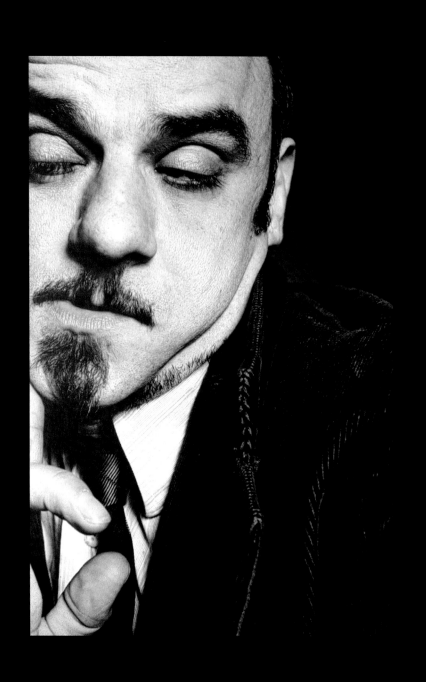

# PROVOCATEURS
# AND RACONTEURS

"*I know that men are the size of stars
. . . we can't apply standards of
measurement—they're false . . . .
There's no way to measure spirit.*"

—MICHAEL MCCLURE, *THE MAD CUB*

Charles Lufran

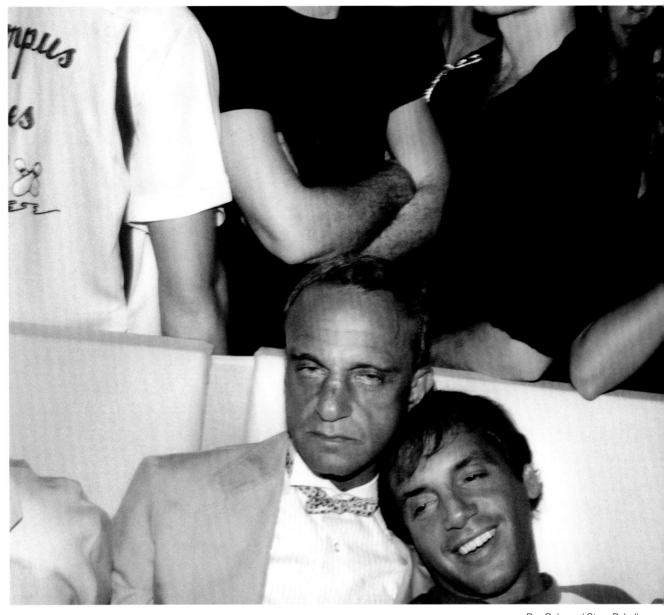

Roy Cohn and Steve Rubell

IN THIS CHAPTER we see extraordinary men from diverse fields who are all known for their accomplishments. Roy Cohn was an evil genius who had worked originally with the fascistic Senator McCarthy, finding "communists" in the 1950s. Here we see him with Steve Rubell, the owner of Studio 54, watching a riot break out as a play by Victor Hugo begins at the Mudd Club. Mayor Ed Koch was good to downtown. He stopped the murderers who were torturing and killing gay men late at night in the trucks parked on West Street across from the Hudson River in Greenwich Village. Muhammad Ali was the people's champion through the 1970s. Timothy Leary was the high priest of LSD. His robes were a little tattered, but he was still a legend and hero of the counterculture. The exuberant but dark Victor Hugo was Warhol's muse in his punk period. John Waters is an underground filmmaker whose films *Pink Flamingos* and *Female Trouble* brought him a strong cult following and introduced artists like Divine into the potent mix of the '70s. Charles Ludlam represented the Theater of the Ridiculous. James Nares, Eric Mitchell, Jim Jarmusch, Nick Zedd, and Amos Poe were all new wave underground film directors out of punk. Nicholas Ray, Kenneth Anger, Jack Smith, Paul Morrissey, and Jonathan Demme are film directors from the '50s, '60s, and '70s. Norman Mailer, Quentin Crisp, Gary Indiana, and Max Blagg are writers.

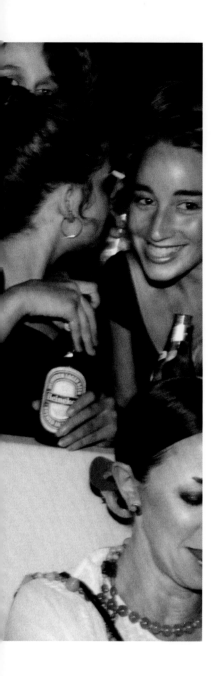

John Waters is among the strongest artists of the Bad Boys. He made his initial impact in the late '60s and early '70s, but his work is an outstanding example of the beat punk ethos. I remember Marcia and I taking him to dinner with William Burroughs. John had affinities with almost every artist in this book, and he was probably most recognized by them (apart from the beats and those who went on with them). Like so many of our subjects, John was primarily a writer.

A number of these people designed or influenced the all-important clubs that made the scene. Steve Mass ran the deep punk Mudd Club. As the resident punk at *Punk* magazine, Legs McNeil was a mighty man and everybody's favorite punk philosopher and catalyst. Anthony Bourdain had the best restaurant on the Lower East Side. Tony Shafrazi ran the hippest art gallery. Gerard Malanga and Rene Ricard were stars of *Chelsea Girls* and good poets. The Kipper Kids and Spalding Gray were cutting-edge comedians. Lester Bangs was the greatest rock writer who ever lived. Fred Brathwaite, aka Fab 5 Freddy, was a bridge to the graffiti artists, rappers, and hip-hop musicians who brought a great, fresh blast of energy downtown. The cross-references, influences, and collaborations between these people formed the delicate mosaic of networks and webs that connected the scene.

Marcia's sensitive portrait of the film director Paul Morrissey reveals him in repose. Separated from the Warhol glitter, he was a prolific artist with his own visions. We owe a debt of gratitude to Morrissey for the stream of sex comedies he made with Warhol, like *Flesh, Trash, Heat*, and *Women in Revolt*. They played a much stronger role in shaping '70s lifestyles than has previously been recorded.

Ray Johnson's New York Correspondence School and Amos Poe's underground films both brought disparate people together: a prime motive of the beat punks.

In 1979 Norman Mailer published *The Executioner's Song*, which seemed to many of us to be his punk novel. In 1974 he had published a book on graffiti. Although hovering between the establishment and the alternative establishment, he lent a good deal of authority to the counterculture by writing intelligently about a number of Bad Boys in Marcia's gallery.

When Marcia photographed Abbie Hoffman he had just emerged from being a fugitive. After her session, he fell asleep on her bed, missing his court date and becoming, once again, a political activist on the lam.

Marcia's lyric portrait of the conceptual artist Tony Shafrazi with a flower in his hair was taken on a day trip to Coney Island. In the 1980s the Tony Shafrazi Gallery in Soho become the showcase of beat punk artists like Keith Haring, Ronnie Cutrone, Andy Warhol, and Jean-Michel Basquiat.

Fred Brathwaite paid homage to Andy Warhol in 1980 when he spray-painted a graffiti rendition of Campbell's soup cans along the whole side of one subway car. The next year he united the worlds of punk, graffiti, and rap by installing the first graffiti art show at the Mudd Club. The more you look into *Punks, Poets & Provocateurs*, the more you find.

Punk was a literate movement, which created a lot of rock writing. Lester Bangs's writing on punk was erudite and kick-ass. He was very funny, and he was really missed. Marcia's tragicomic whiteface Bangs portrait reflects that sadness.

Marcia's Basquiat series is among the book's strongest work. These twisted portraits, owing much to Francis Bacon's painting style, were taken during Basquiat's graffiti period. His writhing body and bared teeth reveal his raw talent, fighting through its own flesh to emerge. It is like the odalisque of Joey Ramone. The difference is that Joey was at the zenith of his career while Basquiat was just getting started. Reflecting Basquiat's painting style, Marcia has made a series of tribal portraits.

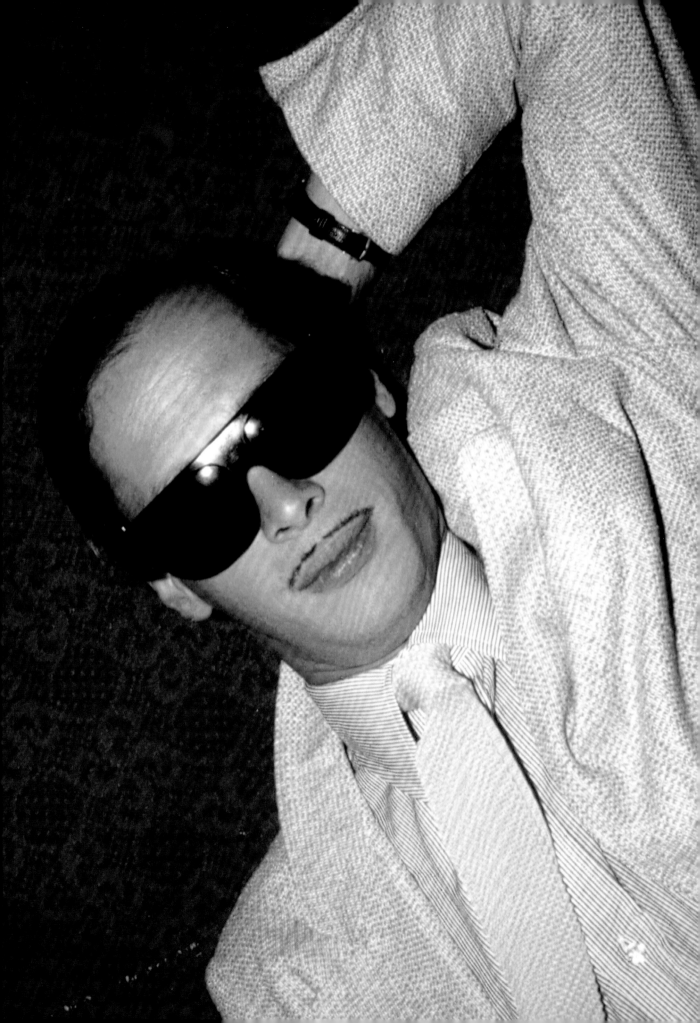

# JOHN WATERS
## SORT OF FAMOUS

BY JOHN WATERS

From *Shock Value: A Tasteful Book About Bad Taste*

I'LL GO ANYWHERE. You have as much fun in a town where you give a lecture as does the person who "rents" you, since this "sponsor" totally manages your life from the minute you arrive. You land in a strange airport and just stand there in the baggage area, trying to look intelligent, until a stranger approaches you and timidly asks, "Are you John Waters?" (A friend who had just completed a book tour and I were discussing this phenomenon, and she added, "Yes, it could be anybody that approaches you—a killer, a kidnapper, a rapist. You don't know him, but you get in his car.") My sponsors usually seem surprised at my relatively normal appearance and blurt out, "*You're* John Waters?" Remembering the ad I saw for videotapes of my films that said "John Waters—his very name is synonymous with fear and nausea," I feel relieved the poor person hasn't started crying or vomiting at the sight of me, and I try to convince them: "Yes, sorry to disappoint you, I *am* John Waters." One sponsor told me, "I thought you'd have bleached hair and wear eye makeup," and I was shocked to realize that some people thought Divine and I were the same person. I gently explain that, luckily, I have no acting aspirations, so I can get away with being more conservative in life. "I bet you're weird," they say hopefully as we walk to their car in the airport parking lot.

"Well, I don't live like the characters in my films," I tell them. Would they expect Alfred Hitchcock to kill people in showers? I wonder.

When we get checked into the hotel room, they sometimes whip out large amounts of marijuana. Since smoking grass only makes me nervous, I politely turn it down, reassuring them that I used to be quite a drug fiend in my youth. They can't get over it: "You don't take dope?" Once they realize the only thing wrong with me is my ideas, we relax and begin to have a normal good time, and I'll hope they take me to the best restaurants and introduce me to the most interesting people in town.

I've never had a hostile reaction from a college audience. The auditorium is usually crowded, and I introduce one of my films and answer questions afterward. I deadpan all of my preposterous opinions on films and filmmaking and feel just like Shecky Greene. The first question is always "Did Divine really eat shit?" and then "Do you have parents?" "Do you live like a normal man in an apartment?" Every once in a while I'll get a lulu like "Is that Edith's real face?" but generally college students today are quite serious and are interested in the financing, distribution, and marketing of my films.

Only once did a member of the college audience get out of hand, and that was at the School of Visual Arts in New York. As I pontificated over trashy movies to a class of art students, a punk ran forward and started biting my arm. I tried to pull away, but he had such a grip with his teeth that he was impossible to shake off. It really hurt, and the thought of getting lockjaw went immediately through my mind. Finally, the professor who had asked me to speak ran to my rescue, pried the student menace off me, and mumbled apologies as he looked in horror at the bite marks on my arm. Realizing the punk was only trying to be friendly, I laughed at this rather strange display of affection and assured all involved that I was okay. After the talk, the punk invited me to come see his band play at CBGB, and that night a bunch of friends and I showed up to catch his act. He came onstage throwing lit firecrackers into the audience, climbed up on a kitchen chair, dove headfirst into a birthday cake, hit himself over the head with a hammer, and dumped a bucket of paint on himself. Then he began to sing, and I realized that his entrance was the best part of the show.

"*John Waters is the Pope of Sleaze*"

—WILLIAM BURROUGHS

John Waters

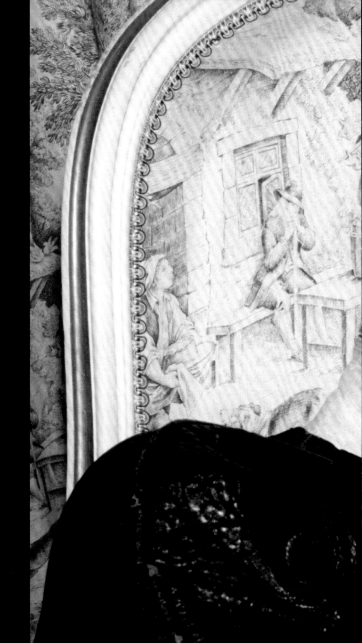

ovation. But one must remember that there is such a thing as good bad taste and bad bad taste. It's easy to disgust someone; I could make a ninety-minute film of people getting their limbs hacked off, but this would only be bad bad taste and not very stylish or original. To understand bad taste, one must have very good taste. Good bad taste can be creatively nauseating but must, at the same time, appeal to the especially twisted sense of humor, which is anything but universal."

"THE FILTHIEST PEOPLE ALIVE,"
*SHOCK VALUE* BY JOHN WATERS, 1981

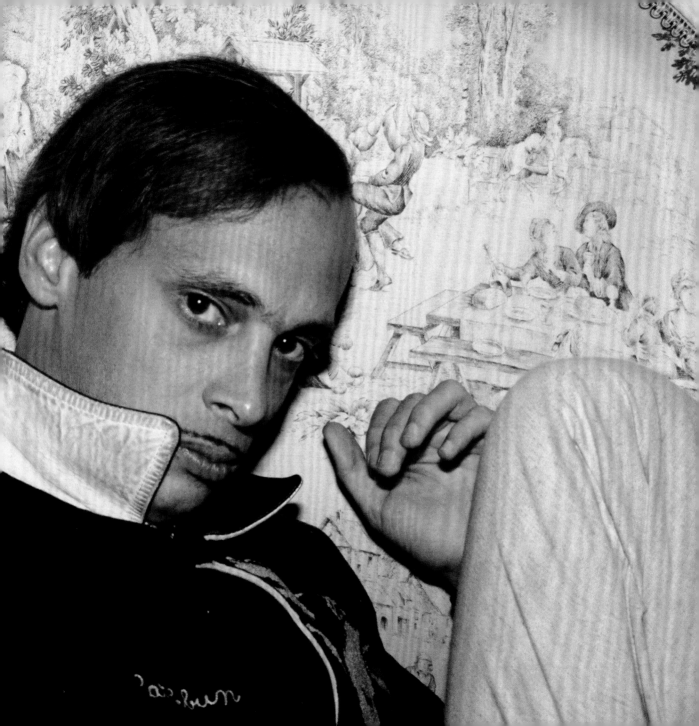

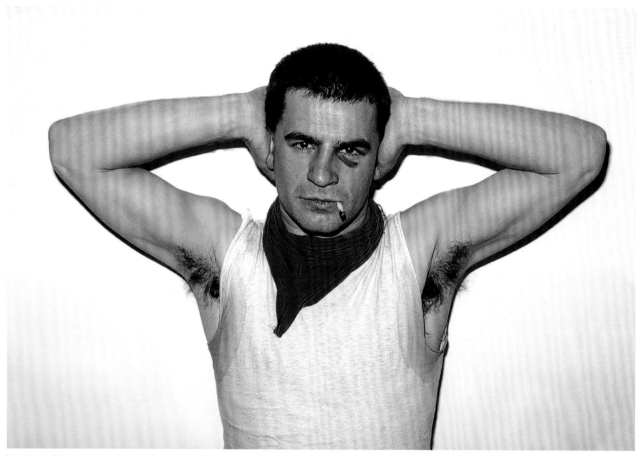

Eric Mitchell (ABOVE), James Chance, Eric Mitchell, and James Nares (OPPOSITE)

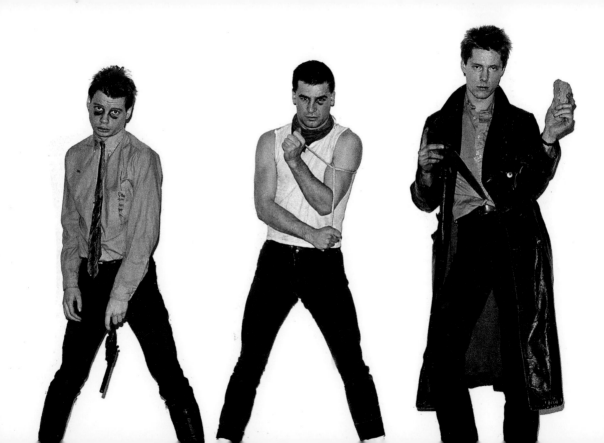

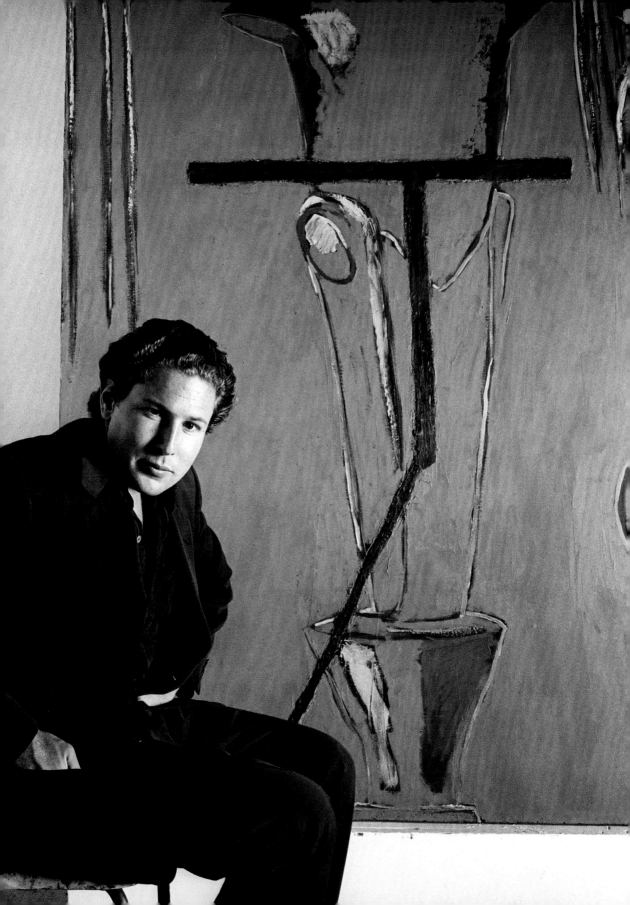

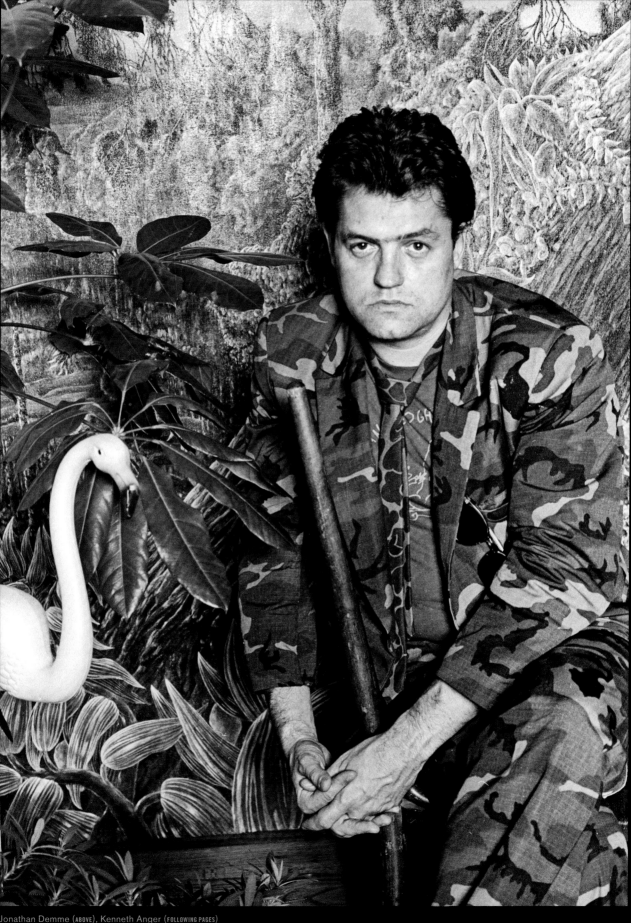

Jonathan Demme (ABOVE), Kenneth Anger (FOLLOWING PAGES)

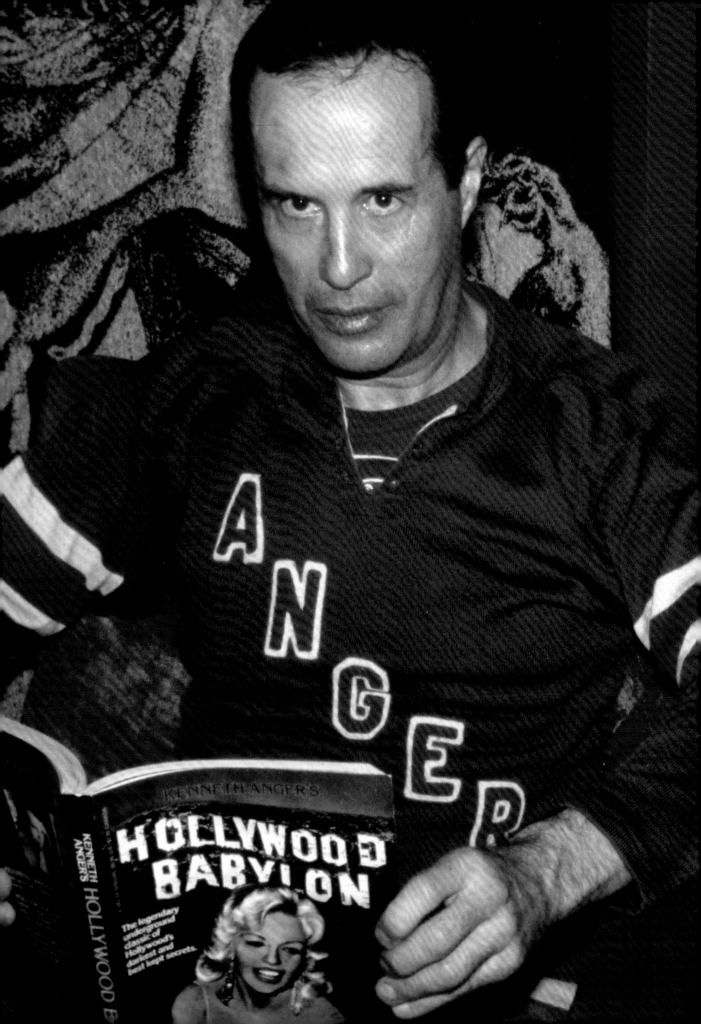

MR. ANGER

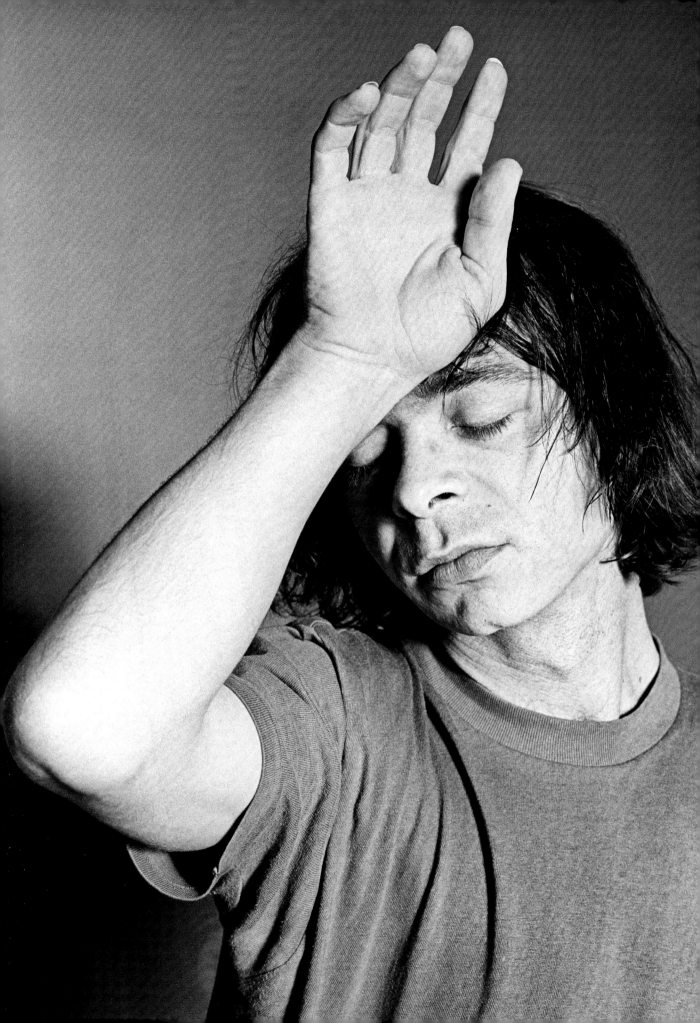

# GARY INDIANA
## NOT SUCH A BAD BOY, REALLY

BY GARY INDIANA

With excerpts from "One Brief, Scuzzy Moment,"
*New York Magazine*, December 6, 2004

NEW YORK WAS NOT A PLACE where being nobody and nothing felt comfortable. For the first and only time in my life, I made a beeline for the people I wanted to meet and become friends with, including most of the people whose names I'd seen in an underground magazine, *X*. Circa 1979, everyone I saw on Second Avenue, day or night, was either someone I knew or someone I recognized: Larry Rivers; punk avatars Richard Hell and Tom Verlaine; filmmaker Nick Zedd; actress Black-Eyed Susan: Jean-Michel Basquiat (who went by his graffiti tag SAMO then); filmmaker Amos Poe; Teri Toye (the most beautiful boy who ever became a girl); and sometimes Debbie Harry. Understand, these familiars didn't graze in packs—there were seldom more than twenty ambulatory individuals scattered between Fourteenth Street and Houston at the same hour.

I lived with Michel Auder on West Broadway, then in Olivier Mosset's loft on Lower Broadway. Eventually I got an apartment on East Eleventh Street that I still occupy when I'm not traveling. In the meantime I met Bill Rice in The Bar on Fourth Street and Second Avenue. We became closest friends, and began performing plays I'd written, in the garden behind Bill's studio on East Third. I'd also met Tina L'Hotsky, queen of the Mudd Club, and started going to the Mudd Club almost every night. It was at the Rock and Roll Funeral Party there that I read an angry poem in front of a big audience, and that got written up in *Rolling Stone*, and suddenly I became a minor celebrity. I directed a play at the Mudd Club, *Alligator Girls Go to College*, which led to other plays that my little company staged at the Performing Garage. In those Mudd Club days I had the reputation of a walking train wreck. The globally hyped, short-lived phenomenon known as the East Village art scene originated in the basement of the building I live in. One day in 1981, through a doorway under the stoop, I noticed Patti Astor rolling paint over dingy walls, in a space. Patti was opening a gallery. In Charlie Ahearn's movie *Wild Style*, she played a reporter whose car breaks down in the Bronx, where she befriends a charismatic group of graffiti artists. Patti's character inserts these artists into the downtown art world.

In my experience, life seldom imitates art and certainly never improves on it, but Patti and her partner, Bill Stelling, did smuggle Harlem and the South Bronx into a veritably albino art scene. The Fun Gallery really was fun. Patti served lava-lamp-colored cocktails. The openings carried the sexy charge of surplus beauty in the room. The place was totally free of pretension. Patti simply didn't care if she made any money: the point was to zap a little soul into the prevailing rigor mortis. Lady Pink, Futura 2000, Daze, and Lee Quinones, among other graffiti artists, as well as renaissance goofball-wit Arch Connelly, were all part of the Fun Gallery. You knew it was all finished when the methadone clinic moved out.

I think people forget that however fucked up we all were, we also worked constantly—when we weren't at Mickey Ruskin's One University Place or Steve Mass's Mudd Club. I never took all the drugs people thought I did. The only drug love affair I had was with amphetamine, which I didn't take to party but to write. Alcohol was a problem for quite a few years. My lippy attitude made me a lot of enemies.

I knew everybody and had sex and/or sampled drugs with most of them. When Reagan came in I had to find a job, so I became the *Village Voice* art critic for two years, and took a lot of acting jobs in Europe. I had a long affair with Ron Vawter, a great actor, and wrote a play for him when he was HIV positive. He performed it until just before he died.

I had a twelve-year, very complicated love affair with the film director Werner Schroeter. Besides Ron, and my cat Lily, who lived with me for thirteen years, Werner was the important love of my life. All these people are dead now: Bill, Tina, Ron, Werner—so many people I cared about have died. You should treasure your own history. William Burroughs once told me, "People like us are lucky because every shitty thing that happens to us is just more material."

Gary Indiana

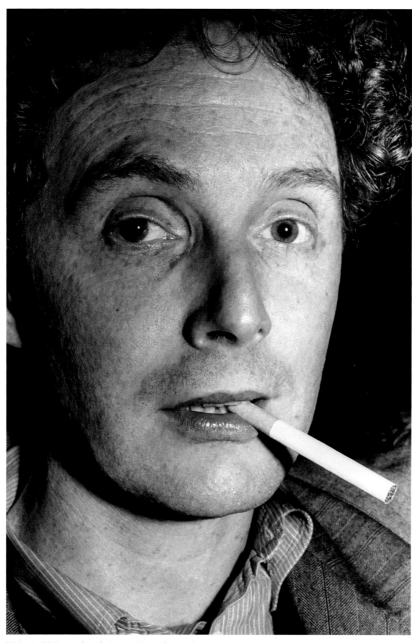

Malcolm McLaren (ABOVE), Danny Fields (OPPOSITE)

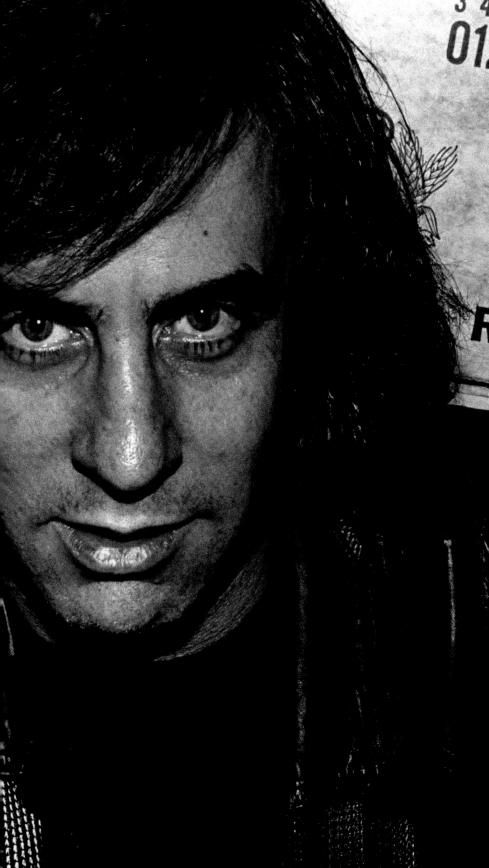

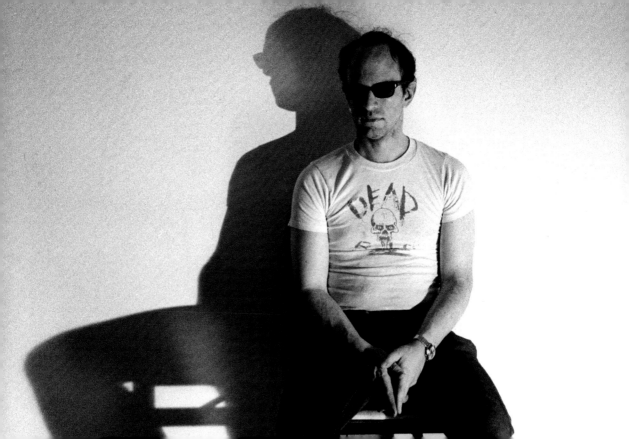

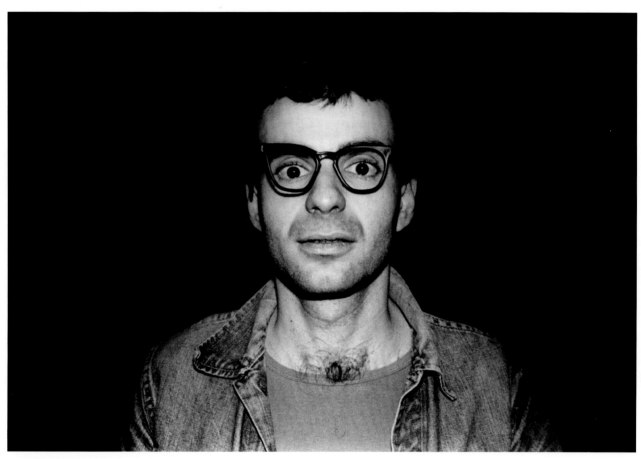

Steve Mass (OPPOSITE), Ronnie Cutrone (ABOVE)
Nick Ray (FOLLOWING PAGES)

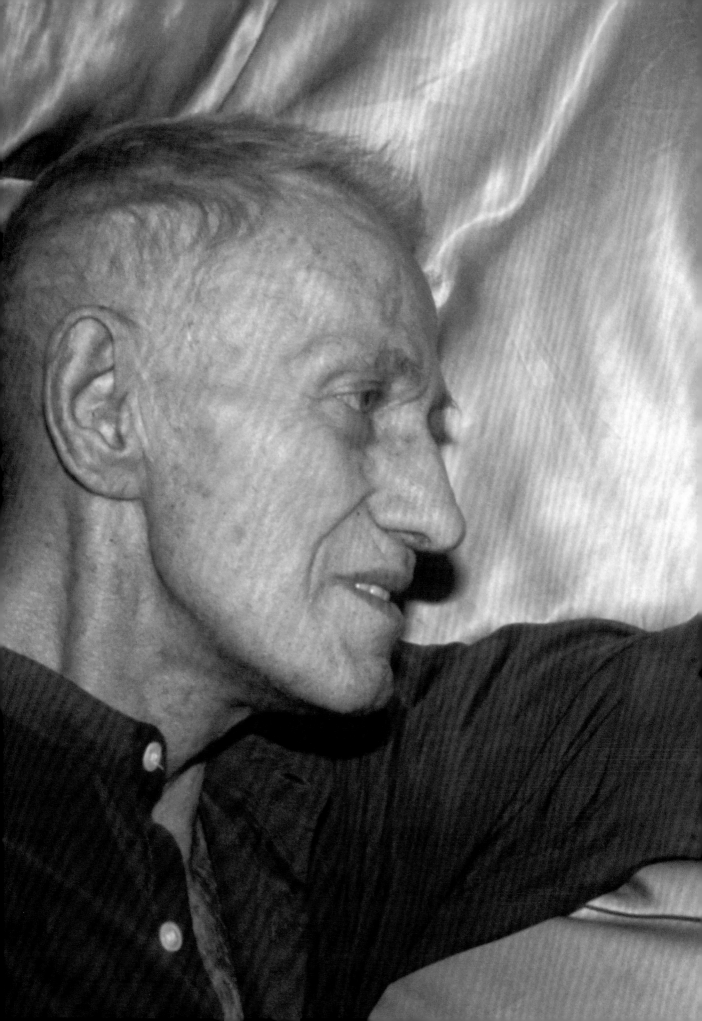

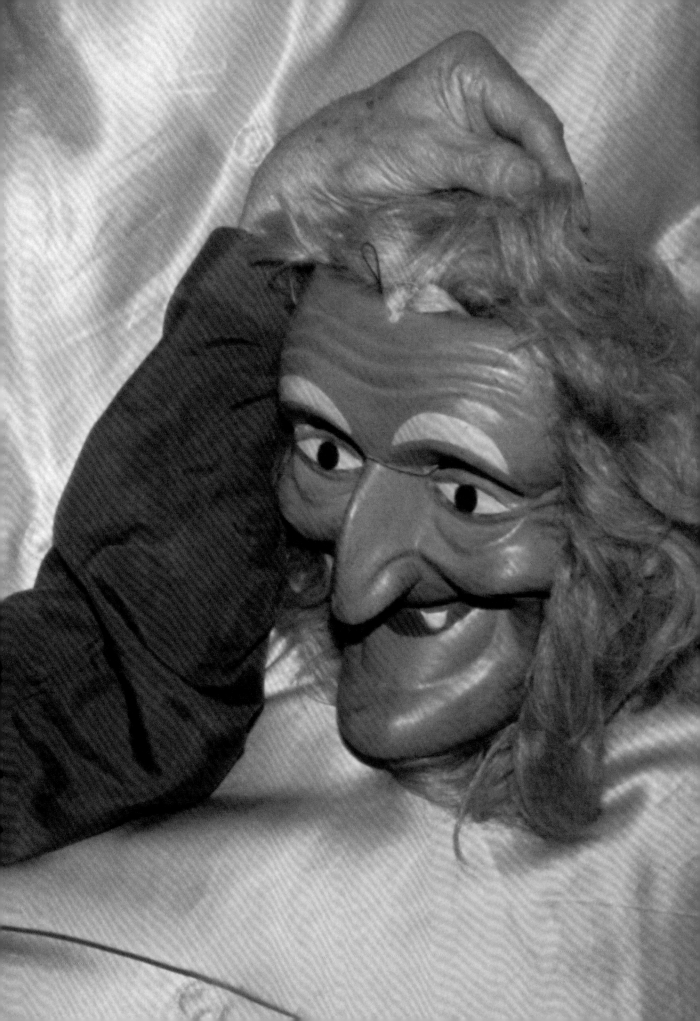

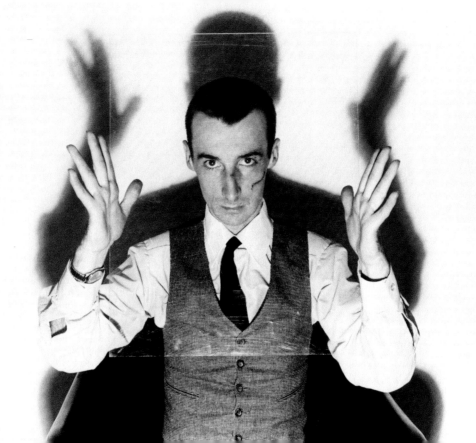

# VICTOR BOCKRIS
## SPEECH TO THE ST. MARK'S POETRY PROJECT AUDIENCE, NEW YEAR'S DAY READING, 2002

*For a person without an extended family in New York, St. Mark's served as immediate neighborhood community and family. In later years St. Mark's became a cradle for some higher rock 'n' roll, New Wave, and performance language. So it had tremendous impact on the centralized progression of rock 'n' roll intelligentsia.*

–Allen Ginsberg, St. Mark's Poetry Project
 from Anne Waldman, *Out of This World*

I FIRST STOOD HERE at this podium on January 1, 1974. I remember the marathon reading that night in particular, because it got a big write-up in the *Voice*. They said it marked the beginning of a new era, and it did. Patti Smith, Jackie Curtis, Robert Wilson, and a number of other people who would become stars of the '70s read that night. But Allen Ginsberg and John Giorno and William Burroughs also sat on these steps. And the greatest thing about that night was how much the younger generation loved the older generation, and how much the older generation would come to love the younger generation. Standing here on this stage and remembering all the years I have come to the St. Mark's marathon readings makes me realize how very much I miss Allen and William and the many other great people who died in the past five years. I miss them because they not only shared with us their wonderful words and visions, but they shared their luminous presences.

But then, as I was walking over here trying to figure out what to read, I suddenly realized that all writers have luminous presences. By which I mean, a presence that is both enlightened and enlightening, and that allows other people to be in its light. It is a presence that is both strong and vulnerable because it needs to allow other minds to walk in and out of its mind. As luminous presences we all have the potential to fill this room for many years to come with as much light as the heroes who came before us–if we can learn how to survive.

We need to be made more aware of the need to learn how to live, because life is very short, and sometimes it goes away too quickly. Andy Warhol said that, talking about how he hoped his work affected people. I can perhaps add a clue to his admonition: in 1965, William Burroughs and Brion Gysin wrote a book called *The Third Mind*, published in 1978. It was about the cut-up techniques and the fact that, collaborating as intensely as they had on the melding of their two minds, they had created an individual third mind. Anybody who is open enough to collaborate with another person has the potential to create a third mind. The best work of the Rolling Stones, for example, is the creation of the third mind born out of forty years of collaboration of Keith Richard and Mick Jagger. "The future of writing may be in collaboration," Burroughs once told me. Not only that, but I know the survival of this planet depends upon our recognition that life is collaboration.

The best way to combat terror is to follow Burroughs through the hole he blew in time into this stark present–to stop living in references to the past, writing what we have already written, fighting wars we have already fought. The only way to do this is to climb out of our angry individual Rimbaud ego suits, which are as obsolete as cowboy drag, and enter the sacred field of collaboration in the heart.

"Minutes to go," Mr. Burroughs wrote in 1959–but who knows what clock he was watching. I, Victor Bockris, tell you that it is not too late: the key is in the window, in the light in the window; the key is in the third mind.

Bless yourselves, love and caress the writers in you, and extend your mind into the luminosity of all minds.

Victor Bockris

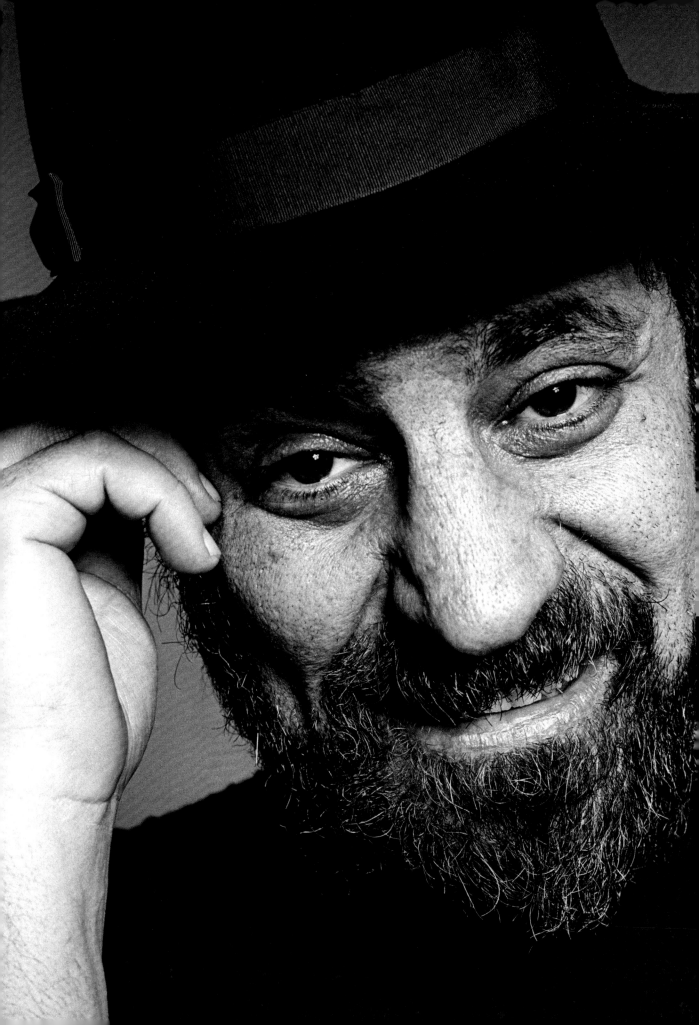

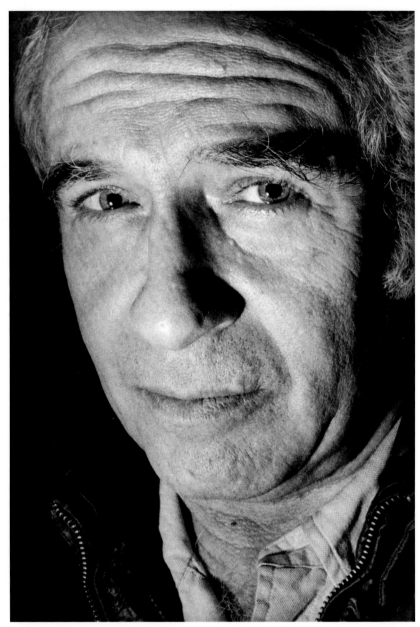

Abbie Hoffman (OPPOSITE), Norman Mailer (ABOVE)

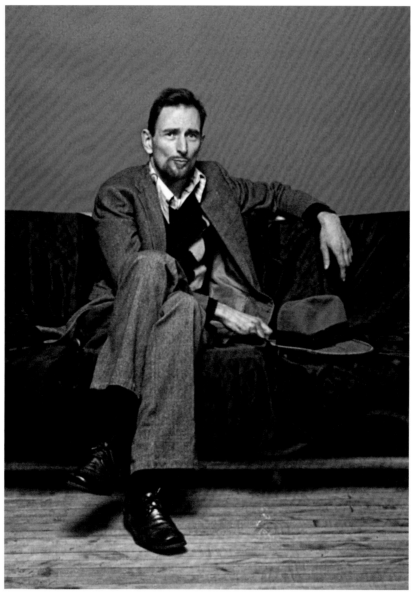

Jack Smith (ABOVE), Christo (OPPOSITE)

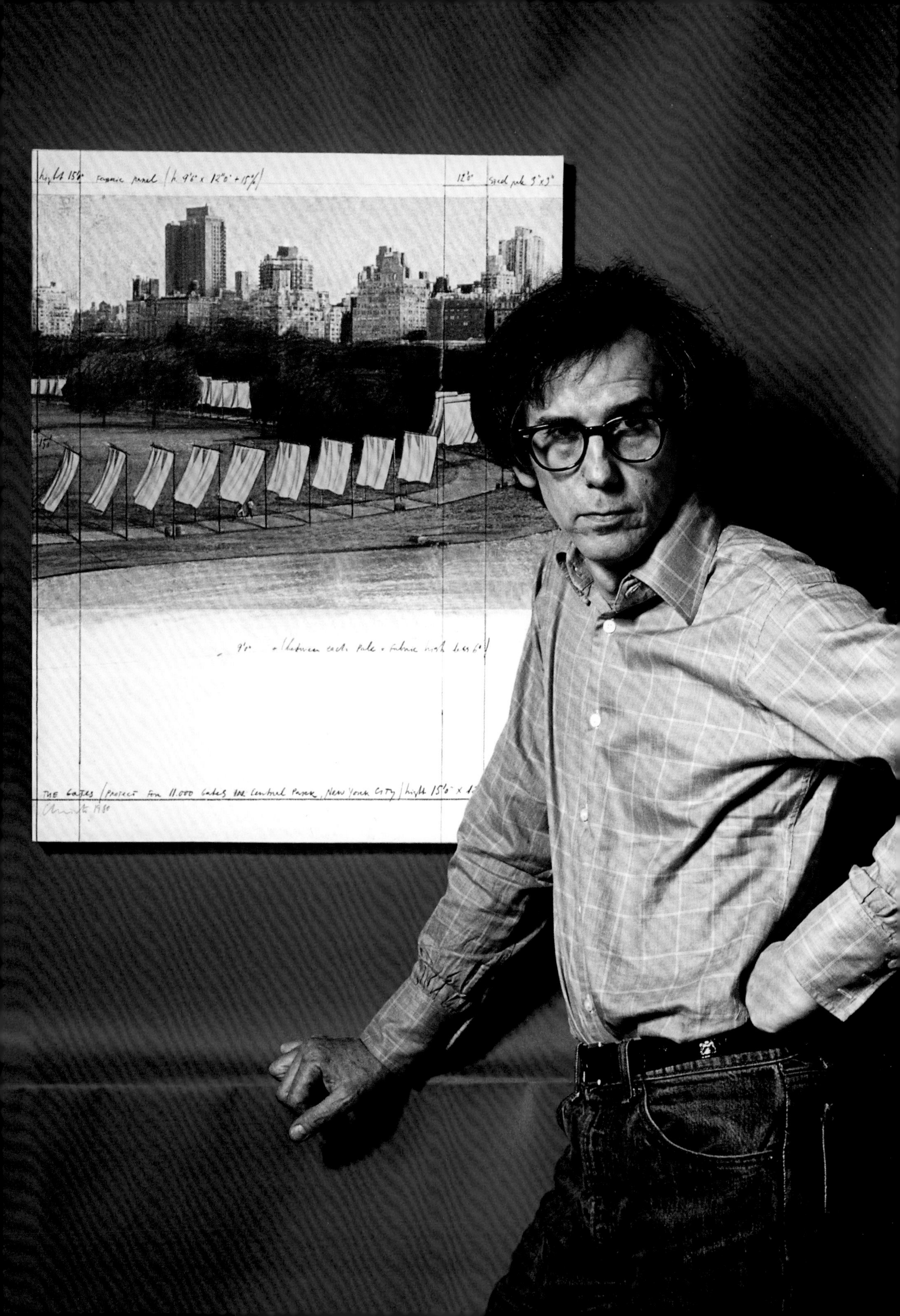

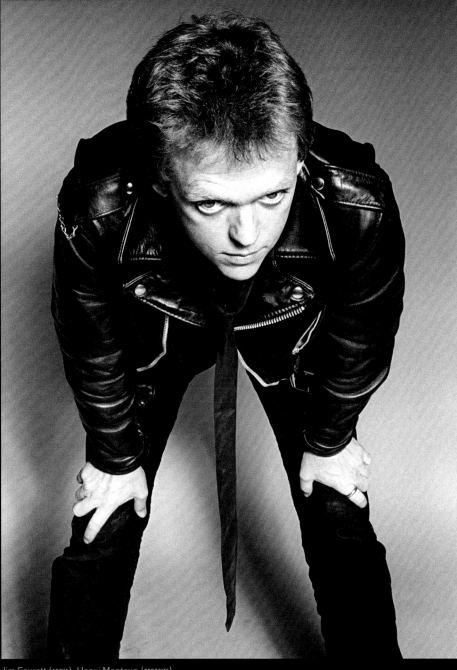

Jim Fouratt (ABOVE), Haoui Montaug (OPPOSITE)

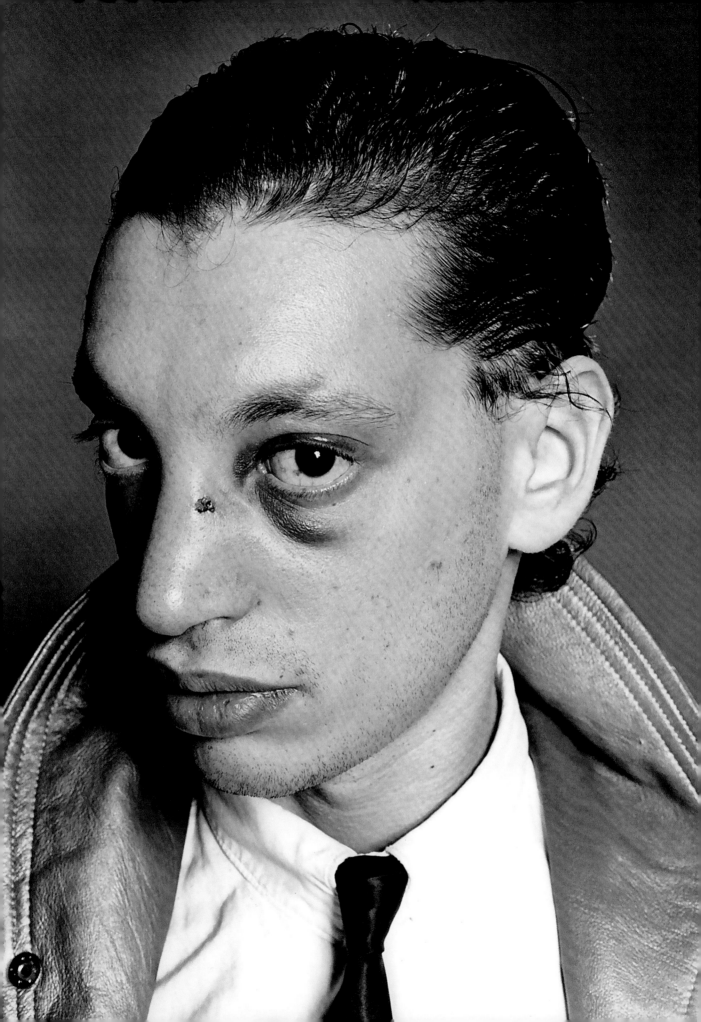

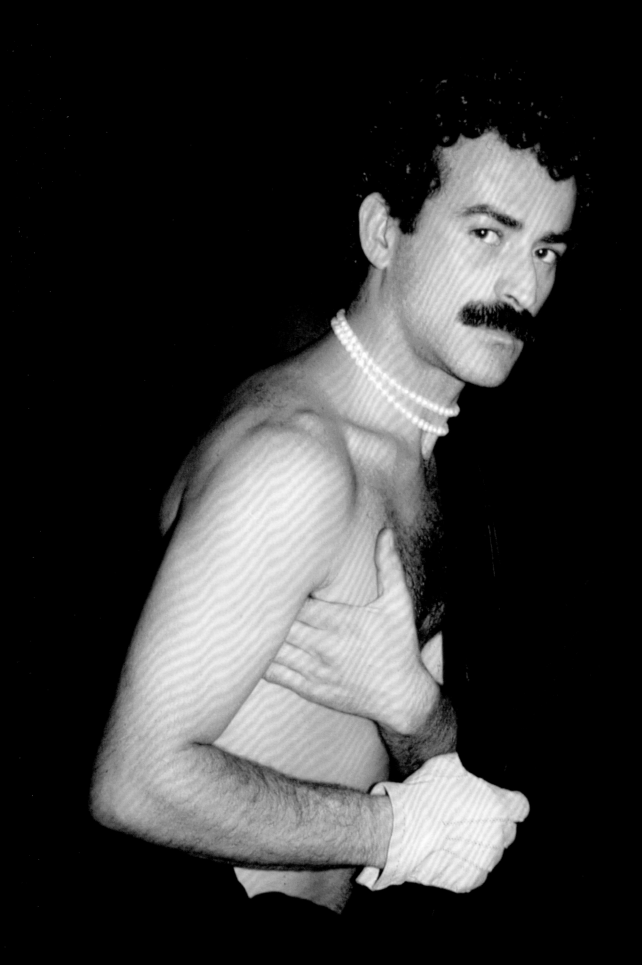

# VICTOR HUGO
## CATALYST OF CHAOS

"VICTOR WAS MUCH MORE than another big dick," wrote Steven Gaines in his lively biography, *Simply Halston: The Untold Story*. Victor Hugo was a unique proto-type of the new tribe: outspokenly gay, strikingly good-looking and incredibly funny. The multitalented young Venezuelan had been working with America's number one fashion designer, Halston, since 1974. "Victor was brilliant, zany, exciting, and dan-gerous," Gaines continued. "Because of him, Halston would forever live his life on the edge—on the edge of legality, or propriety, and of sanity."

"The person that Halston loved, more than his own life, was Victor Hugo," Gaines quoted Peruchio Valls, a mutual friend, as saying. "And the love of Victor Hugo's life was Halston."

"Victor soon became the third point of a triangle between Warhol and Halston," Gaines explained. "They had known each other for years but they were both so shy they shied away from each other," Victor Hugo recalled. "I said, 'Men, you have such a great tender love for each other I cannot be in between you,' and I put them together, but they had their doubts. It was just so painful."

Victor's best friend, Benjamin Liu, stated, "They were two queens at the heights of their careers who made it to the top of their industries at the same time so there was a lot of the queendom. . . . I thought it was a peculiarly American, almost healthy kind of business competition. And Victor had the best of both worlds in many senses, but he also created tremendous energy and creativity for both of them."

Victor Hugo's main role was as the court painter's jester. With his irrepressible cocaine-fueled energy, Victor had a gift for live theater, especially for entrances. It was like Victor to arrive by seaplane at a Montauk dinner party in a sequined jock-strap, or to show up at Studio 54 in an ambulance, jump off a stretcher, and begin to dance. He was also a voluble talker in a thick Venezuelan accent, which most peo-ple—including Andy—found almost incomprehensible. In the manner of all royal fools, he mocked Andy, calling him "the Queen of the Shallow." But he was impressed by Andy's attitude toward life.

Hugo was Warhol's sexual anthropologist. In 1977, Victor became both procurer and model for Warhol's *Torsos* and *Sex Parts* paintings, a series of explicit, verging on pornographic, canvases depicting male backs, buttocks, penises, and thighs.

Hundreds of photographs were taken over 1977, from which Warhol selected several of the least openly sexual shots of Victor and his friends for the *Torsos* silk-screens; six of the more explicit photos became the *Sex Parts* series the following year. Victor Hugo fawned over Andy's creations, while at the same time joking with Halston that Andy "needs to get off."

He was never Andy's lover, but through the mid 1980s the abstinent War-hol experienced sex vicariously through Victor's repeated adventures. According to Steven Gaines, "Victor turned into something of a sexual muse for Warhol, who would frequently sponsor Victor's purchase of hustlers or bar tricks and attend and photograph sexual sessions with them." Victor Hugo recalled, "Andy was jerkin' off in the bathroom in between taking pictures."

Victor Hugo

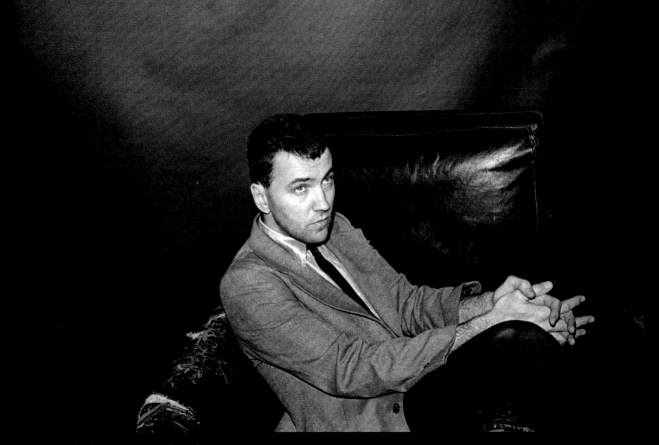

Diego Cortez (ABOVE), Gerard Malanga (OPPOSITE)

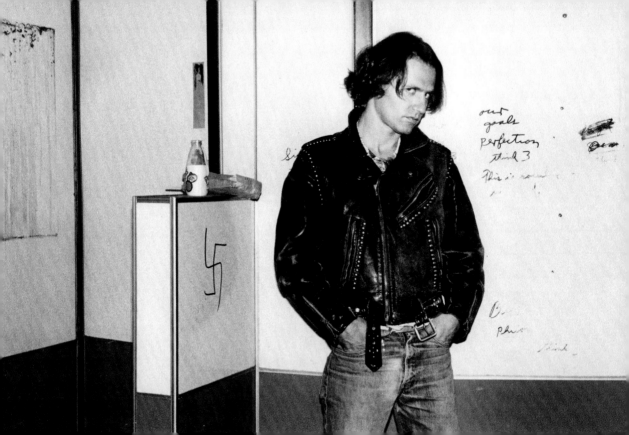

Quentin Crisp (OPPOSITE)

Paul Morrissey (FOLLOWING PAGES)

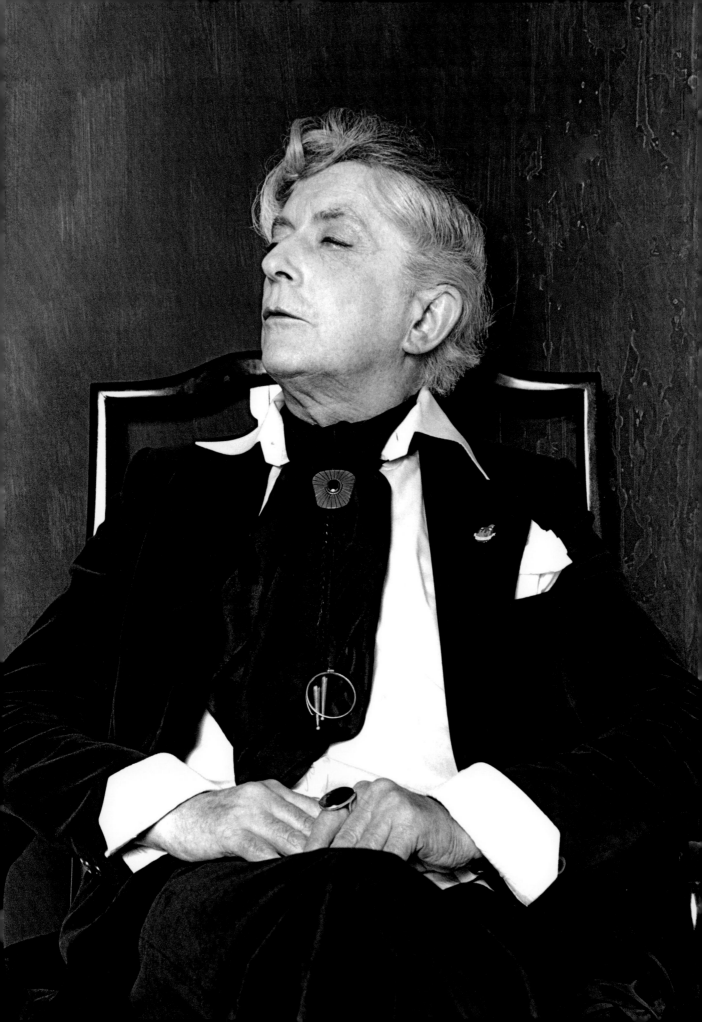

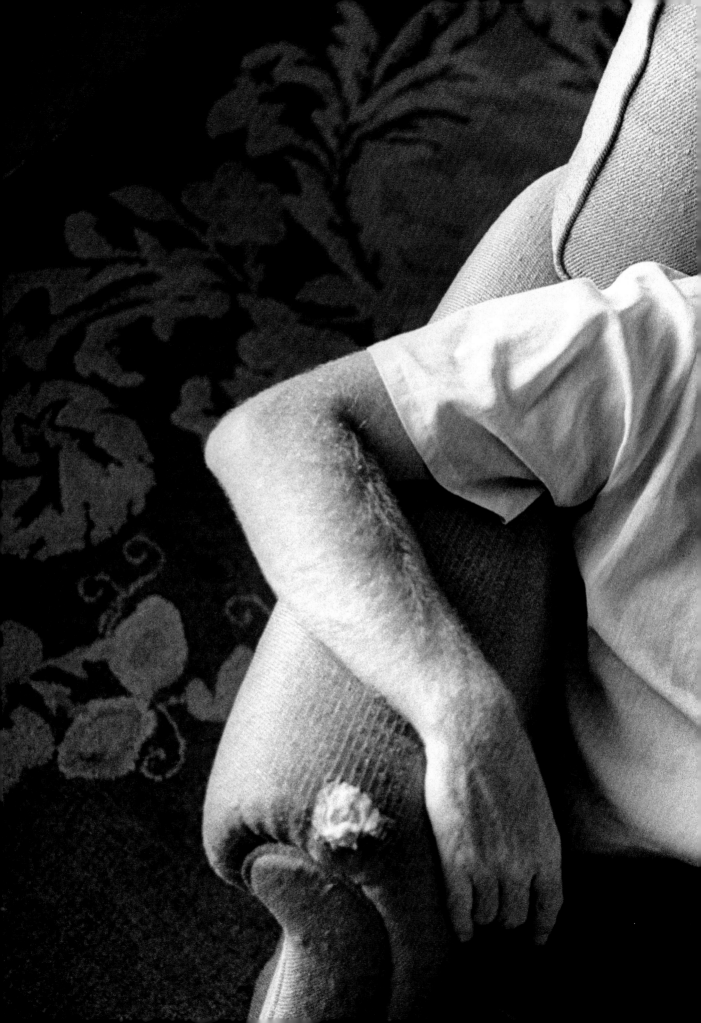

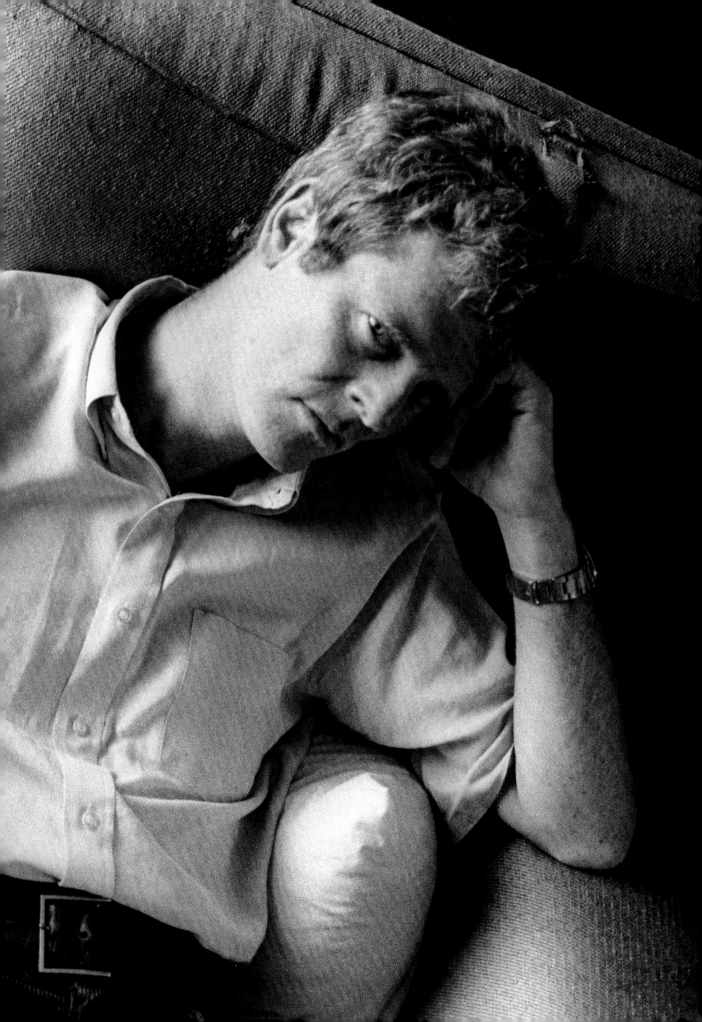

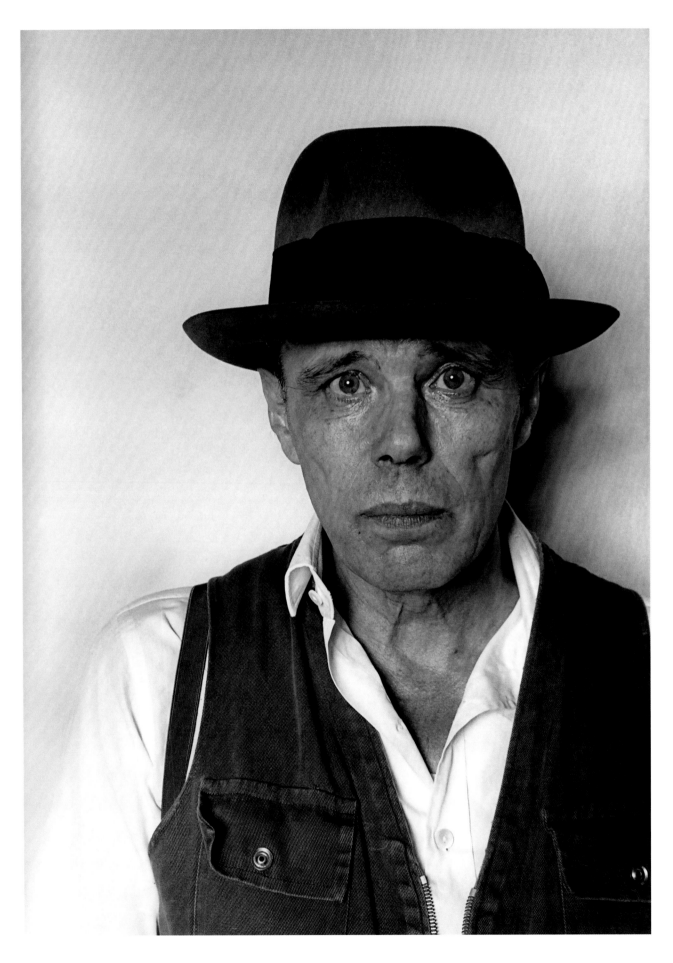

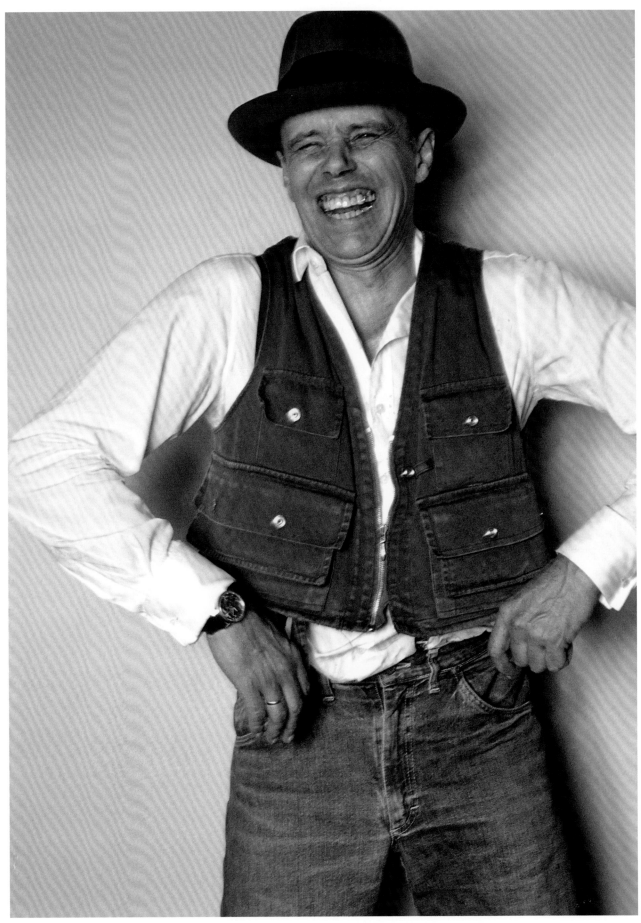

Joseph Beuys

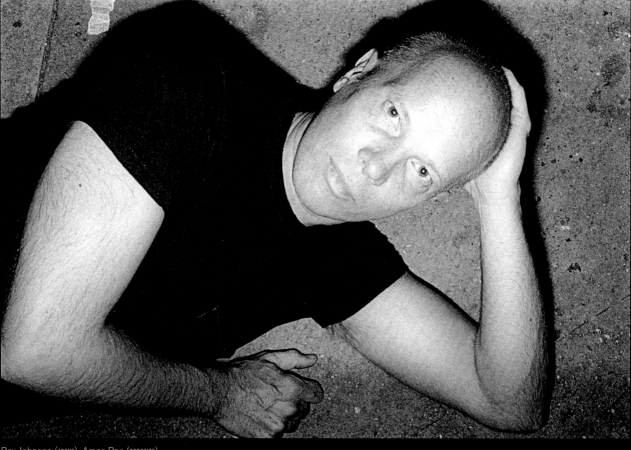

Ray Johnson (ABOVE), Amos Poe (OPPOSITE)

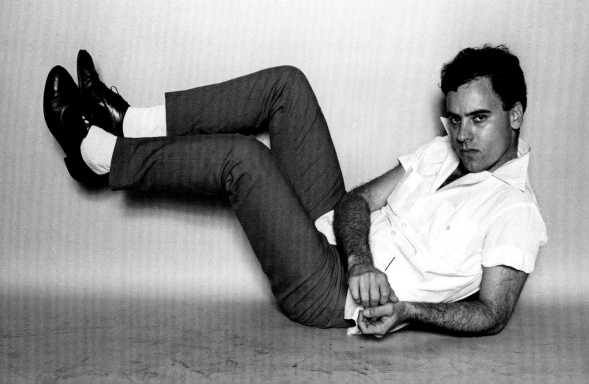

# LEGS MCNEIL
## RUNNING WITH LEGS

AS THE RESIDENT PUNK at *Punk* magazine, Legs McNeil was the scene's soul and its hip philosopher. "The great thing about punk was that it had no political agenda," he wrote in his and Gillian McCain's seminal book on New York punk, *Please Kill Me: The Uncensored Oral History of Punk.*

It was about real freedom, personal freedom. It was also about doing anything that's gonna offend a grown-up. Just being as offensive as possible. Which seemed delightful, just euphoric. Be the real people we are. You know? I just loved it.

I remember my favorite nights were just getting drunk and walking around the East Village kicking over garbage cans. Just the night. Just the night.

Legs's birthday, 8:30 p.m. at his girlfriend Lori's apartment: my roommate Jeff Goldberg and I put our heads together on Legs's birthday present. What could we get him? A *watch*, we decided, what a great idea, and rushed out and spent $25 on a Timex, a manly model, which we then bestowed on him with speeches worthy of Dean Martin: the beginning of a new life, et cetera. You're a big boy now, et cetera.

Legs pretty much refused to take it out of the box. He stuffed it in his jeans. It fell out. He stepped on it, picked it up, pretended it didn't work. It was like giving the wrong girl a doll. Some girls spot the point of it right off. "I don't want a fucking doll!" they yell. "I don't wanna take care of a fucking baby!" Legs was rejecting time, rejecting giving up, rejecting the acceptance of any kind of routine. It was sort of heroic, in a way.

Throughout these years Legs was like my blood brother. He only had one problem. He was incorrigible with girls. I used to tell him, "Legs! It's gonna fall off!" Thus it was that I was poleaxed to meet the girl he settled down with (!) in a deluxe apartment in the sky. Legs and Lori were a cute couple. They certainly looked good together, and you got a sort of good feeling from being with them together. It was fun. She was funny. She always had drugs or could lead you to them. She was strong. She could run with us. It went on for a long time. But it was, of course, always a troubled relationship in the field of stories about drunk, Irish punks in black leather jackets who electrify the lives of beautiful, sexy, hip middle-class Jewish girls from New York, or anywhere.

I mean, you'd all be having a good time at Arturo's, with plans to go to CBGB with the Ramones in fifteen minutes, when suddenly Lori and Legs would be running down the street. You'd carry on, but sort of miss them and wish they hadn't rushed off. A couple of hours later, coming out of the club, you would see them speeding by in a cab, passionately making out. It was an epic relationship.

Legs and I had a ritual. On the way up to Lori's apartment, we used to kneel down in the elevator and say a prayer of thanks to God for the body of Susan X. She was the single most beautiful girl on the punk scene for about six months. That was before she got beat up by her English speed-dealer boyfriend, who used to get hung out the window by his feet if he didn't pay his supplier on time, and then get thrown on a kitchen floor covered with broken glass, naked. She thought she deserved the beatings.

Legs and I knew her before we had discovered this flaw in her character. There were no flaws on her body, no flaws and no clues. You had no idea where she had come from. She was a cream dream and she was intelligent, too, actually probably much too intelligent for Legs; too intelligent for me, too. She would probably think that Legs was more intelligent than I was, and perhaps she was right from her own perspective, but I don't think so.

Legs McNeil (OPPOSITE)

Tony Shafrazi (FOLLOWING PAGES)

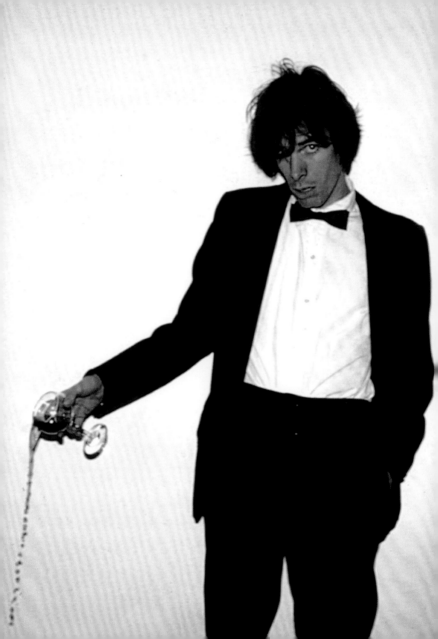

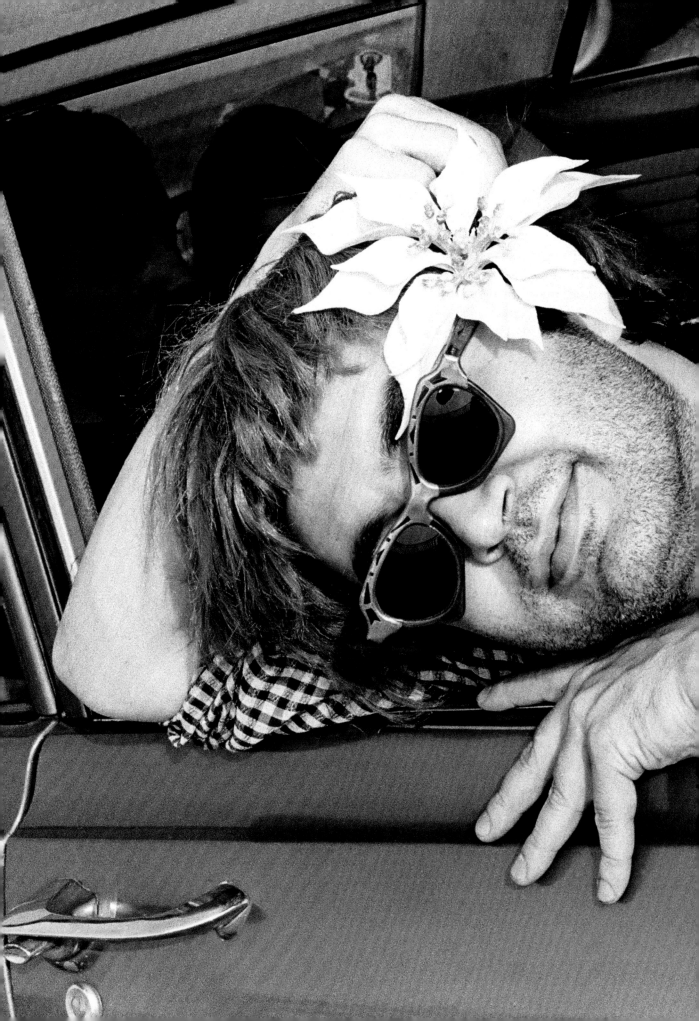

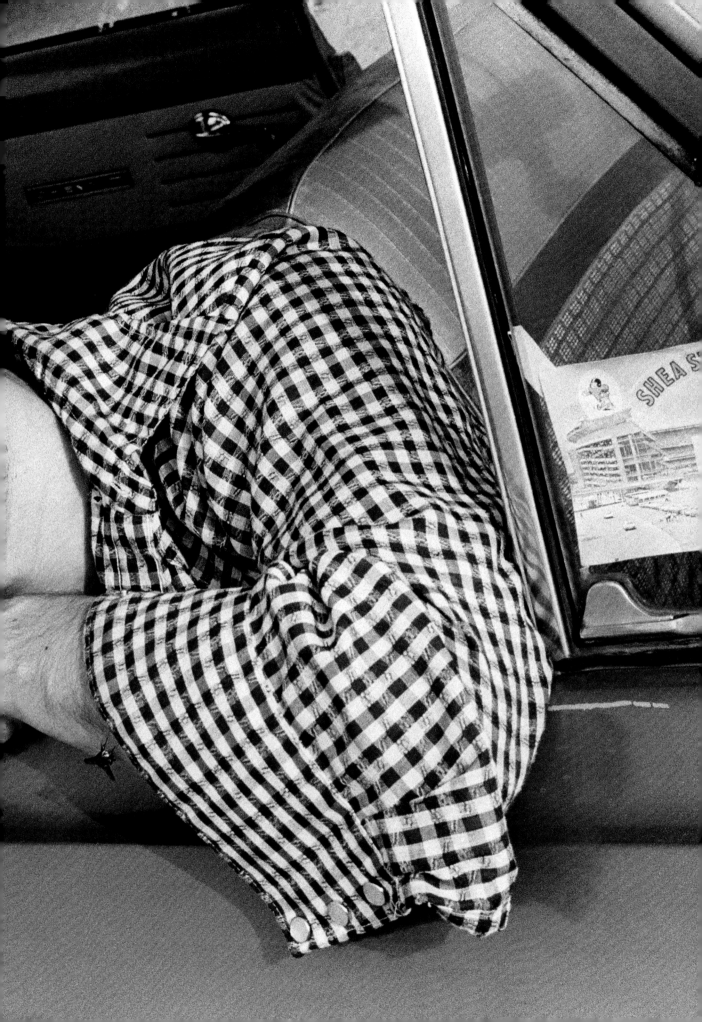

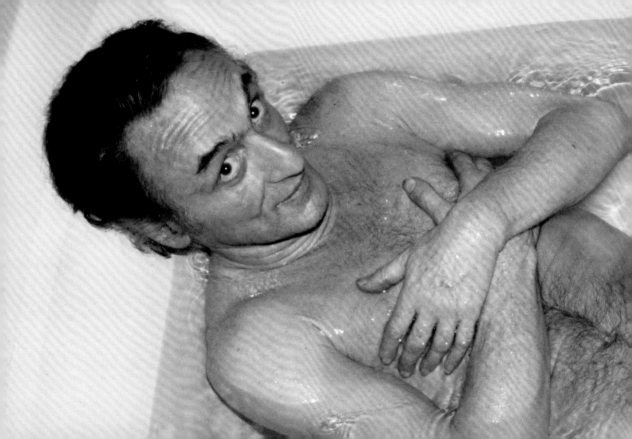

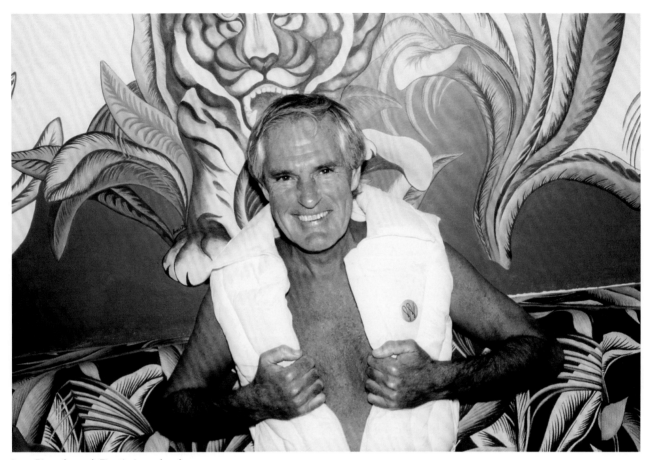

Larry Rivers (OPPOSITE), Timothy Leary (ABOVE)

the dry-goods area and on the banquettes, fifty-pound flour sacks being popular staging areas for after-work copulation. We'd bribe the doormen and security people of all the local nightclubs and rock-and-roll venues with steak sandwiches and free snacks, so that after we'd finished with our pleasures at the bar, we'd bounce around from club to club without waiting on line or paying admission. A squadron of punk rocker junkie guitar heroes ate for free at the restaurant—so we got free tickets and backstage passes to the Mudd Club, CBGB, Tier Three, Hurrah, Club 57 and so on. And when the clubs closed it was off to after-hours where we'd drink and do more drugs . . . "

—ANTHONY BOURDAIN
FROM *KITCHEN CONFIDENTIAL: ADVENTURES IN THE CULINARY UNDERBELLY*, 2000

Anthony Bourdain

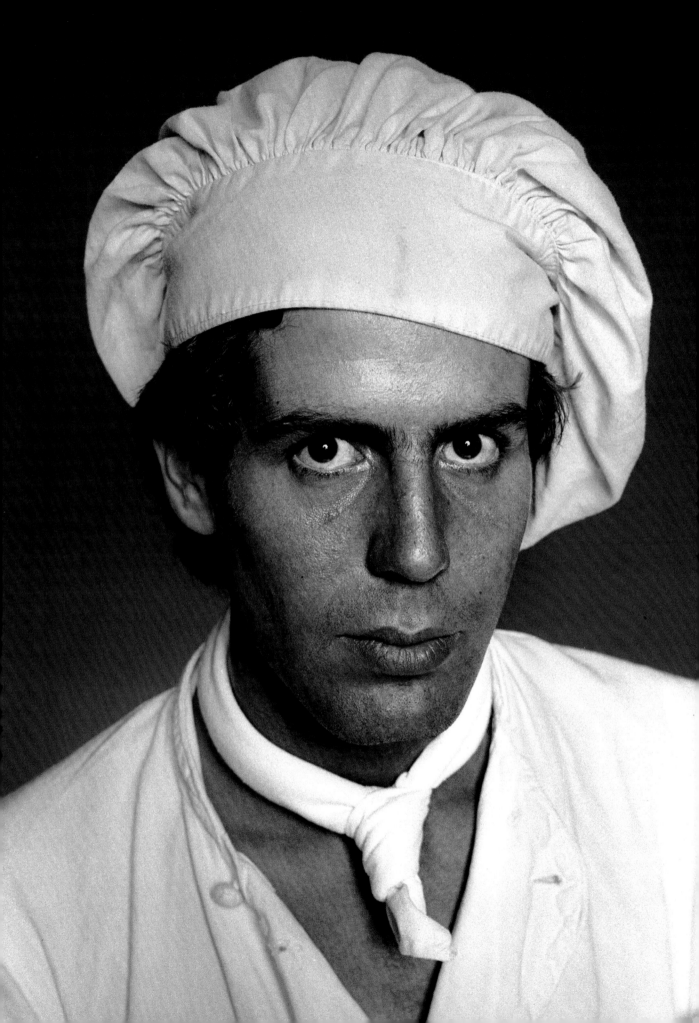

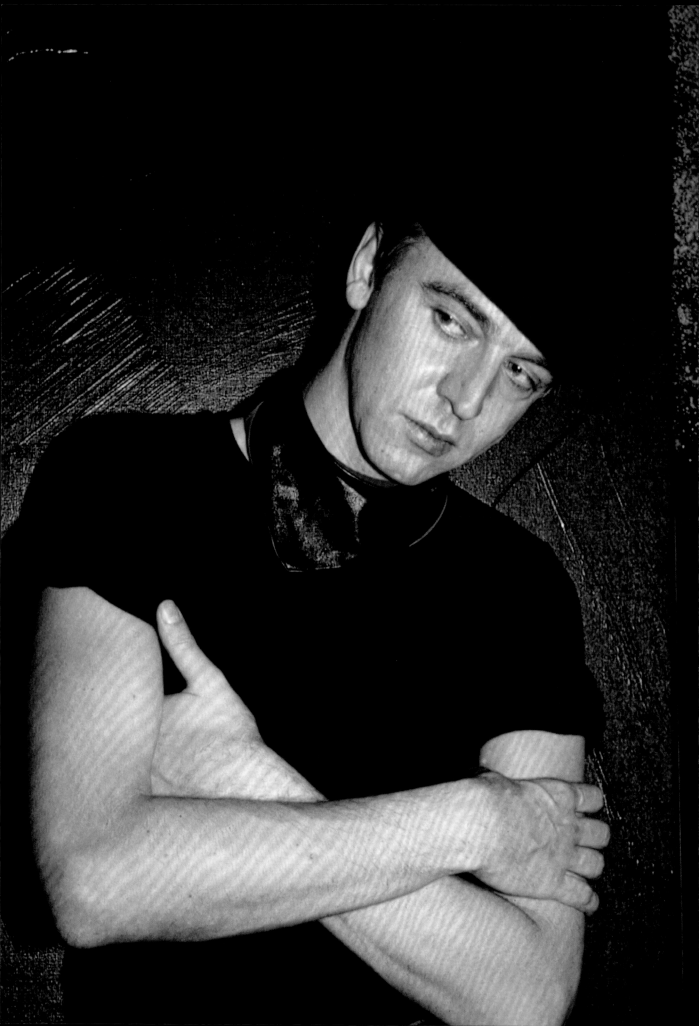

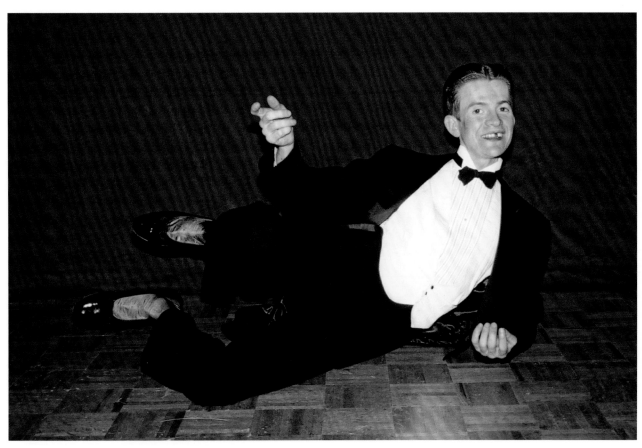

Rene Ricard (OPPOSITE), David McDermott (ABOVE)

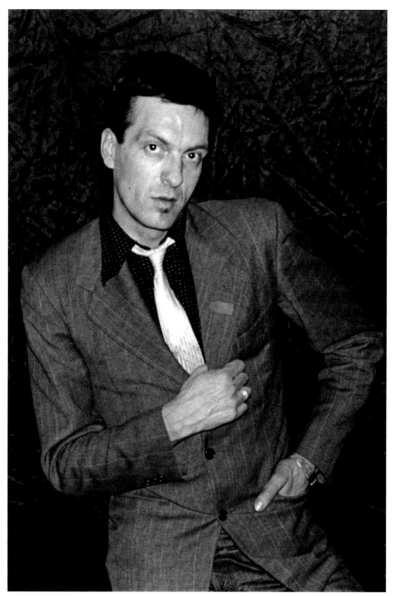

Max Blagg (ABOVE), Tommy Gunn (OPPOSITE)

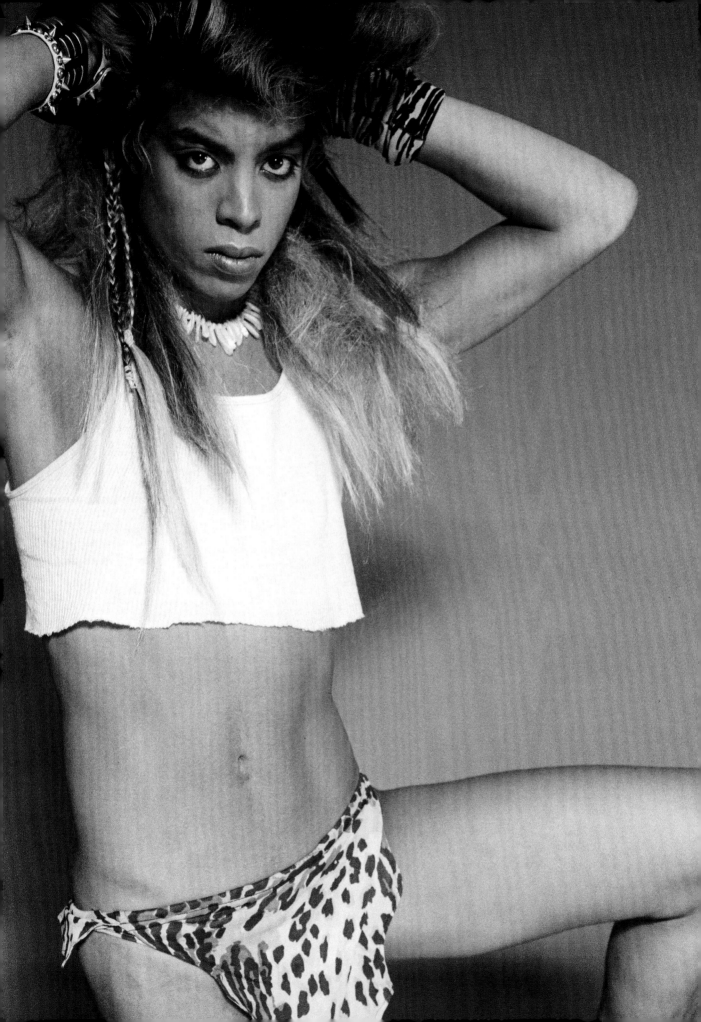

Fred Brathwaite (Fab 5 Freddy)

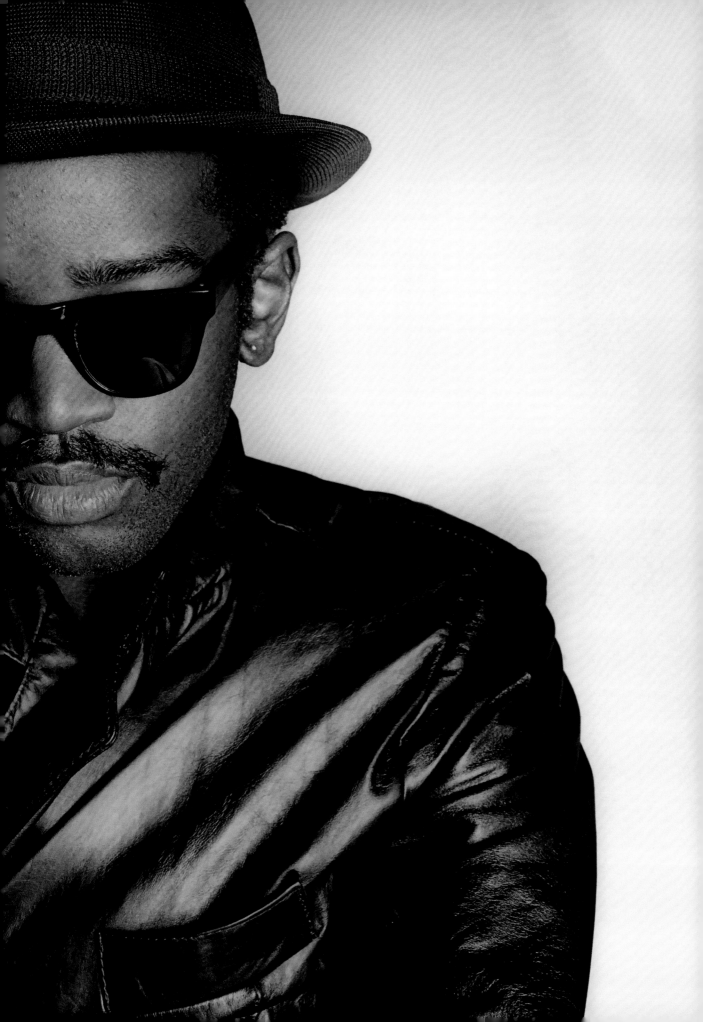

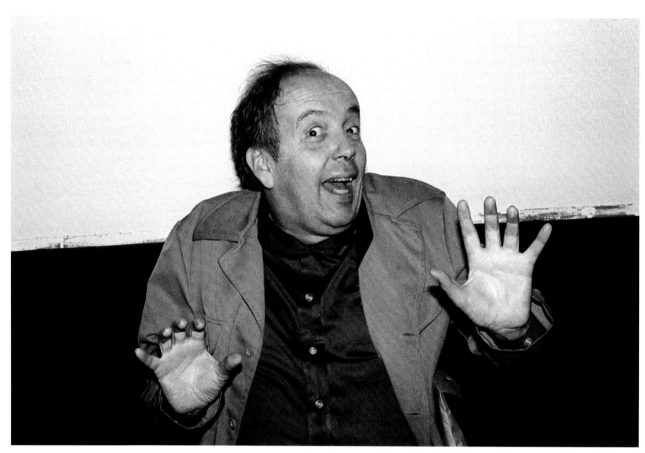

Taylor Mead (ABOVE), Jackie Curtis (OPPOSITE)

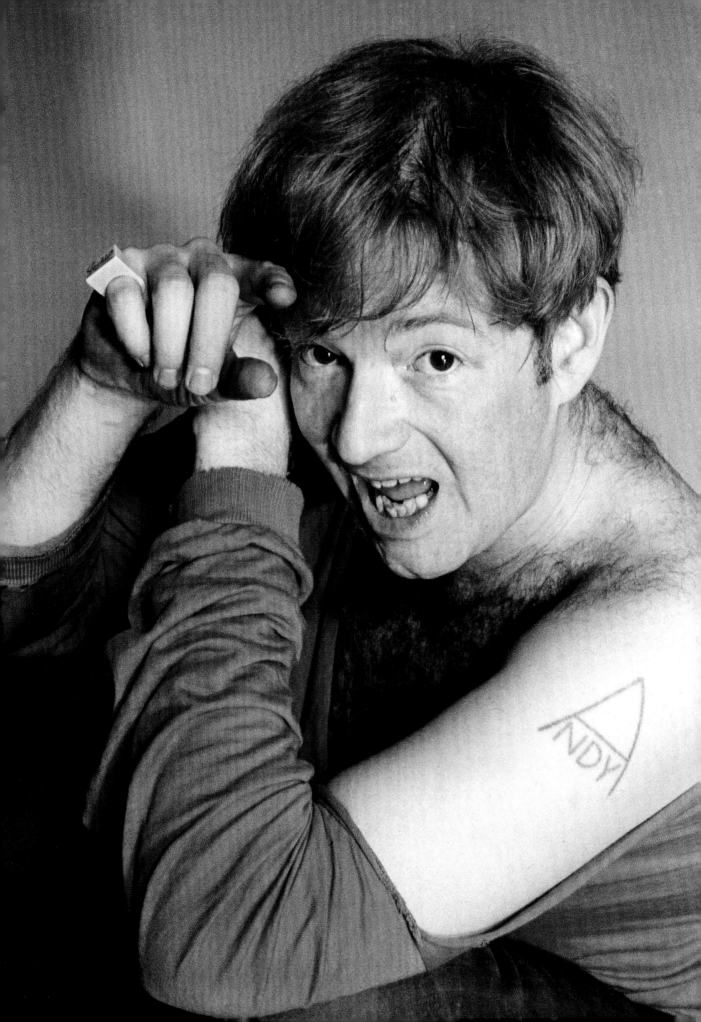

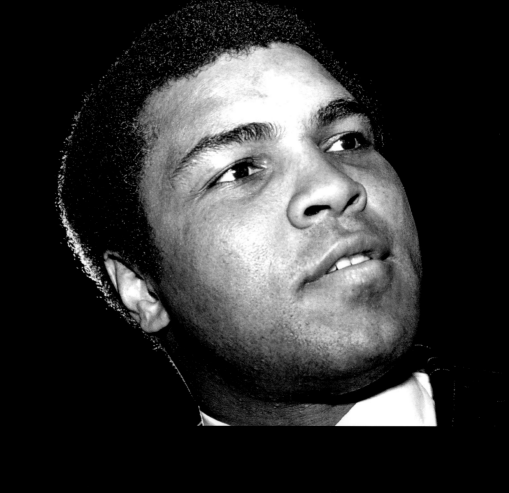

# MUHAMMAD ALI
## RAPPING WITH THE PRINCE OF SLAM

BY VICTOR BOCKRIS

From *Muhammad Ali: In Fighter's Heaven*, 1974

ALI SITS BACK IN HIS CHAIR, looks up calmly, and says, conclusively: "Imagination. See, I fly. They stand still. . . . I suggest to myself that I'm going to do this and do that, and I do it. I believe I'm gonna get him in this round; I practice it. And I believe I can do this, and do it. Confidence. Confidence. Every man wants to be determined. Every man wants to believe in himself, every man wants to be fearless. And when I display this, it attracts people; they come to see if I can do it. Many of them envy you, because they want to do it, and they can't. Many of them like it; many of them don't like it. Many like you for it. See? . . .

"Take me, for example. I attract people. Pretty girls from all over the country charter planes to my fights because I say things that attract them: 'I'm beautiful! I'm too pretty to be a fighter! Look at me! I'm the prettiest fighter! There ain't never been a fighter so beautiful!' And they just say, 'He's crazy!' They know I'm pretty." Ali is beginning to enjoy himself. Grinning broadly, he acts out the role of each person.

"Then I attract the redneck white folks that don't like black people: 'I'm the greatest!'" he yells, rolling his eyes with his fist in front of his face. "'That nigger's too arrogant; he talks too much!'

"Then I attract the black militants that don't like the whites: 'Yeah! Tell 'em, brother. Tell them honkies, brother!'

"Then I got all the long-haired hippies, because I don't go to war. I ain't goin' to Vietnam.

"Then I attract the Muslims, because of the name Muhammad Ali. Then the Israeli, who don't get along with the Muslims, might come to see me get whipped, because I'm a Muslim. And the Muslim's gonna root for me, because he don't want the Israeli to get his wishes. So you add it all up, I got a helluva crowd. Personality."

He read another poem, commenting on it as he went along:

Life is a fair trade where all adjusts itself in time.
If his wealth is in the bank, and not in his knowledge,
Then he doesn't possess it, because it's in the bank.

"Ain't that beautiful? A man with no money can get it. They had me broke at one time. I was fighting and thinking and writing and I came back. A lot of people lose their money; but with no mind, they don't get it again." Ali read the poem a second time, putting a gentle emphasis on "because it's in the bank."

Since he refused his induction to Vietnam and changed his name from Cassius Clay to Muhammad Ali, declaring support for Elijah Muhammad and the Black Muslim movement, Ali has emerged as a man with a message. And it is not about boxing; he really didn't want to talk about that any more. Whenever I brought it up, he steered the conversation back to what he now considers his major tasks: writing, running the camp, thinking. Boxing was a metaphor, a chest of tools into which he could reach for illustrations, something in which he was expert, but disinterested.

"Why are you successful?"

"I would say determination to be successful in whatever field you endeavor. Then hope, in whatever field you determine, to be successful. Hope comes from the determination to achieve something. So therefore, this determination in itself can be a very great power. The goal which a person determines to reach is small in comparison to the power that he gains in the process of determination. And in itself, belief is another thing which a lot of men don't have, belief. Many things could be accomplished if we only believed. I was determined that I would be successful. . . . I believed. Number One is Allah, A-L-L-A-H. God is the number one reason to whom I give credit for my success."

Muhammad Ali

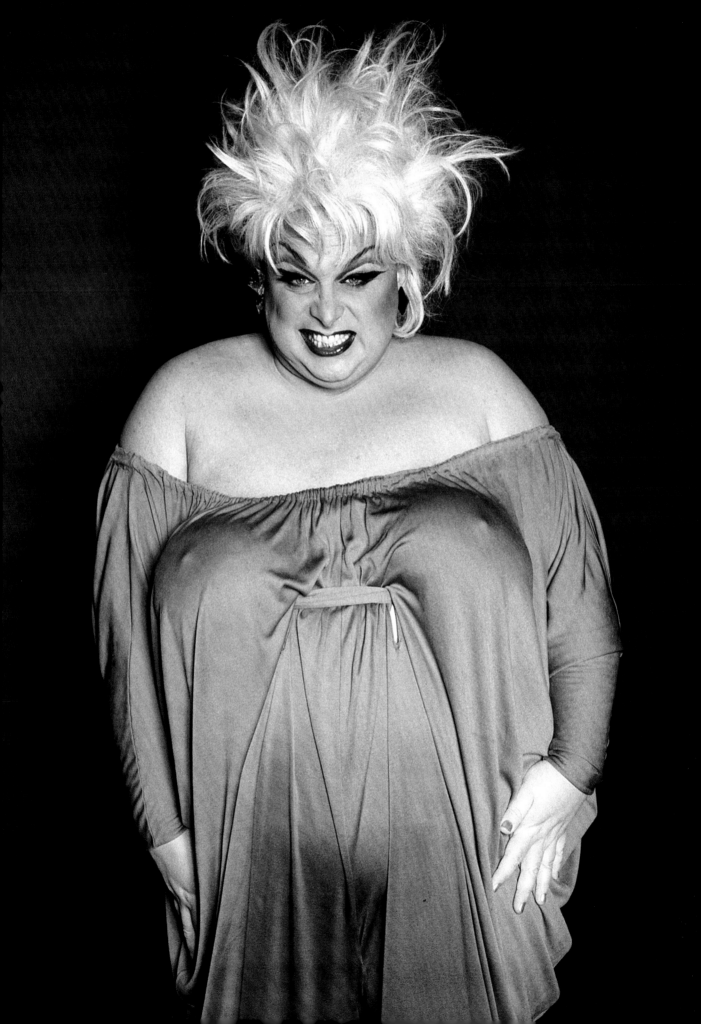

# DIVINE
## THE MOST BEAUTIFUL WOMAN IN THE WORLD

BY JOHN WATERS

From *Shock Value: A Tasteful Book About Bad Taste*

UNDERNEATH DIVINE'S COCKEYED GLAMOUR lives a serious actor who wants nothing more than to work every day. If getting publicity can result in a job offer, Divine is certainly game. If hired, he will give you his all without any moral objections to the script. He's eaten dog turds, crawled through pig shit, mainlined eyeliner, eaten guts, and risked arrest by appearing in my films, but I've never once seen him throw a star trip.

Divine is certainly no transvestite. He says he sometimes dreads getting in drag but realizes these flamboyant outfits are his "work clothes." The only time he goes through the drag ordeal is for a play, movie, or personal appearance. Thank God, he is also not a female impersonator—I can hardly imagine him making people suffer through Judy Garland or Carol Channing imitations. Divine is simply an actor who usually is cast as a woman. He seems comfortable living his "interpretation of a man" and says he is quite satisfied with his natural "plumbing." He recognizes the limitations of his illusion and tries to solve all his drag headaches before they become a producer's problem. After the heels of his spikes had crumbled under his weight for the umpteenth time, he decided to have an unbreakable steel pair made for him by special order. Unfortunately, when they arrived, he slipped them on and discovered they weighed over twenty pounds each and he could barely lift his legs to walk.

Divine has been so convincing on film that some of the public assume the offscreen Divine to be the same as his onscreen personality. This is, I suppose, a compliment to Divine's acting ability—but after all, I don't make documentaries. If Divine really were like the characters he portrays, he would have been locked away in a mental institution years ago.

Today (1981), Divine lives quietly in a Manhattan penthouse off Fifth Avenue with his longtime roommate, Phillip. Divine still goes out to all the parties, but he realizes this is really just another aspect of "work." In private, he much prefers a pound of grass and a small circle of friends. He still gives occasional big parties, but usually just serves champagne and chocolates. Rarely does his old Jayne Mansfield, publicity-hungry behavior surface—but when it does, It's more subtle. When he attended Harvey Milk's funeral in San Francisco, he purposely sat directly behind Governor Brown and made the national news. But at least he hadn't crashed: he had been a friend of Harvey's. Divine is similar to many of the old-time movie stars in that he spends all his money immediately, and we joke that if he made a million dollars this week, he'd be broke the next. His drag fever has almost vanished, and I keep trying to convince him that the best possible offscreen look for him would be a well-tailored black wool men's suit, white shirt, and black tie.

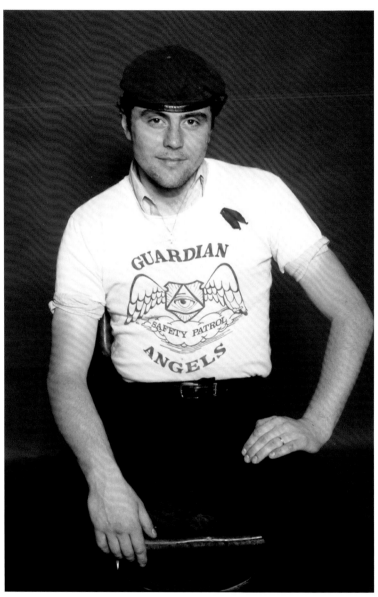

Curtis Sliwa (ABOVE), Mayor Ed Koch (OPPOSITE)
Jean-Michel Basquiat (FOLLOWING PAGES)

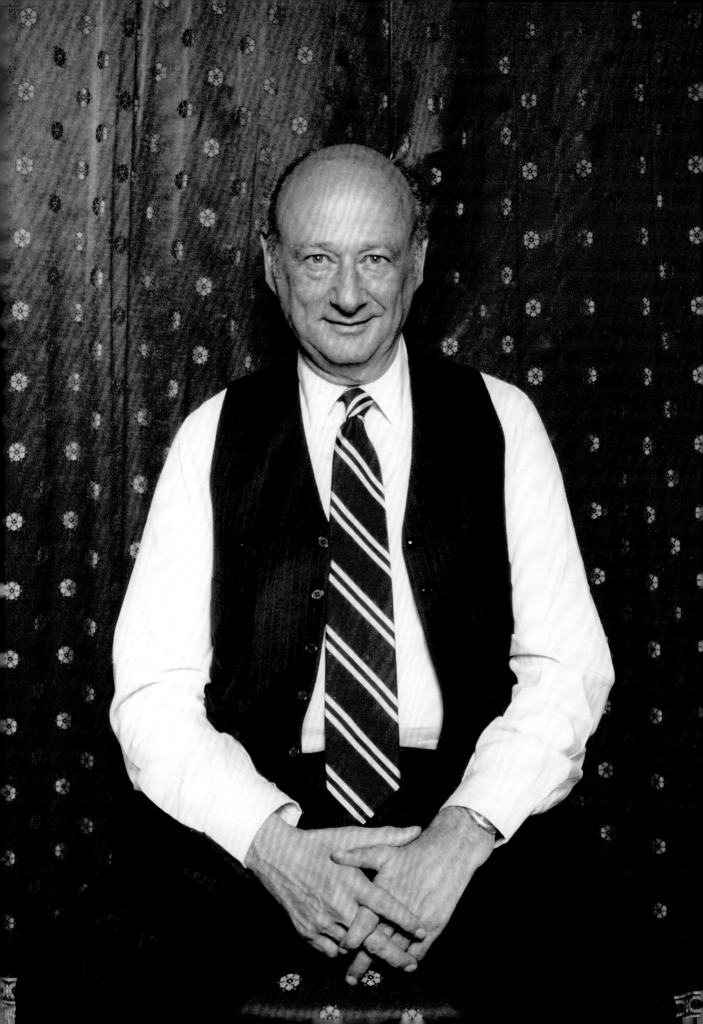

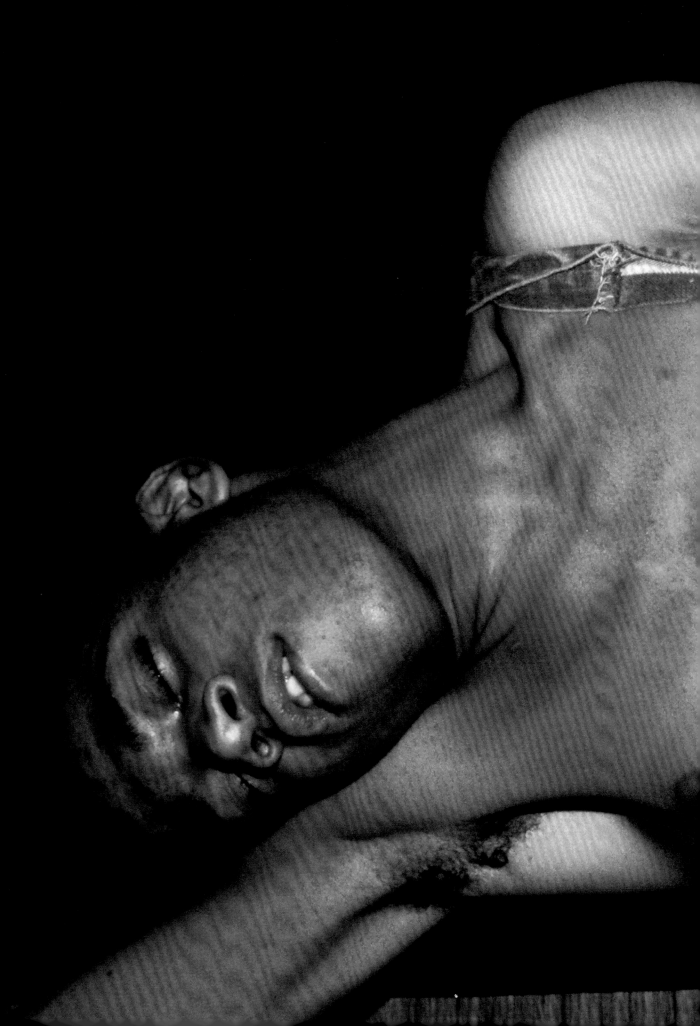

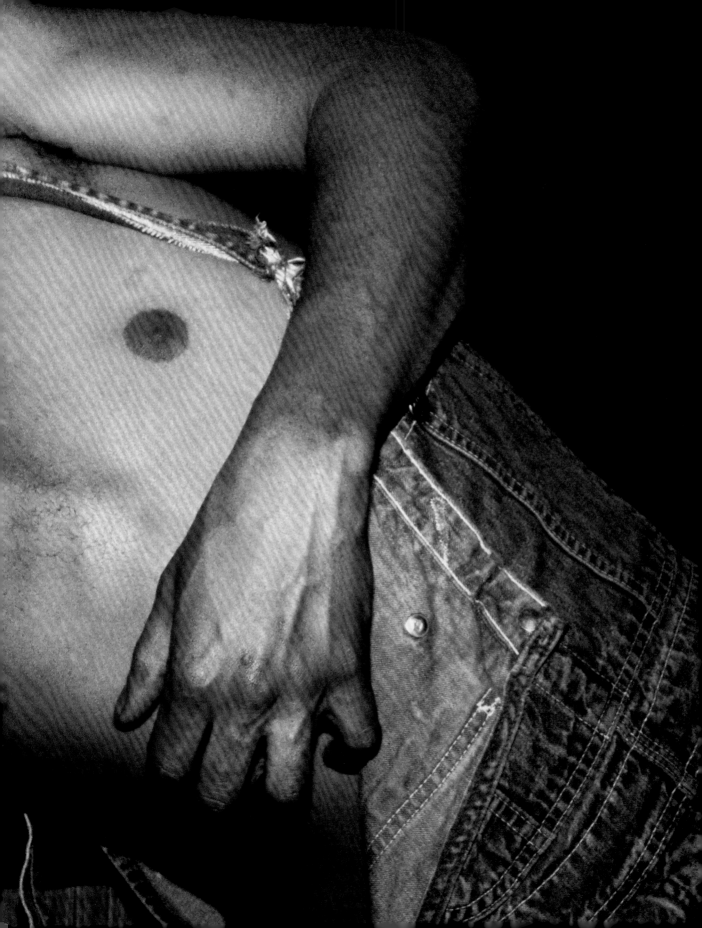

# JEAN-MICHEL BASQUIAT
## THE REVOLUTION OF 1981

From, "The Life and Work of Basquiat," *Gadfly*, May–June 2000

THE GRAFFITI ARTIST JEAN-MICHEL BASQUIAT was among the most radical new powers to emerge in New York. Once again, behind the fame we find a writer. Basquiat began his career as a writer. Because his writing was an important part of his work, it is necessary to examine what he wrote.

In 1977, when Basquiat was a junior in a special New York institution, City as School High School, he teamed up with a fellow student to invent a philosophy-cum-religion called SAMO. SAMO first appeared in a satirical sketch in the school's paper, *Basement Blues Express*, where it was introduced as a faith in which "we do all we want here on earth and then rely totally on the mercy of god on the pretence that we don't know . . . " In an accompanying page of blurbs, one convert announces, "I used to be hooked on speed. Now that I found SAMO I found the truth."

Basquiat never graduated from high school. In a classic caper that introduced the rascal in him before the entire audience of his fellow students and teachers, he pied the principal at the end of the principal's commencement address. Afterward, Basquiat saw no point in returning for his senior year. Instead, after a period of incubation spent hanging out in Washington Square Park dropping acid and smoking pot, he devoted the second half of the year to introducing the SAMO texts to the inhabitants of the Lower East Side and the burgeoning Soho art world. Appropriating the City As School concept, he spray-painted such SAMO sayings as "SAMO as an end 2 Vinyl punkery" and "SAMO as an alternative 2 placing art with the 'radical chic' set on Daddy's $funds" all over the Lower East Side and Soho, turning their walls into canvases.

According to his own account, he was primarily a wordsmith whose original concerns were literary. At his purest, he was a poet. After leaving home for good in 1978, he had no money to purchase painting supplies and was forced to throw himself on the mercy of strangers for a place to live. The first period, which lasted into 1981, climaxed with his finest poems, including "The whole livery line bow like this with the big money all crushed into these feet"; "Pay for soup / Build a fort / Set that on fire"; "Origin of cotton"; and the sublime "Jimmy Best on his back to the suckerpunch of his childhood files."

When Basquiat hit his stride as a painter in 1982, watching him paint was like watching Ali fight. The audience was an important factor in his work, and he often painted in front of critics, dealers, collectors, and friends. After rapidly achieving the financial success to live out his fantasies, his scenario rarely differed. Wherever he was, in his loft or in a studio provided by his gallery in a foreign city, two or three assistants would build his stretchers and prepare his canvases. Meanwhile, three large canvases, measuring anywhere from eight by six feet to sometimes fifteen feet long, would be set before him, flat on the floor or up against a wall. Situated at convenient locations around the space would be a mound of top-quality cocaine on a large piece of tinfoil, several ashtrays containing large spliffs of the strongest marijuana, which, like Burroughs on a writing binge, he would regularly visit, and an open bottle of red wine costing $500. Battered copies of Burroughs's *Junky*, Kerouac's *Subterraneans*, and *Bird Lives!*, a biography of Charlie Parker, lay next to expensive art books on Cy Twombly and Leonardo da Vinci. A state-of-the-art boom box flooded the space with beautiful, pulsing jazz by Miles Davis, Charlie Parker, and Ornette Coleman.

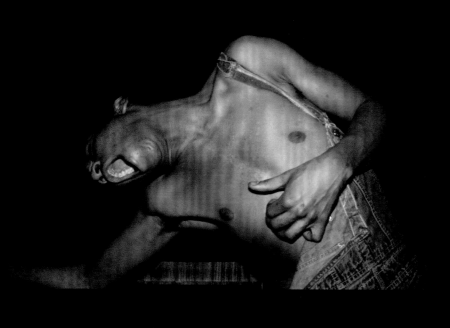
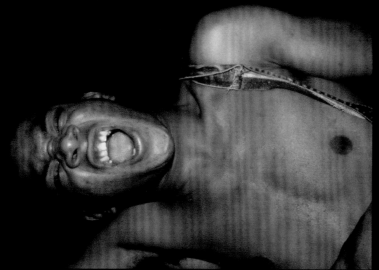
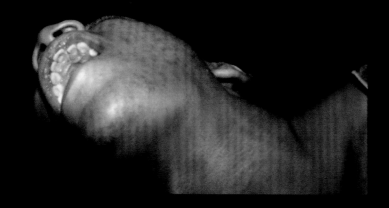

Wearing a new Armani suit, elegant shirt, and tie—but with bare feet—he would enter the brightly lit space. While painting, Basquiat would dance, backpedaling from one canvas to another, his hands at waist level, ready to snap out a line without stopping or deliver a punch of paint. Like Kerouac, he believed in spontaneous composition and would never change a line once he started it. In this manner—while the mound of cocaine slowly disappeared, joints were crushed out in ashtrays, one bottle of wine was replaced by another, and his suit was splattered red, black, yellow, and gold—Jean-Michel would paint until all three canvases were completed to his satisfaction. This sometimes meant filling a canvas with a brilliant work only to paint entirely over it, producing an even more brilliant work. He once worked for three days without stopping.

Basquiat's similarity to Warhol is astonishing. Both men believed their original impulse to make art came from their mothers. Each had a serious childhood illness that kept him out of school for a significant period of time. Like Warhol, Basquiat had his spleen removed as a result of violence. Both broke into the privileged art world as invaders, starting their careers with three-year runs, unloading their image banks and becoming internationally famous in the process. As Warhol had done before him, Basquiat completed a stunning series of approximately one thousand paintings in a span of three years, knocking out all the young contenders on the way to the title. In the concluding chapter of her biography *Basquiat: A Quick Killing in Art*, Phoebe Hoban writes,

> The SAMO sayings were a distilled version of the themes he would repeatedly return to in his later work: racism, materialism, capitalism, pop culture, mortality . . .
>
> Basquiat's work, like that of most of his peers, was based on appropriation rather than draftsmanship. In contrast to most of his peers, the images he appropriated—whether they were from the Bible or a chemistry textbook—became part of his original vocabulary, alphabet letters in an invented language, like notes in a jazz riff, or phonemes in a scat song. Basquiat combined and recombined these idiosyncratic symbols throughout his career: the recursive references to anatomy, black culture, television and history are his personal hieroglyphics. Critics have compared his aesthetic to sampling, as if this child of the media were a highly tuned antenna who received, and then broadcast, urgent bits of message, loud and clear.

Like another Bad Boy, the writer Stephen Crane (*The Red Badge of Courage*), who had lived on the Lower East Side in the 1870s, Jean-Michel thought living in New York was like living in a war, where you might be killed tomorrow. He lived each day as if it were his last, drinking from the deepest cups of pleasure, making the greatest art possible. Basquiat's paintings exploded on canvas in 1981 as he took off on a three-year streak that would establish him as one of the best artists in the world. With a painter as good as Basquiat, it isn't the content that grabs your attention, but the shock of the work's strength and the ferocious conviction with which it is delivered.

The poet and art critic Rene Ricard, who played a vital role in establishing the new art stars of the 1980s, referred in a 1981 *Artforum* article to Basquiat's initial burst of painting as "The Revolution of 1981" and bestowed upon him the immortal title of "The Radiant Child."

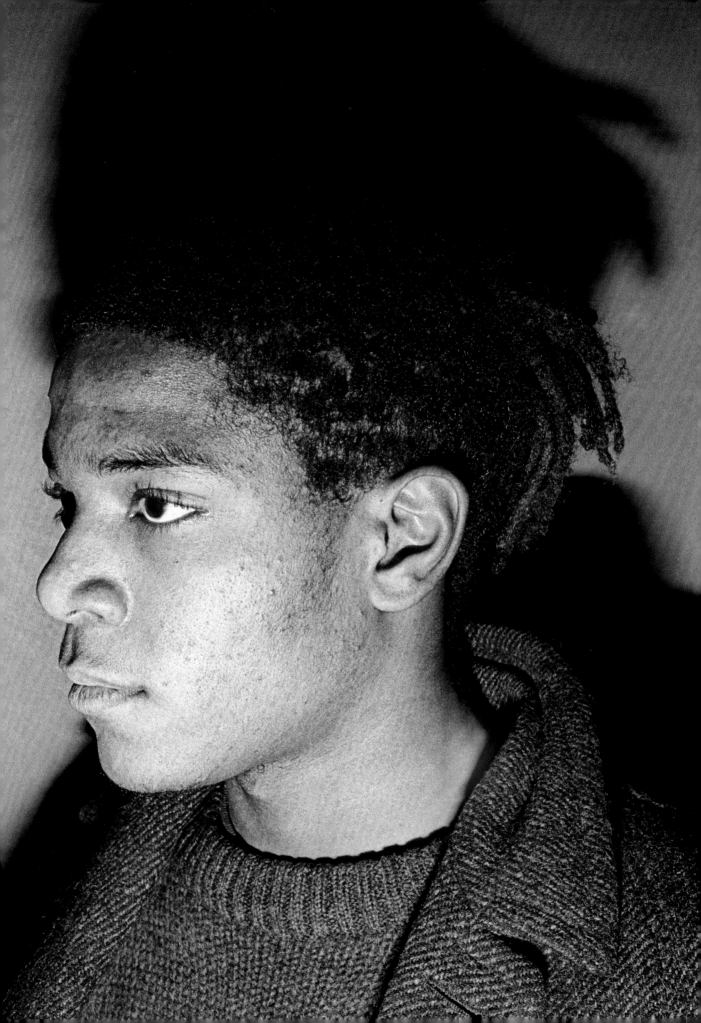

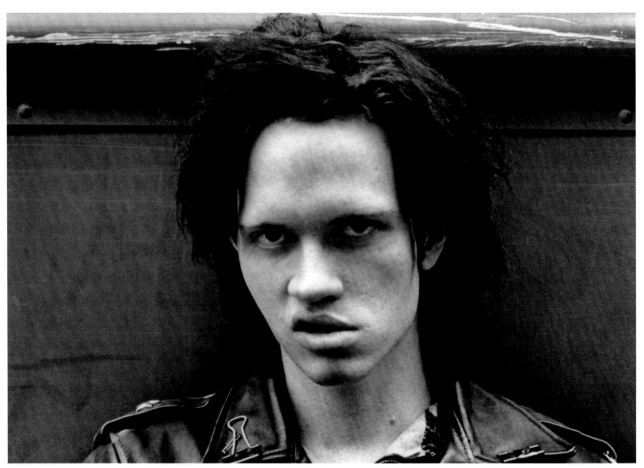

Nick Zedd (ABOVE), Jim Jarmusch (OPPOSITE)

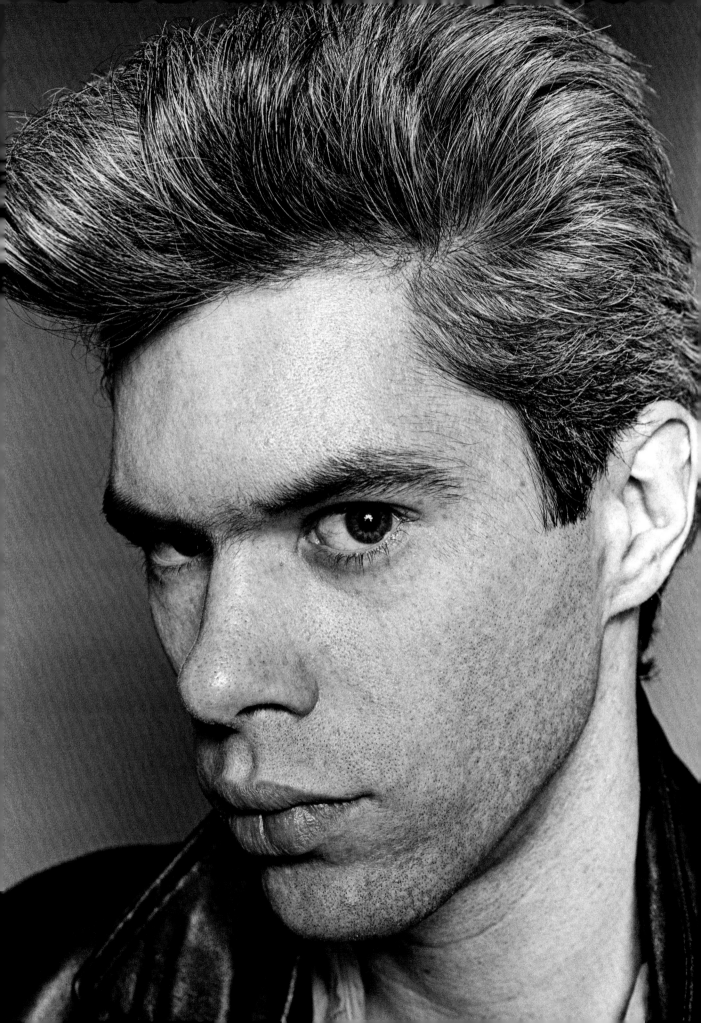

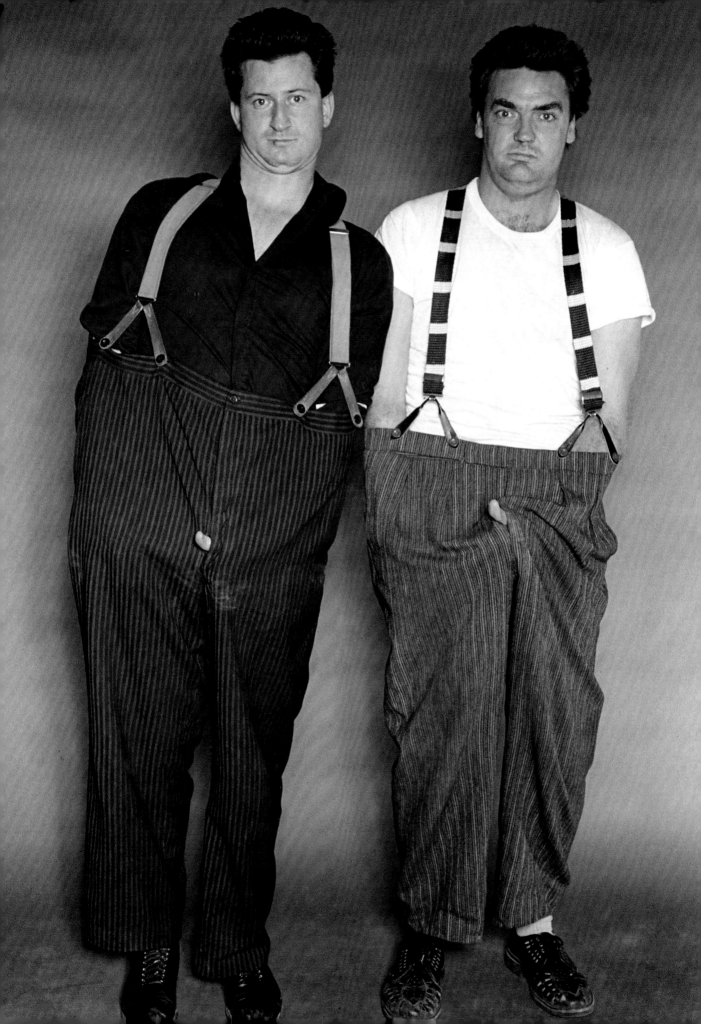

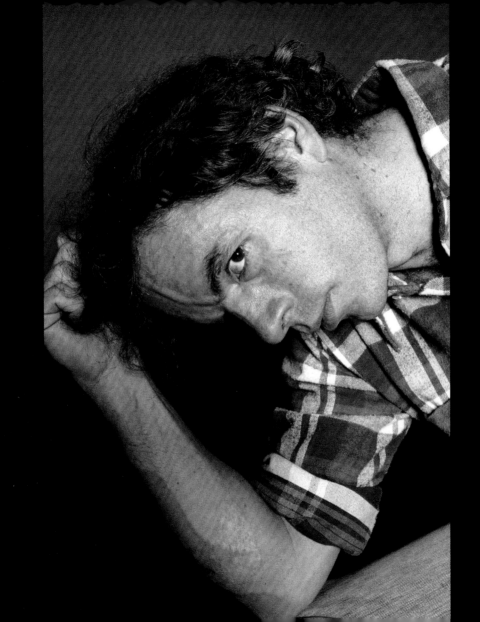

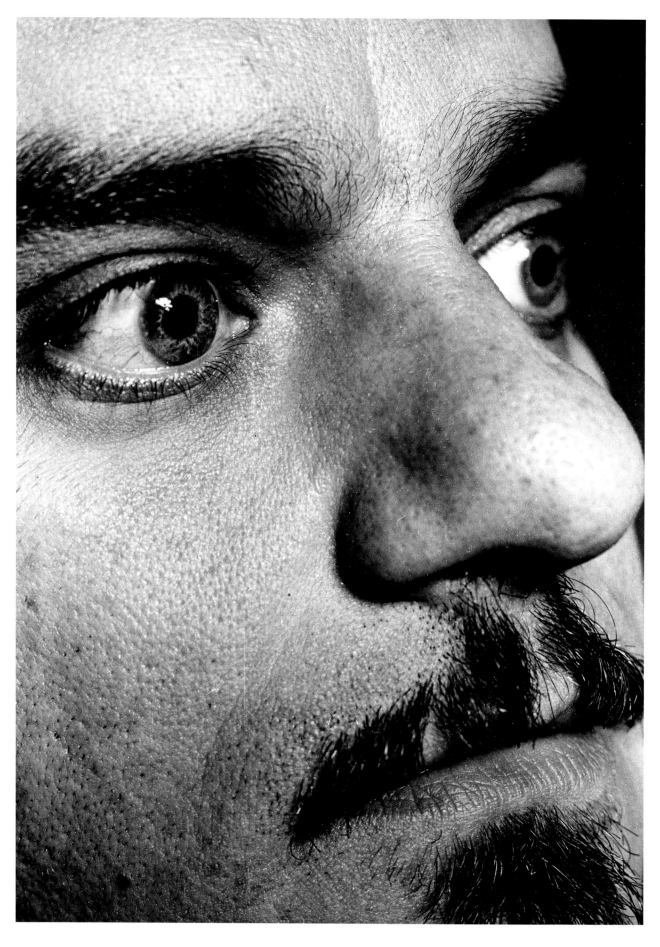

Charles Ludlam

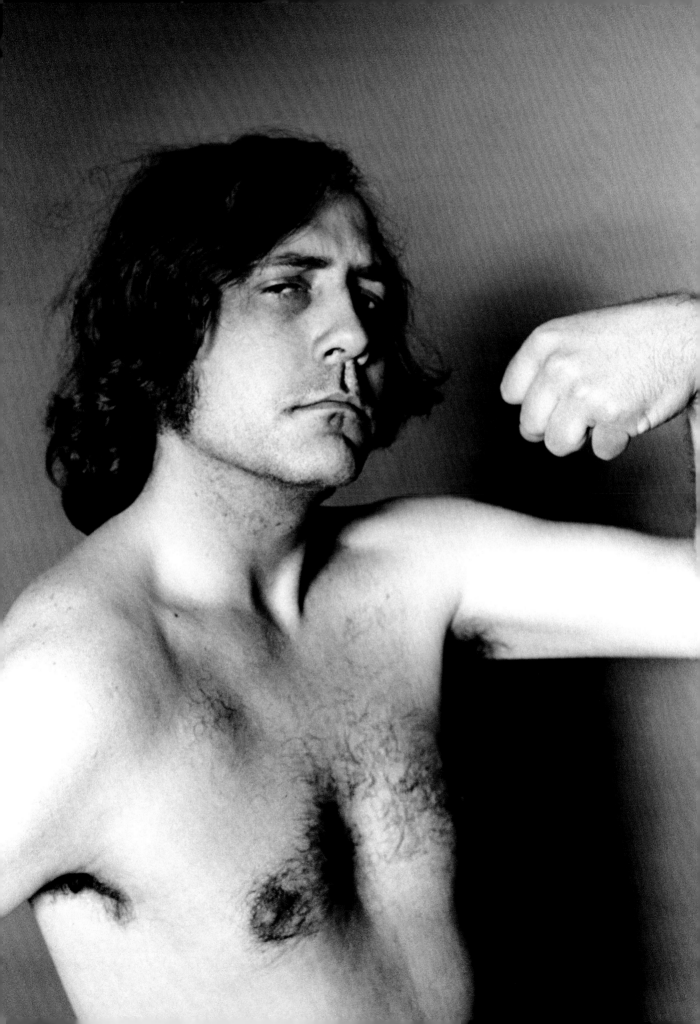

# LESTER BANGS
## BAD BOY OF PUNK LITERATURE

*It's not exactly that records might unhinge the mind, but rather that if anything is going to drive you up the wall it might as well be a record. Because the best music is strong and guides and cleanses and is life itself.*

—Lester Bangs, *Psychotic Reactions and Carburetor Dung*

LESTER BANGS CAME UP in the vanguard of the little-recognized rock writers' movement that picked up from the beats, using those artists' passion and realism to celebrate the healing powers of rock 'n' roll. It was Bangs's personification of the music, his total commitment, that put him on a higher plane than the others.

The marriage of Lester Bangs and Greil Marcus, who edited Bangs's signature collection, *Psychotic Reactions and Carburetor Dung: The Work of a Legendary Critic: Rock 'n' Roll as Literature and Literature as Rock 'n' Roll*, was a crowning moment in rock literature. As Marcus reports in his introduction, Bangs half-jokingly described himself as

> obviously brilliant, a gifted artist, a sensitive male unafraid to let his vulnerabilities show, one of the few people who actually understood what was wrong with our culture and why it couldn't possibly have any future (a subject I talked about/gave impromptu free lessons on incessantly, especially when I was drunk, which was often, if not every night), a handsome motherfucker, good in bed though of course I was so blessed with wisdom beyond my years and gender that I knew this didn't even make any difference, I was fun, had a wild sense of humor, a truly unique and unpredictable individual, a performing rock 'n' roll artist with a band of my own, perhaps a contender if not now then tomorrow for the title Best Writer in America (who was better? Bukowski? Burroughs? *Hunter Thompson*? Gimme a break. I was the best. I wrote almost nothing but record reviews, and not many of those. . . . )

"Lester was the great gonzo journalist, gutter poet, and romantic visionary of rock-writing—its Hunter S. Thompson, Charles Bukowski, and Jack Kerouac all rolled into one," wrote Jim DeRogatis in his pioneering biography *Let It Blurt: The Life and Times of Lester Bangs.*

> Out of tune with the peace 'n' love ethos of the sixties and the Me Generation navel-gazing of the seventies, he agitated for sounds that were harsher, louder, more electric, and more alive, charting if not defining the aesthetics of heavy metal and punk. Where others idealized the rock 'n' roll lifestyle or presented a distant academic version of it, he *lived* it, reveling in its excesses, drawing energy from its din, and matching its passion in prose that erupted from the pages of *Rolling Stone*, *Creem*, and the *Village Voice*. In the process he became a peer of the artists he celebrated, brash visionaries and dedicated individualists such as Captain Beefheart, Iggy Pop, Patti Smith, Richard Hell, and most of all Lou Reed.

According to DeRogatis, twenty years after Lester wrote approvingly about the Sex Pistols, John Lydon returned the compliment.

Lester was a madman, and I used to really like his writing," the singer said. "Although it could be perceived as nasty, there was always a sense of fun in it. This is why British music journalism adopted that style, but they got it wrong. It just turned into something nasty. Lester questioned things, and you'll find the majority of people don't like to question what they just take for granted.

Lester played with the furies and paid the price, dying in 1982, around the same time as John Belushi. Perhaps he was thinking about himself when he wrote his 1979 obituary of Sex Pistols bass player Sid Vicious, which was later published in *Throat Culture* magazine:

> We all had a bit of Sid's hide, I guess, but wasn't he such a willing victim? The Gary Gilmore of rock 'n' roll. . . . I'm just completely fed up with cheap nihilism especially when it starts acting trendy. I know society is sick and life is getting more complicated by the second, but if all you've got to say is get fucked life sucks you stink I stink who cares I'm bored whip me beat me kick me there's nothing else to do then I think you and everybody else would be a lot better off if you just kept your fucking mouth shut in the first place, not to mention [kept] your self-destructive habits to yourself instead of parading them around like the red badge of courage or something.

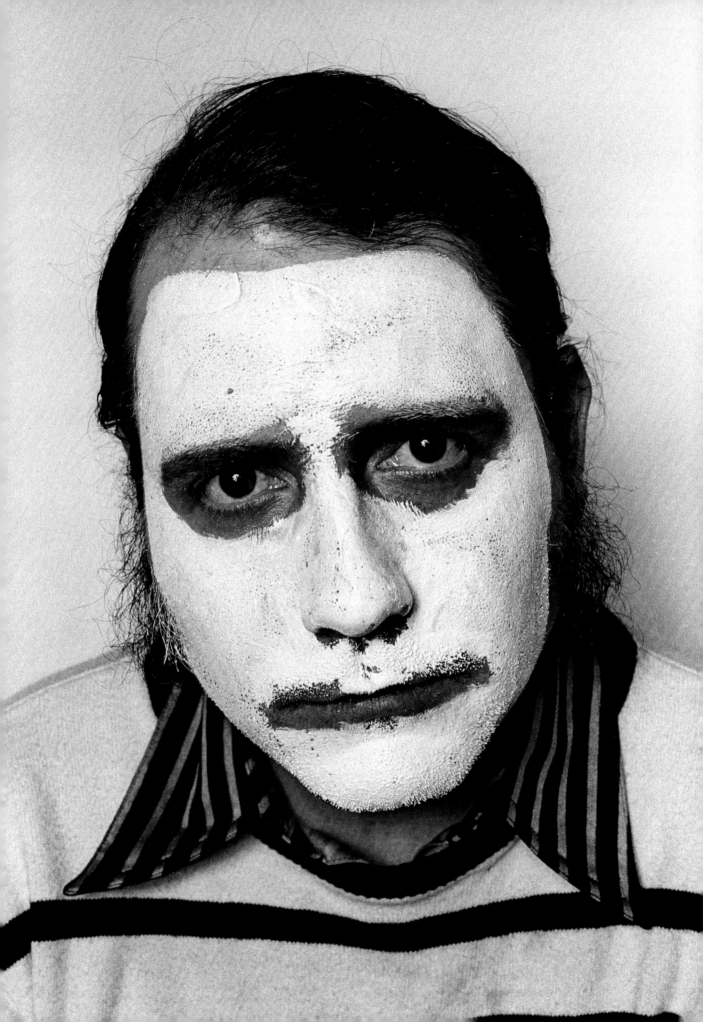

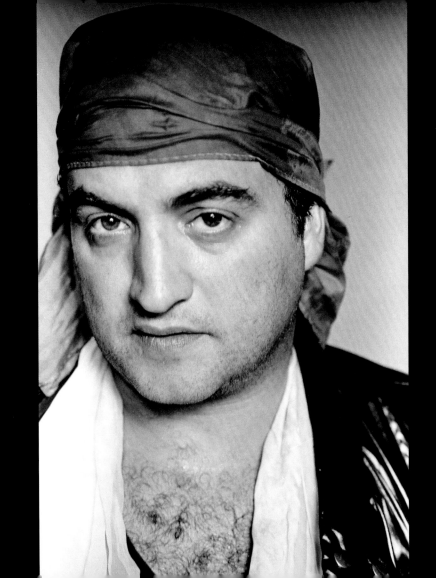

# ANOTHER BAD BOY NAMED JOHN

## JOHN BELUSHI

"*Acting coach Del Close saw in*

*Belushi an instrument—a trainable,*

*ticking, badboy time bomb.*"

*—BOB WOODWARD, WIRED: THE SHORT*
*LIFE AND FAST TIMES OF JOHN BELUSHI*

John Belushi

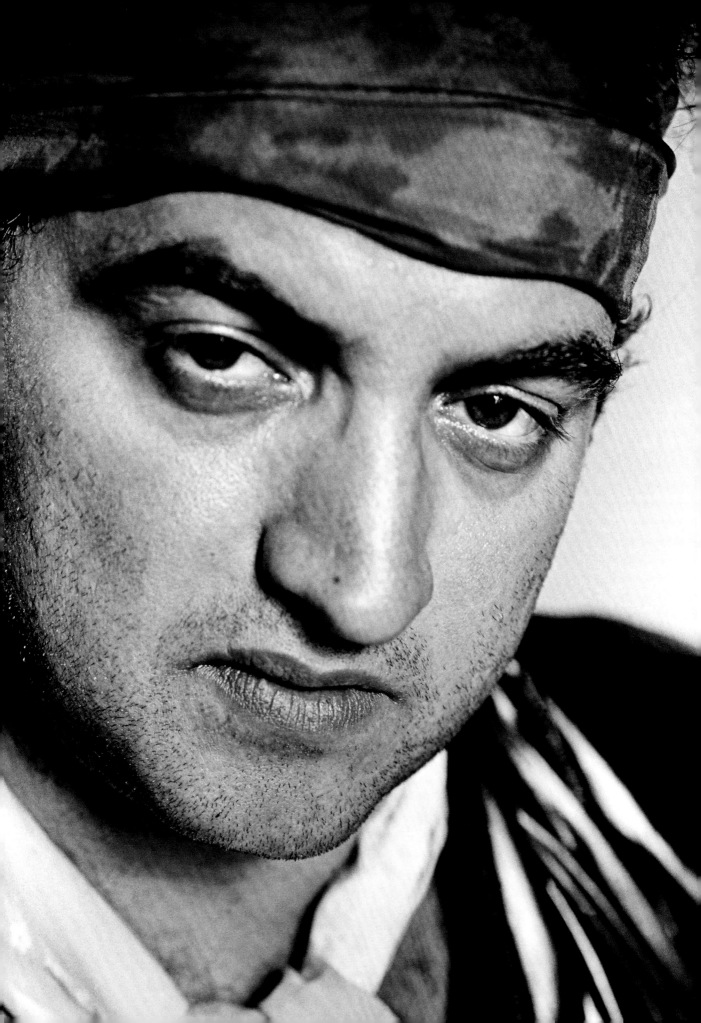

ON SEPTEMBER 13, 1981, John Belushi gave Marcia Resnick what would turn out to be his last photo session. It came about after they bumped into each other at the after-hours club AM-PM, around 3 a.m. After catching up on recent activities, Marcia poked John in the ribs and queried, "When are we going to do a photo session?"

"How about now?" he replied.

Unbelievably, instead of seizing the opportunity, she presumed he was joking and partied on for another couple of hours. Imagine her surprise when upon returning home around 6 a.m. she discovered John waiting in a limousine with an entourage in front of her studio at 530 Canal Street.

This was one of those occasions on which both artists made the best possible use of the circumstances. John was twenty-four hours into a two-day binge without sleep. Marcia was exhausted and looking forward to going to bed. They went to work with raw nerves exposed. At first, she was amazed by how uncomfortable John seemed to be in front of her still camera when he was so fluid in television and movies. He was, she sensed, unsure of himself, and he asked for props.

Steven Spielberg, who'd directed John in the film *1941*, had loved the way expressions flowed over John's face. Marcia shot two rolls of 35 mm black-and-white Tri-X film. Belushi rapidly produced a series of expressions for Marcia's shoot, in the course of which, with a good deal of passion and feeling, he delivered a retrospective of his career.

Two years after John Belushi's death, Bob Woodward, who'd made his name writing about the fall of Richard Nixon, published *Wired: The Short Life and Fast Times of John Belushi*. Chapter Fifteen contains several pages about Marcia's photo session. Woodward described the climax of the session.

> He dodged the camera, turning his head. Resnick clicked away, still searching for the right shot. She inched forward, so close the lens caught only his head, then only his face: There was the Bad Boy, the exhaustion and frenzy captured. . . .
>
> Resnick had a strong intuitive feeling about getting someone's picture at just the right time. There was something that people exuded almost subconsciously. She hovered a fraction of a second and snapped. "That's it."

Viewed as a whole, these sixty images are a vivid record of John Belushi's journey from a handsome, romantic pirate to a cool and classic Bad Boy, ending on a series of unmistakable death masks. In an essay about Marcia's 1987 show of her Belushi portraits at the University of Texas, the critic Alan Sondheim asked, "Is Resnick's series in fact Belushi's most powerful work?"

In *Wired*, Woodward wrote,

> On October 16, 1978, John Belushi's face was spread over America, staring defiantly over his toga from the cover of *Newsweek* under the headline: "College Humor Comes Back."
>
> . . . John was quoted: "My characters say it's okay to screw up. People don't have to be perfect. They don't have to be real smart. They don't have to follow the rules. They can have fun. Most movies today make people feel inadequate. I don't do that."
>
> [*Newsweek* wrote,] *"He is a bundle of conflicting emotions. Yes, he wants success, money, and stardom, but the punky kid in him recoils at the prospect of it all. . . . "*
>
> *John Landis was quoted: " . . . If he doesn't burn himself out, his potential is unlimited."*

"One day, I remembered that the week before he died John had made a flippant remark about heroin," wrote Judy Belushi in *Samurai Widow*. "It was after our argument about his being out of control. A little while later he apologized and admitted

*"One need not know that Belushi is doing (and doing in) Joe Cocker to relish his extraordinary limb-twitching performance. He looks as if he were plugged into an electric socket. Tripping over his legs, he falls down with a thud and never stops playing while vainly attempting to lift himself from the floor feet first."*

—MEL GUSSOW, REVIEW OF *LEMMINGS*, *NEW YORK TIMES*, 1973

John Belushi

243

I was right: he was abusing himself again and needed to stop. Sitting on the couch, he rubbed his face as if trying to wake up. 'I don't know what got into me this morning. What did I take last night, heroin?' He'd said this in such a funny way that we both laughed, and that seemed to diffuse the tension between us."

In a special issue of *Rolling Stone* on John Belushi, Hunter Thompson said: "Even though he was a bit of a monster, he was our monster, as well as a damned good person you could count on for help in dark times."

And Mitch Glazer, who had written the *Crawdaddy!* cover story on John back in 1977 that labeled him "The Most Dangerous Man on Television," pinned John in this bittersweet memory:

> Late summer of 1978. The backyard . . . was carpeted in yellow fuzz; thick curtains of it had blown down from the tree in the Belushi courtyard. The wicker couch and the man asleep on it were covered in gold pollen. After a while, John, a white cap covering his eyes, began to shift positions on the small couch. He kicked his legs: nightmare running. He bolted up abruptly, eyes open, yellow fluff sticking to his eyelashes, to his hair. "I gotta get off the island . . . I don't wanna be here!" he shouted. Then calmer, now awake: "Shit, I just had the weirdest nightmare. Did you ever see *Pinocchio*? Remember," he said, brushing the flowers from his face, "Remember that island for bad boys that Pinocchio went to? All those kids cursing and drinking . . . Pretty soon they all began turning into donkeys. God, it was horrible. I mean, in my dream it was happening to me." John jumped up from the couch. "I kept telling 'em I didn't wanna be a bad boy anymore, but they wouldn't listen."

In March 1982, six months after their session, Marcia met John at Christopher Giercke's loft. She gave Belushi one of her postcards from *Re-visions*, an image of her model Laurel Rubin. On the back, she wrote a phone number. (In retrospect, John's affection for Laurel had clinched his decision to give Marcia the photo session.) Resnick had not been prepared for what she witnessed at Christopher's space. "That was really something," she recalled.

> Somebody had coke and he had some coke that was unusable—it was poison. Nobody wanted to take it, but John was right into it. He was shoveling it into his nose. At first it was funny; I mean, it was tragic.

> When I showed him the contact sheets, he was walking down the stairs to the limousine waiting to take him to the airport and a plane for Los Angeles. He just did not know what to do with them. He said, "These are terrible," and handed them back to me, but I knew he had not really seen them. Who knew that only a few days later he would be dead?

I remember the night John Belushi died. I heard about it at Mickey Ruskin's One University Place. I've never been a violent person, but on the way home I kicked out the windshield of my girlfriend's car. Then I trashed my bedroom, broke my typewriter, burst into tears, and asked my roommate to hug me. Marcia went to her favorite bar, drank herself into oblivion, and woke up in a hospital to see her parents' anguished faces hovering over her. John Belushi's death signaled the end of an era. It would have long-lasting results. To quote the great Ralph Ellison, writing about the death of Charlie Parker and other musicians, "Our memory of some of the more brilliant young men has been touched by the aura of death, and we feel guilt that the fury of their passing was the price paid for the art they left us to enjoy unscathed."

> **"There was John in his swimming suit, bouncing on the diving board—up and down, up and down. In one burst he soared up as high as possible, kicked his feet, landed his ass on the end of the board and flipped over into the water.**
> **'Albanian oak,' Dan Aykroyd said. 'Yes,' Lorne Michaels replied. Belushi was nonperishable."**
>
> —BOB WOODWARD, *WIRED*, 1984 (SAID IN 1976)

John Belushi (OPPOSITE AND FOLLOWING PAGES)

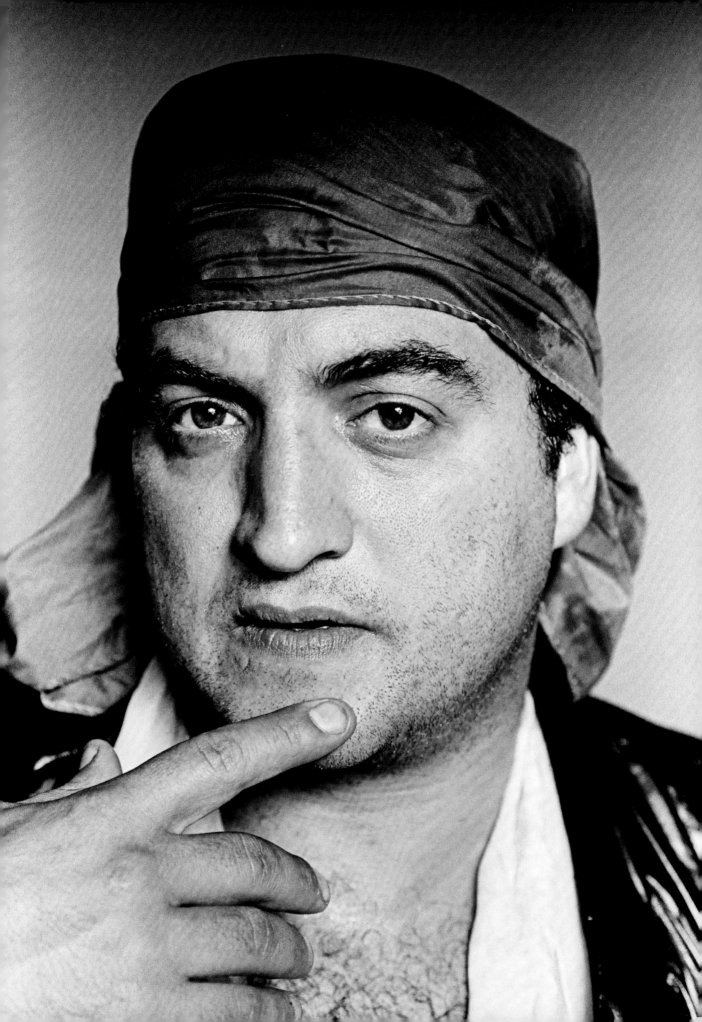

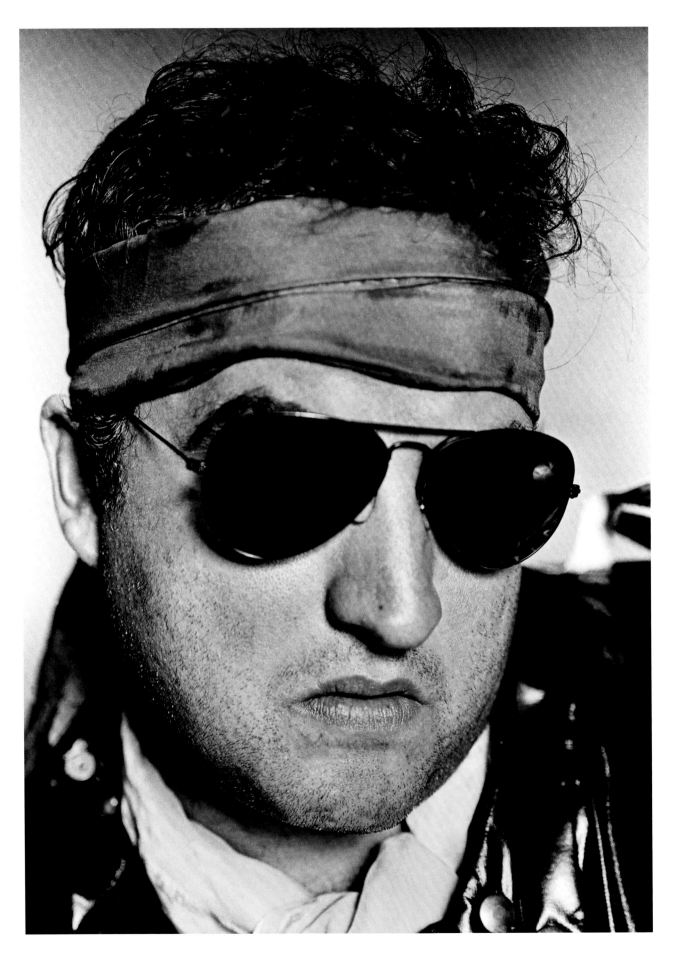

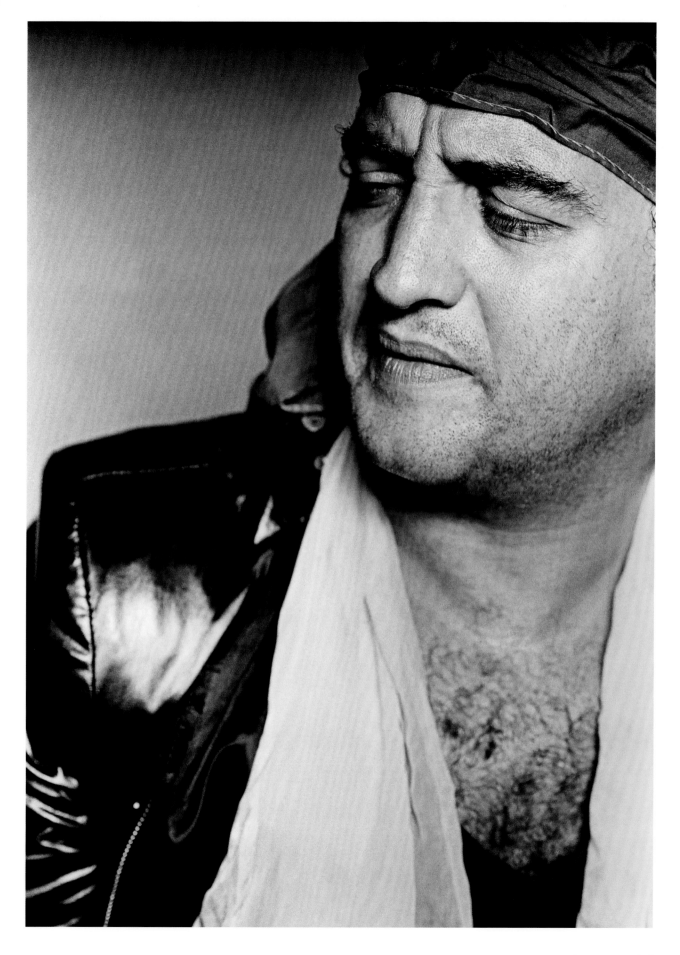

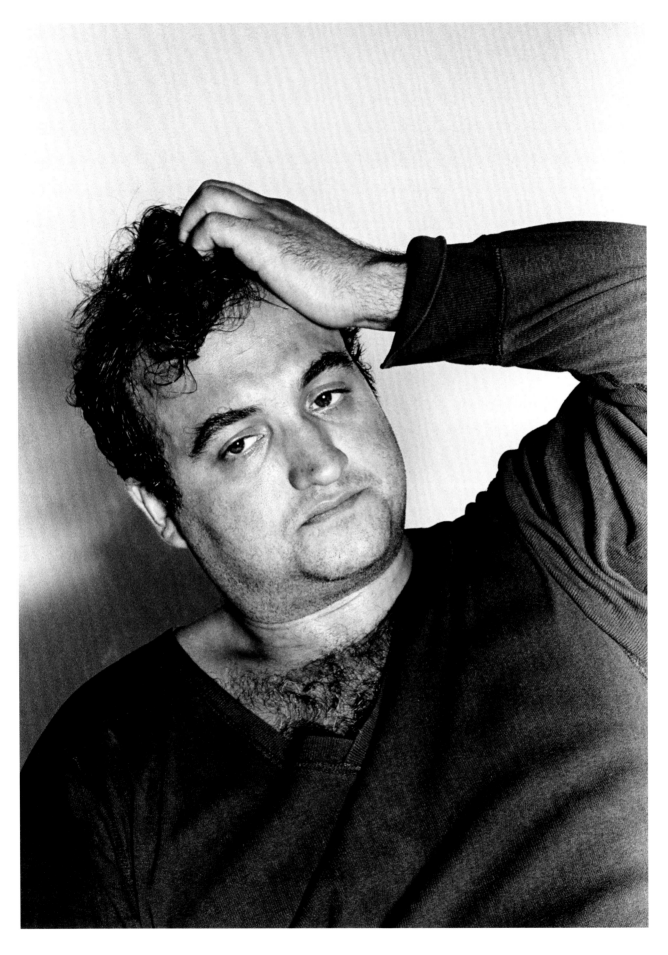

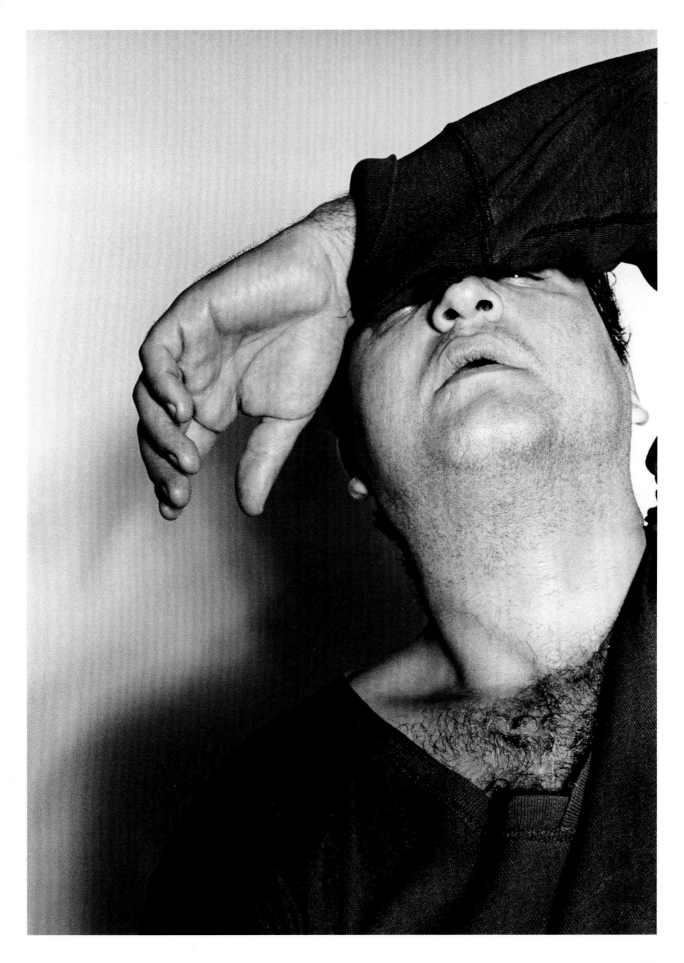

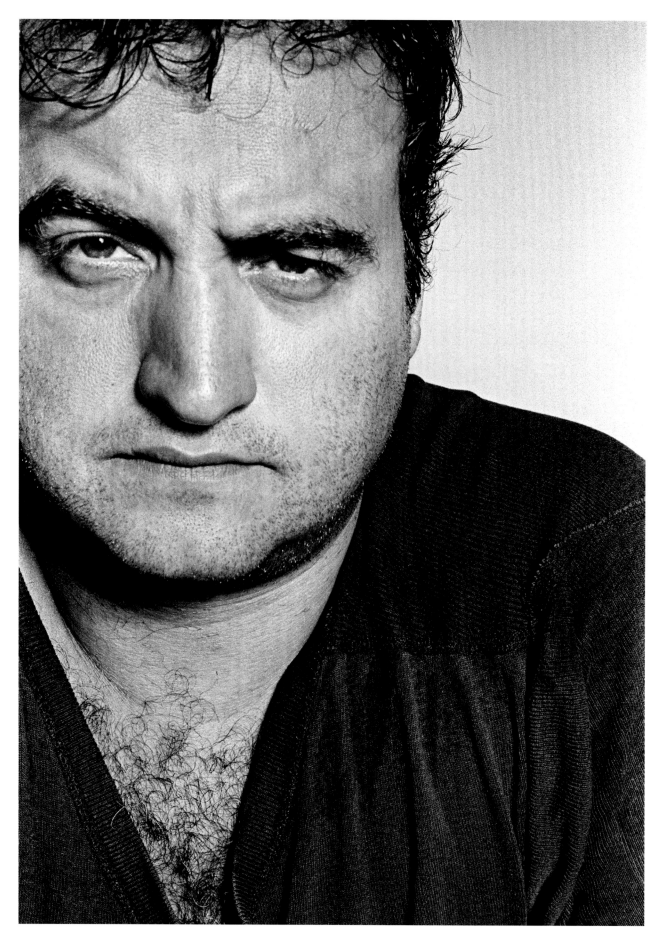

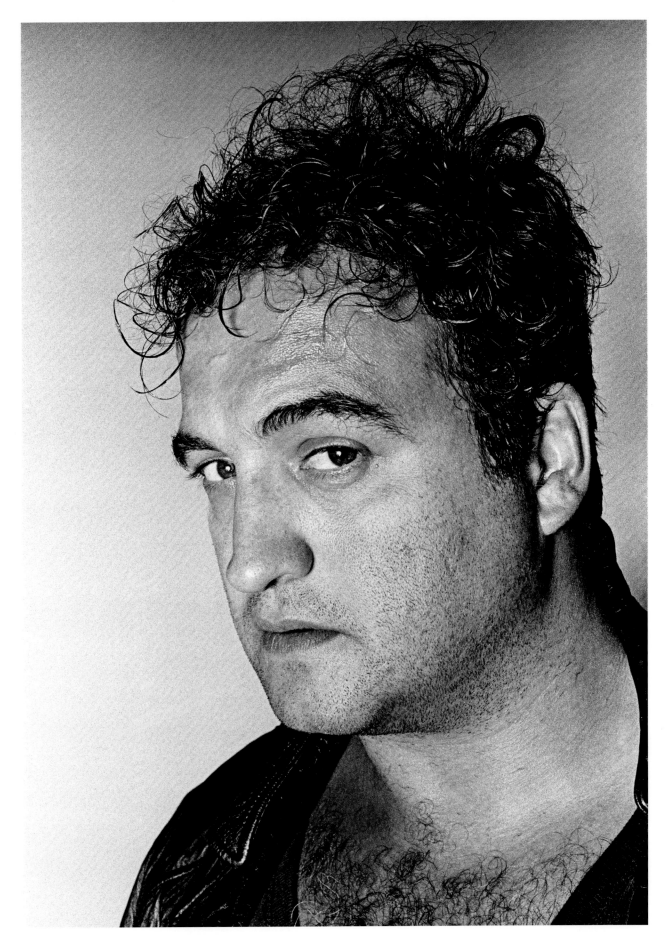

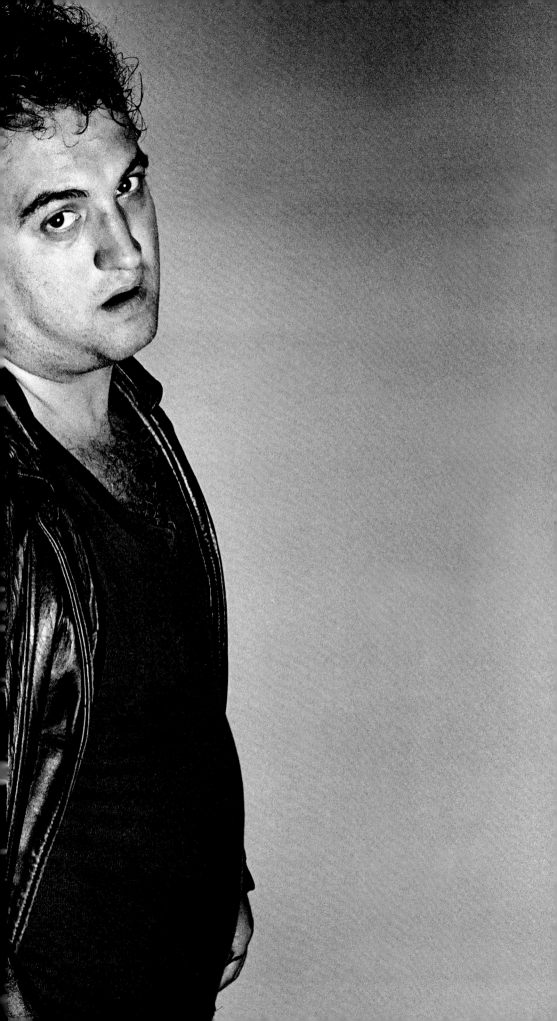

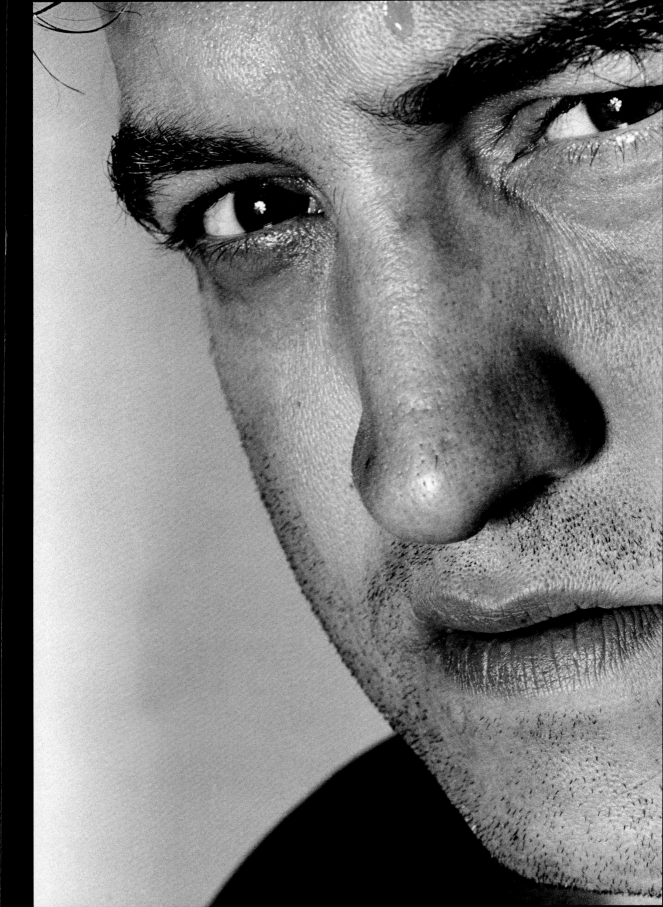

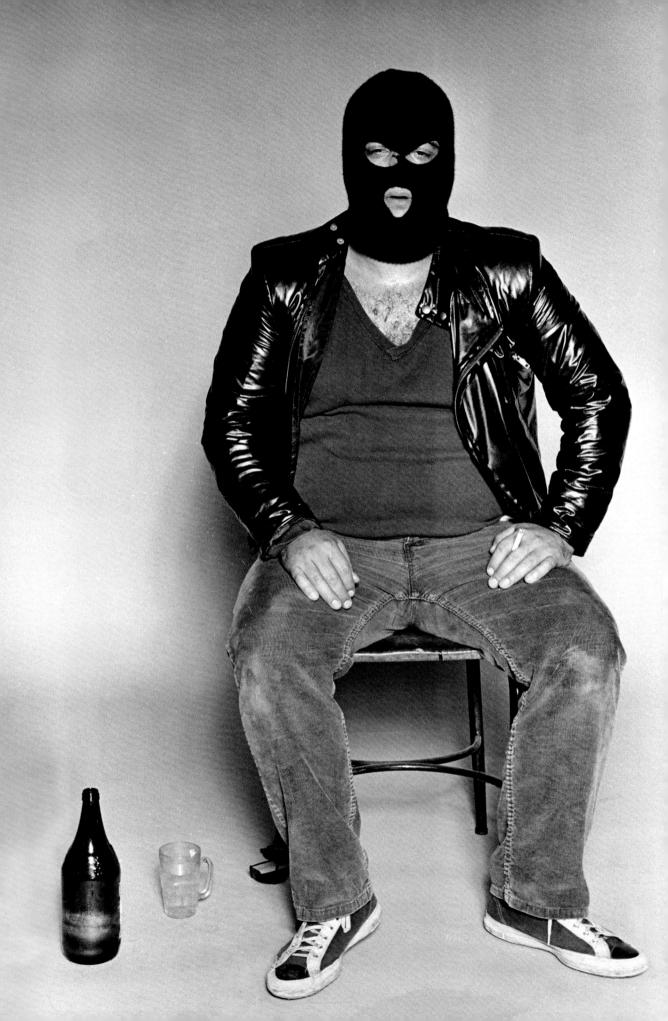

"*Resnick felt that John was again trying to outfox the camera. A mannequin off to the side had a dark wool ski mask over its head. John put it on so that only his mouth and eyes showed through. He sat in a chair and looked like the anonymous executioner, fat and sinister . . . Click, click, click, click.*"

—BOB WOODWARD, *WIRED*, 1984 (SAID IN 1976)

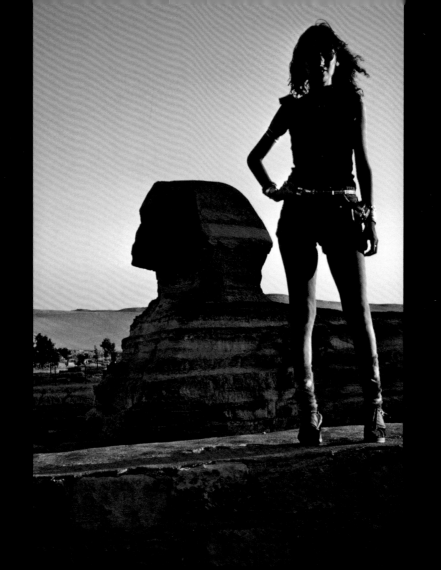

# BAD GIRL

## ORDEAL IN EGYPT

"Men look at women. Women watch themselves being looked at. This determines not only most relations between men and women but also the relation of women to themselves. The surveyor of woman in herself is male: the surveyed female."

–JOHN BERGER, WAYS OF SEEING

Marcia Resnick

# ORDEAL IN EGYPT

BY MARCIA RESNICK

IN JULY 1977, I was gripped with the desire to be elsewhere. I felt rootless and uncomfortable. I needed to leave New York and decided to run away to exotic lands. From Greece, I took a boat heading to Alexandria, on the north coast of Egypt. The boat left at 8:00 on a Monday morning, and I spent the whole day wandering around the deck. I met some Americans and Scandinavians. Not knowing Arabic and not wanting to travel alone, I befriended an Egyptian. His name was Hamdi. He was once a soldier and he immediately had a mysterious hold over me—he made me take a nap, he made me eat, he made me not eat. We communicated in Italian, though I had never spoken Italian before in my life. I would make up the words. He never understood what I was saying, and I understood him sometimes. He promised me I could stay with him in his parents' house in Cairo, and he would take me to Luxor, and we would drive in his father's car, and he would show me around Cairo, and he would take me to the pyramids. He told me he was a "commerciante," a commercial businessman. When I told him I was an "artist," he grinned devilishly. He then got angry and told me that while I was with him I must never tell anyone that I was an "artist," especially his mother.

We got off the ship at 8 a.m. on Tuesday. He made me promise not to talk to anybody and he warned me about four hundred times to hold on to my handbag because "brutos" and "assassinos" were out there waiting for me. I had all these lovely fantasies about Egypt, but now I was just scared that all these rip-off artists would be grabbing at my bag. I warned my American and Scandinavian friends from the boat, "Watch out! Hamdi told me about the brutos and assassinos!" They thought I was crazy and decided among themselves that Hamdi was putting me in harm's way and that I wasn't going to live. Hamdi left me somewhere to watch his bags. It was like a movie. The place was teeming with people in exotic costumes speaking Arabic. I was excited. We had to traverse an endless walkway to customs while little kids kept asking to carry our bags. His two bags were filled with electronic equipment and other stuff he was smuggling in. They were unbelievably heavy and felt like ten tons of rock. Even he couldn't carry them. Finally Hamdi dumped his bags, plus my two bags, onto the back of this poor child. My mouth dropped open. He was telling the kid to hurry up and the child was totally scrunched over, carrying these bags to customs.

We finally got to customs and the kid was blue, really blue, and I said, "Listen, I can carry my own bags. You really can't do that to him." And then Hamdi gave him like maybe half a cent and the kid started to yell and scream and Hamdi started to yell and scream. This happened at least a hundred times. Every time there was a financial exchange, Hamdi would totally rip the person off and the yelling and screaming thing would start.

Then ensued about four hours of sitting and waiting at customs for Hamdi, who had apparently imported a huge washing machine and refrigerator from Milan; I guess this was one of his first jobs importing stuff. It was very easy for me to get through customs. I just sat there watching all the hustle—hundreds of people yelling and multitudes of sinister-looking men in white robes, fighting and acting aggressive. It made Times Square on New Year's Eve in New York seem tranquil. It was dreadful and depressing and hot. Here I was, an American Jew in Egypt, but I kept the Jewish part a secret. Hamdi was an Egyptian. He faintly resembled Omar Sharif. He had fought the Israelis in the October 1973 war; he'd been shot in the head. He had a two-inch bullet hole scar slightly above his left eye. He was subject to migraine headaches and, as it would turn out, irrational, violent, destructive temper tantrums.

Finally, we escaped the melee and found a taxicab. Originally we were going to go to Cairo straightaway. Instead, he said, "Now we're going to go to a hotel." But first he had the cab drop us off at this little tailor shop with pictures on the walls of ladies and men wearing 1920s American fashions. Fabulous Egyptian cotton was on the shelves and a big ceiling fan was spinning around and spiderwebs were lodged in every corner.

Apparently this was the shop of a relative. A group of men were sitting around and Hamdi kissed them all hello. My hands were really dirty, and I went upstairs and washed them.

I was wearing a long black skirt and a black T-shirt because Hamdi had insisted I cover my entire body in public. I looked insipid and pale. He introduced me by my first name and as an American. I was thirsty, so he bought me a vile lemon soda. Then we got into another cab with two of his relatives and he brought me to a seemingly abandoned hotel.

We went into a suite of rooms and put our bags down. Hamdi said, "Wait here and I'll get something to eat." He brought back four loaves of bread, some prosciutto, two kinds of cheese, olives, and hot peppers. When he made me take off all of my clothes except my panties and T-shirt, I was afraid he was going to rape me on the dirty bed, but he hardly touched me. It was so strange. He said that his head was reeling from two and a half days on the boat and from carrying impossible-to-carry bags. Then I noticed baby cockroaches crawling around on the floor, and huge ones, and other crawling insects of every kind, everywhere, all over everything, and bugs on the bed. I ran around the huge, empty, offensive rooms, stifling tears.

I drank some water from the sink. I began to overreact and imagine that I was going to get typhoid. My stomach turned and I was really frightened. When I saw mice in every room, I wanted to cry, and I tearfully yelled at Hamdi something I thought he might understand: "*Mickey Mouse!*" I stood in the corner of the room and screamed and screamed and I said, "*I have to get out of here right away! I'm getting out of here right away!*" And I ran into the other room and made myself vomit up all the food all over the floor of this horrible hotel with all these cockroaches and mice. I saw a cockroach crawling in my bag and I felt disgusted. Why was I there? It was so sleazy—especially sleazy because I was convinced that Hamdi and his cousin had conspired to bring me there so that Hamdi could molest me. I continued to scream. I felt wretched and alone. I wished I'd gone off instead with the Americans or Scandinavians I'd met on the boat.

I told Hamdi I was leaving immediately for New York and that I had never been in a place so repulsive. Watching my face, he began to understand. I tried to make as many loathsome, grotesque expressions as possible. He had changed his story. He had, of course, lied. He had told me that he would drive me to Luxor and Aswan and that I would stay with his family in Cairo. Now he said we would stay in a hotel in Cairo because his mother and father were in Aswan and he didn't have their apartment key. That's when I really started to get very scared, because all the promises had started to break down. "Uh-oh." I thought. "I've been had." But I was not in a position to escape; I was alone, I really didn't know where to go, and it was so late I couldn't go to a tourist hostel. I thought, " I'd better stay with him until tomorrow."

Pointing to a painting on the wall of the filthy room, I pantomimed painting motions with my hands and once again said to him that I was an artist. Since I'd met him, I'd told him over and over again that I was an artist, and he'd kept insisting that I mustn't tell anyone that. Now I asked, "Why can't I tell anyone I'm an artist?" I figured either he was stupid or I was inept. Suddenly he lit up and explained that he'd thought, when I'd said that I was an artist, that I was saying I was an exotic dancer, which is why he'd taken me to the hotel in the first place.

Finally he said, "Okay! Okay!" and he grabbed all of our bags and we left the hotel and got into a taxi and started to look for another hotel. We went from one hotel to the next and to the next, but they were all filled. When we finally found a hotel room, it was exorbitant. It cost something like twelve dollars. I refused to pay that much, even though we were going to share the expense. I knew we could get a much cheaper place. And Hamdi said, "Well, let's look at the room." It was huge and had fourteen beds. I madly ran around the room, saying, "Great! This is really fabulous! I'm going to spend six dollars so I can stay in a room with fourteen beds! How many people do you see? You see one, two people!" And I started to rant in improvised Italian, mixed with English and Spanish and whatever other language I could think of. I yelled at the guy who was going to charge us twelve dollars and told him that we'd pay half as much for the room and that would be it. Obviously he wasn't going to give us the room for that amount, because the room was the kind that could be rented to a family of fourteen hundred people, because they always stuffed about thirty-two people into each individual bed in Egypt. By the time we got out of there, we were at our wits' end.

It was about 9 p.m. So we jumped into another taxi. It was very hot. I was really hungry and thirsty. I wanted some ice cream, and Hamdi bought me ice cream, but the taxi was about to go, so I ate the whole plate in record time, just stuffed it all down, and suddenly I was riding full speed into the night on the way to Cairo.

The taxi was a huge car with a lot of other people in it, all men. Hamdi would never allow me to sit next to another man, so he sat next to the driver and made me sit next to the door, positioned in the "death seat." The taxi sped along at about a hundred miles an hour down a long, dark, straight road, passing trucks on the right and on the left. It was pitch black outside. The other passengers were utterly silent, and all you could hear was the noise of the car and the wind rushing by outside. Along the roadside were men in white robes, which fluttered in the breeze created by the fast-moving cars. Their arms were extended as they hitched for rides. They were like apparitions—so many of them, on and on, on this road. It seemed like a surreal dream. The driver was obviously very skilled, as he was able to finesse the taxi at such a high speed on a road that seemingly had no traffic regulations. I kept reminding myself of my "death seat" predicament as we drove toward Cairo.

I was feeling incredibly pressured from everything that had happened that day. I didn't want to close my eyes, because how would you want to die when you crash: with your eyes wide open, or your eyes closed? That was the basic question: do you want to see it happening, or do you want to be unaware?

Then suddenly the car jolted to a halt, made a left turn, and drove into a greasy-spoon café and truck stop. Men with beady eyes and rotten teeth, wearing white robes and turbans, sat at rickety bridge tables. They sipped tea with huge quantities of sugar, further decaying their teeth.

When we reached Cairo Hamdi mysteriously produced the key he'd previously claimed not to have, and brought me to the seedy apartment of his aged parents in a tacky part of the city. For a week he made it impossible for me to leave, locking my camera and other important possessions in a closet. He insisted that the men in Cairo were "*brutos*" and "*assassinos*" and that such men were really fond of "artists" like myself, and they would devour me if I went outside. His mother and sisters cooked me large, exotic meals. Even Cleopatra never had such good food. In the end, I escaped my abductor by planning a trip to Luxor, the ancient city of Thebes, which he miraculously agreed upon. I think he wanted me to appreciate his country's heritage. (He also may have wanted to marry me.) He let me have my camera, but kept a few of my possessions so I would return to him, which I didn't. I celebrated my newfound freedom by wandering the streets of Luxor, wearing hot pants decorated with the faces of Cleopatra and Nefertiti.

This perplexing ordeal inspired my fascination with Bad Boys and led me to take the photographs in this book.

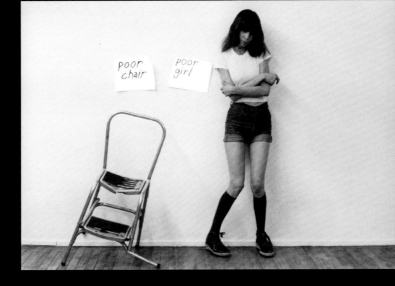

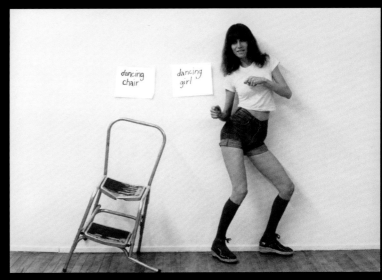

Marcia Resnick

# AFTERWORD
## MESSAGES FROM
## THE INTERIOR

BY ANTHONY HADEN-GUEST

SO YOU HAD YOURSELF QUITE A TIME at Marcia Resnick's haunted house party, right? It's a gathering at which the guests are proudly or painfully self-aware—where not even the most famous, the most notorious, or the neediest are allowed to slip into something comfortable, like the well-upholstered body armor of a pose.

Resnick does not achieve this truthfulness by a kind of ambush, the way that Richard Avedon so often did. There's a trust here. Now this is necessarily true of all photographers who work successfully in rock and roll, but they are iconographers. That is their job description. With Marcia Resnick, you are getting messages from the interior, notes from a fellow traveler, and this creative complicity unites images as formally varied as Johnny Thunders regarding his face in a handheld mirror, James Chance in a whiter-than-white tux and a blacker-than-black tie, Steve Rubell snuggling up to Roy Cohn, and Tony Shafrazi with a Hollywood stubble and a lily nestled in his wig, vamping like Cleopatra on a barge or a caterpillar in your salad.

The pictorial truth-telling comes through in the dead-on portraits. Resnick catches David Byrne blowing a Magrittean cloud of smoke, and John Lydon in an unexpectedly cheerful mood. Her photo of Mick Jagger, Andy Warhol, and William Burroughs, in the Burroughs bunker, sends out a wave of worlds-in-collision reality. Occasional, chillingly offhand details tell further truths. A syringe sticks out of Johnny Thunders's Sinatraesque black straw hat. Eric Mitchell, James Chance, and Haoui Montaug all have black eyes—Montaug's perhaps sustained while working the door at Danceteria. "People would always come to me to be photographed when they had a black eye," Resnick says.

Of course, talent and self-destruction are not necessarily codependent, as the presence of Julian Schnabel, Christo, Mick Jagger, and James Brown in these pages makes clear. But sagas of brilliance on autopilot to nowhere have always been featured in the story of art. The gossip addicts we've all become tend to find them more interesting than the routines of, say, Anthony Trollope, who kept office hours when writing his novels, or Wallace Stevens, who wrote his coruscating poetry in his time off from his job as an executive for a Connecticut insurance company.

And yes, Resnick's Bad Boys pose, but their poses do not conceal reality. They are reality. Stiv Bators of the Dead Boys is on his knees, wearing a black shirt and red tie. David McDermott postures on the floor, turtle-like, in a tux. Klaus Nomi is in Greek-coin profile, in a black waistcoat and black leather pants; long black gauntlets cover his arms and his fingernails are painted black. Then we have the extraordinary moves of Jean-Michel Basquiat. I call them "extraordinary" because they seem to be both baroque and realistic glimpses of anguish.

Resnick's pictures sometimes recall paintings—Joey Ramone's long, pale face looks like an El Greco face, and in one terrific shot Walter Steding's luminous eyes remind me of a Margaret Keane—but this is clearly a matter of congruence rather than intention. There is equally clearly no reference in the Basquiat photographs to the work of that proto–Bad Boy, Caravaggio, but one is reminded that, as Mick Jagger has observed in these pages, "There is nothing new under the sun, dear," and there have been Bad Boys for as long as . . . well, for as long as there have been boys.

Renaissance artists changed names as often as the punks. According to one story, Caravaggio, born Michelangelo Merisi, killed a man while still a teenager in Rome. He became a hugely successful artist, but killed again and fled the city. According to another tale, the Pope approved a contract taken out on his life. Nonetheless papal

> **"The aim of every artist is to arrest motion, which is life, by artificial means and hold it fixed so that a hundred years later, when a stranger looks at it, it moves again."**
>
> —WILLIAM FAULKNER,
> *THE PARIS REVIEW*,
> SPRING 1956

lawyer Laerzio Cherubini commissioned him to paint *The Death of the Virgin* for his family chapel. The church fathers rejected the painting when they discovered that Caravaggio had used a famous whore as his model, but it was bought by the Duke of Mantua.

Punks always have had their patrons. The cause of Caravaggio's death, in his late thirties, remains a mystery. A recent theory is that he was poisoned by the lead in his paints. Similarly, Marcia Resnick's Bad Boys—a significant part of her life and art—were workaholics, often provoking their early demise.

Verifiable data about the Bad Boys of times gone by is scarce. It's all hearsay, rumorville. Shakespeare's contemporary, the great dramatist Christopher Marlowe, was in his late twenties when he was stabbed to death in a Deptford tavern. Rumors that he had moonlighted as a spy have swirled ever since. Nobody knows.

Mystery also cloaks another proto–Bad Boy, Arthur Rimbaud. (Thomas Miller, one of Resnick's models, borrowed the last name of Rimbaud's lover and became Tom Verlaine.) It was known that Rimbaud gave up poetry before he was twenty-one, and became a trader, explorer and gunrunner in Ethiopia. He died in his late thirties, but there were Rimbaud sightings in Africa for years.

Fabian Lloyd, the nephew and ardent supporter of Oscar Wilde, took the name "Arthur Cravan" and was nicknamed "Colossus" for his size. He was a prankster, performance artist, brawler, and briefly the light heavyweight boxing champion of France. He wrote and published *Maintenant!*, a blistering art magazine that was admired by Marcel Duchamp and Francis Picabia. (One capsule review suggested that Marie Laurencin painted like she needed a good fuck.)

When World War I broke out, Cravan skedaddled to New York, where he became part of the Duchamp circle and married the beautiful avant-garde poet Mina Loy. They left for Mexico when America entered the war. Mina Loy went to Paris when the war ended, to await her husband. But he seemingly vanished without leaving Mexico. Dadaists would report sightings of the surely-not-too-hard-to-spot Colossus for years, but he has been as engulfed in mystery as Caravaggio, Marlowe, or Arthur Rimbaud.

William Hogarth, the British artist and pitiless portraitist of Bad Boys in such scarifying series as *A Rake's Progress*, made hardcore visual references to "the pox"—syphilis—and made two prints, *Beer Street* and *Gin Lane*, in which he contrasted cheerful drinkers of beer with human ruins—a mother addicted to hard liquor, dropping her infant to its presumed death. A new Hogarth would advance the plot, replacing the pox—an inconvenience, now, until a strain resistant to antibiotics takes us back in time—with AIDS. The great Klaus Nomi was one of the first well-known AIDS victims. That new Hogarth could invent a Pot Place and a Smack Alley. We know upon which street most of Resnick's Bad Boys would most likely be found. Jerry Nolan and Johnny Thunders, whom we see together in one haunting Resnick photograph, died before their time, within a year of each other, and are buried in the same cemetery.

So to the future, and indeed the present: it's hard to imagine Marlowe, Caravaggio, or Rimbaud—or, come to that, the gaunt heroes of the Mudd Club, in its darkly glorious days—flourishing in the polychrome world of social media and blogs. The same is equally true of Marcia Resnick's Bad Boys. Could the murky doings in clubland have survived iPhone photographs, directional transmitters, and God knows what gizmos are shortly to come?

Bad Boys in times to come will have to discover new ways to bud, bloom, and head off into the dark. As they will, as they will. In the meantime, *Punks, Poets & Provocateurs* is like a core sample in a rich archaeological dig, made during a time when some dared, few cared, some died, and piercings (along with a full arm tattoo) weren't just another dress code.

# CAST OF CHARACTERS

**MUHAMMAD ALI** (219) Three-time world heavyweight boxing champion and poet who became a leading figure in the anti–Vietnam War movement when he refused to be drafted.

**KENNETH ANGER** (172-173) Underground experimental film director of the homoerotic *Scorpio Rising* and *Inauguration of the Pleasure Dome*, and author of the gossip masterpiece *Hollywood Babylon*.

**SCOTT B** (22) With Beth B, an independent no wave film director.

**LESTER BANGS** (236, 239) journalist and musician who wrote for *Creem* and *Rolling Stone*. His brilliant, though often irreverent, writings proved him to be one of rock's greatest arbiters. 1948–1982

**JEAN-MICHEL BASQUIAT** (224-225, 227, 229) Graffiti artist whose tag was SAMO. He became internationally renowned for neoexpressionist paintings celebrating African-American heroes like Charlie Parker, Muhammad Ali, and Miles Davis. 1960–1988

**STIV BATORS** (64, 102) Lead vocalist for Dead Boys, whose album *Young Loud and Snotty* contained the punk hit "Sonic Reducer." Bators also founded the band Lords of the New Church. 1949–1990

**JOHN BELUSHI** (240, 242, 245-254) Consummate comic actor and musician known for performing on the television show *Saturday Night Live* and in hit movies like National Lampoon's *Animal House* and *The Blues Brothers*. 1949–1982

**CHUCK BERRY** (77) One of the first and greatest vocalists, songwriters, guitarists, and performers in the history of rock. His classic hits include "Johnny B. Goode," "Rock and Roll Music," and "Maybellene."

**JOSEPH BEUYS** (198-199) Visionary sculptor, performance artist, and educator whose politically charged art and social philosophies have influenced many the world over. 1921–1986

**JELLO BIAFRA** (113) Lead vocalist for the West Coast band Dead Kennedys, a left-wing hardcore punk band whose acerbic lyrics, in songs like "Holiday in Cambodia," shocked right-wing detractors.

**MAX BLAGG** (212) Dapper downtown poet and writer whose books include *From Here to Maternity* and *Pink Instrument*, and whose interview with Iggy Pop appears in this book.

**VICTOR BOCKRIS** (12, 38-39, 182) Author of biographies about cultural luminaries including Andy Warhol, William Burroughs, Debbie Harry, Lou Reed, Keith Richards, Patti Smith, and John Cale.

**ANTHONY BOURDAIN** (209) Chef, author of books including *Kitchen Confidential: Adventures in the Culinary Underbelly*, and host of cable television's *Anthony Bourdain: No Reservations*. Bourdain ran New York kitchens including One Fifth Avenue, Sullivan's, and Brasserie Les Halles.

**FRED BRATHWAITE (AKA FAB 5 FREDDY)** (215) Graffiti artist, rapper, VJ, and actor who catalyzed the infusion of hip-hop culture into the downtown art scene.

**JAMES BROWN** (128-129) Vocalist referred to as the Godfather of Soul. Brown was known for his energetic dancing style and classic hits including "Papa's Got a Brand New Bag," "It's a Man's Man's Man's World," and "Super Bad." 1933–2006

**WILLIAM BURROUGHS** (10, 18, 24, 27, 28, 31-33, 37, 38-39, 42, 59, 60, 62-63) Leading member of the beat generation's inner circle, which included Jack Kerouac, Allen Ginsberg, and Gregory Corso. Burroughs was the greatest visionary of the counterculture; his influential books included *Junky*, *Naked Lunch*, and *Cities of the Red Night*. His New York City living quarters on the Bowery were referred to as the Bunker. 1914–1997

**RICHARD BUTLER** (122) Lead vocalist and songwriter for the Psychedelic Furs, whose albums include *Forever Now* and whose songs include "Love My Way."

**DAVID BYRNE** (11, 86-88) Lead vocalist and songwriter for the Talking Heads. After hits like "Love —> Building on Fire," Byrne began a career as a soloist and mixed-media artist and collaborated with Brian Eno on *My Life in the Bush of Ghosts*.

**JIM CARROLL** (90) Poet, musician, and author of the autobiographical *Basketball Diaries*. Carroll performed with the Jim Carroll Band; his song "People Who Died" was on his album *Catholic Boy*. 1949–2009

**JAMES CHANCE** (19, 127, 169) Lead vocalist, songwriter, and saxophone player for the no wave band the Contortions; he also performed as James White in James White and the Blacks.

**CHRISTO** (187) Influential artist known (with longtime partner Jeanne-Claude) for wrapping buildings and coasts, and for installing *The Gates* in New York City's Central Park in 2005 (a project first proposed in 1979).

**CHEETAH CHROME** ( 64, 156) Guitarist for Dead Boys.

**ROY COHN** (162) Notorious attorney and power broker. 1927–1986

**GREGORY CORSO** (27, 40) Poet and youngest member of the beat generation's inner circle. His books of poetry included *The Vestal Lady on Brattle* and *The Happy Birthday of Death*. "Marriage," "Bomb," and "The Whole Mess . . . Almost" are some of his most popular poems. 1930–2001

**DIEGO CORTEZ** (21-22, 192) Art curator who founded the Mudd Club with Steve Mass and Anya Phillips in 1978.

**QUENTIN CRISP** (195) English writer and gay raconteur whose memoir *The Naked Civil Servant* became a movie starring John Hurt. 1908–1999

**JACKIE CURTIS** (217) Actor, director, playwright, Warhol superstar, and glam artist who often performed in drag and who wrote and performed in the plays *Vain Victory*, *Femme Fatale*, and *Glamour, Glory and Gold*. 1947–1985

**RONNIE CUTRONE** (179) Artist and assistant to Andy Warhol. Cutrone painted large-scale images of American cartoon characters. 1948–2013

**JONATHAN DEMME** (171) Internationally acclaimed director of films including *The Silence of the Lambs* and the Talking Heads concert film *Stop Making Sense*.

**WILLY DEVILLE** (130) Vocalist and songwriter for Mink DeVille, whose albums included *Return to Magenta* and *Le Chat Bleu*. DeVille was known for his suave demeanor and cool looks. 1950–2009

**DIVINE (aka HARRIS GLENN MILSTEAD)** (220) Actor and drag queen who starred in John Waters films including *Pink Flamingos* and *Hairspray*. 1945–1988

**TOMATA DU PLENTY** (101) Lead vocalist for the West Coast band the Screamers. 1948–2000

**BRIAN ENO** (73) Musician in Roxy Music, collaborator with Robert Fripp and David Byrne, music producer for the Talking Heads, and creator of *No New York*, a no wave compilation album featuring the Contortions, Mars, DNA, and Teenage Jesus and the Jerks.

**DANNY FIELDS** (177) Music journalist, photographer, music industry insider, and major influence in the punk rock scene, managing the Ramones and bringing them to England, where they influenced bands like the Clash and the Sex Pistols.

**JIM FOURATT** (188) Writer, gay activist, and club manager for venues including Hurrah and Danceteria.

**KINKY FRIEDMAN** (108-109) Vocalist, songwriter, mystery novelist, and politician. Friedman founded the satirical country-western band Kinky Friedman and the Texas Jewboys.

**ROBERT FRIPP** (20) Guitarist for the English rock band King Crimson and creator of the Frippertronics technique, employed in collaborations with Brian Eno on albums of ambient music.

**ALLEN GINSBERG** (27, 35, 37-39) Poet in the beat generation's inner circle. Ginsberg was a political and spiritual activist who championed gay rights, free speech, marijuana legislation, and world peace. His poem "Howl" paid homage to his fellow beats. 1926–1997

**JOHN GIORNO** (38-39) Poet, performance artist, and neighbor of William Burroughs. Giorno developed multimedia poetry events; he founded the nonprofit production company Giorno Poetry Systems and the phone-based service Dial-A-Poem in order to connect poetry to new audiences.

**MICHAEL GIRA** (133) Artist and musician who founded experimental noise bands Circus Mort and Swans.

**PHILIP GLASS** (91) Influential composer known for a minimal music style using repetitive, mesmerizing structures. Glass has collaborated with artists including Robert Wilson (*Einstein on the Beach*) and Ravi Shankar (*Passages*).

**ROBERT GORDON** (123) Rockabilly vocalist and member of Tuff Darts. During his solo career, Gordon collaborated with Chris Spedding and Link Wray.

**JAMES GRAUERHOLZ** (38-39) Writer, editor, and beat generation aficionado. Grauerholz was William Burroughs's assistant and is executor of his estate.

**SPALDING GRAY** (233) Actor, playwright, and performance artist who cofounded the Wooster Group and whose personal monologues became films including *Swimming to Cambodia* and *Monster in a Box*. 1941–2004

**TOMMY GUNN** (213) Doorman and club promoter at NYC venues including the Cat Club, AM-PM, and the Limelight.

**BRION GYSIN** (43) Painter and performance artist who, with William Burroughs, co-wrote *The Third Mind* in which the authors rediscover the cut-up technique of writing. 1916–1986

**RICHARD HELL** (97-98) Poet, writer, songwriter, vocalist, and musician in the Neon Boys, Television, the Heartbreakers, and Richard Hell and the Voidoids. Hell acted in the music film *Blank Generation*; his song "Blank Generation" was a punk anthem.

**ABBIE HOFFMAN** (184) Activist and author who founded the Youth International Party *(Yippies)*. Hoffman was one of the Chicago Seven activists at the 1968 Democratic National Convention. 1936–1989

**KRISTIAN HOFFMAN** (117) Keyboardist, vocalist, and songwriter for the Mumps and musical director for Klaus Nomi. His writings about Nomi are in this book.

**H.R. (aka PAUL D. HUDSON)** (78) Lead vocalist for Bad Brains, an African-American hardcore thrash-punk-reggae band from Washington, DC, whose albums include *Rock for Light* and *I Against I*.

**VICTOR HUGO** (190) Venezuelan window dresser and boyfriend of fashion designer Halston. Hugo procured men for and posed for some of Warhol's paintings—in particular, *Sex Parts*. 1950s–1993

**GARY INDIANA** (174) Author, playwright, and art critic; his play *Alligator Girls Go to College* was performed at the Mudd Club. He contributed a text to this book.

**MICK JAGGER** (13, 53, 55-57, 62-63) Lead vocalist for the Rolling Stones, songwriter, entrepreneur, and androgynous male icon. Among his many songs are "(I Can't Get No) Satisfaction," "Sympathy for the Devil," and "Brown Sugar."

**JIM JARMUSCH** (231) Independent film director known for *Permanent Vacation*, *Down by Law*, and *Stranger than Paradise*, starring John Lurie.

**GARLAND JEFFREYS** (83) Vocalist and songwriter known for his song "Wild in the Streets."

**DAVID JOHANSEN** (74) Lead vocalist and founding member of the New York Dolls. Johansen was an actor and had a solo music career as Buster Poindexter.

**DR. JOHN (AKA MAC REBENNACK)** (79) Known as the Night Tripper. Dr. John introduced the world to New Orleans funk in his albums *Gris-Gris* and *In the Right Place*.

**RAY JOHNSON** (200) Collagist, pop artist, and founder of the New York Correspondence School (a mail art network). 1927–1995

**ARTHUR "KILLER" KANE** (93) Bass guitar player for the New York Dolls. 1949–2004

**LENNY KAYE** (115) Music journalist, composer, and guitarist with the Patti Smith Group. Kaye coreleased *Nuggets*, a compilation album of garage rock singles.

**THE KIPPER KIDS** (232) Harry and Harry Kipper were Martin von Haselberg and Brian Routh, an improvisational, slapstick, avant-garde performance art duo.

**ED KOCH** (223) Charismatic mayor of New York City from 1978 to 1989. 1924–2013

**WAYNE KRAMER** (75) Guitarist, songwriter, and vocalist for Detroit's politically left-wing rock group MC5. Their song "Kick Out the Jams" was a punk rock anthem. Kramer also was in Gang War with Johnny Thunders.

**TIMOTHY LEARY** (207) Psychologist and writer whose experiments with LSD and psilocybin at Harvard led to his advocacy for psychedelic drugs. His maxim "Turn on, tune in, drop out" was made popular in the 1960s. 1920–1996

**ARTO LINDSAY** (114) Guitarist who cofounded the no wave band DNA. Lindsay also performed with the Lounge Lizards and the Golden Palominos.

**RICHARD LLOYD** (95) Guitarist, songwriter, vocalist, and founding member of the new wave band Television. Lloyd is also a soloist, known for his album *Alchemy*.

**SYLVÈRE LOTRINGER** (38-39) Literary critic, cultural theorist, educator, and founder of *Semiotext(e)*, a scholarly journal elaborating on the epistemology of semiotics. In New York City in 1978, Lotringer staged the Nova Convention, a three-day homage to William Burroughs.

**LANCE LOUD** (103) Lead vocalist for the Mumps and star of *An American Family*, a pioneering 1973 reality television series. 1951–2001

**CHARLES LUDLAM** (160, 234) Playwright, actor, director, and avant-garde theater innovator. Ludlam founded the Ridiculous Theatrical Company, among whose plays was *The Mystery of Irma Vep*, in which cross-dressing prevails. 1943–1987

**WALTER LURE** (92) Guitarist and vocalist for the Heartbreakers, whose one studio album was *L.A.M.F.* ("Like a Mother Fucker").

**JOHN LURIE** (118-119) Artist, saxophone player for no wave band the Lounge Lizards, and actor in films including *Stranger than Paradise*, *Down by Law*, and *Permanent Vacation*.

**JOHN LYDON** (19, 104, 107) Lead vocalist and songwriter for Public Image Ltd (known for the albums *Metal Box* and *The Flowers of Romance*). As Johnny Rotten, Lydon was lead vocalist for the Sex Pistols (known for *Never Mind the Bollocks, Here's the Sex Pistols*). He was irreverent in both incarnations.

**NORMAN MAILER** (37, 185) Novelist, journalist, essayist, playwright, screenwriter, film director, friend of the beats, cofounder of the *Village Voice*, pioneer of New Journalism, and recipient of a National Book Award and two Pulitzer Prizes. 1923–2007

**GERARD MALANGA** (193) Poet, photographer, assistant to Andy Warhol, and actor in many of Warhol's films.

**PHILIPPE MARCADE** (153) Lead vocalist for the Senders.

**STEVE MASS** (178) Owner of the Mudd Club.

**DAVID McDERMOTT** (211) Artist and vocalist who hosted the *New Wave Vaudeville* show at Irving Plaza.

**MALCOLM McLAREN** (176) Performer, impresario, and manager of the Sex Pistols and the early New York Dolls. 1946–2010

**LEGS McNEIL** (203) Author and resident punk and cofounder of *Punk* magazine with John Holmstrom. With coauthor Gillian McCain, McNeil chronicled punk's history in *Please Kill Me: The Uncensored Oral History of Punk*.

**TAYLOR MEAD** (216) Poet, writer, actor, and Warhol superstar who performed in Andy Warhol's *Lonesome Cowboys*, in many of Anton Perich's videos, and in Jim Jarmusch's *Coffee and Cigarettes*. 1924–2013

**ERIC MITCHELL** (168-169) Director of no wave films including *Underground U.S.A.*; actor in Amos Poe's *Unmade Beds* and *The Foreigner*.

**HAOUI MONTAUG** (189) Writer, doorman at NYC venues including the Mudd Club, and cabaret producer of *No Entiendes*. 1952–1991

**PAUL MORRISSEY** (196-197) Wrote, cast, edited, filmed, and directed many of Andy Warhol's films, including *Chelsea Girls*, *Trash*, *Flesh*, and *Heat*.

**MARK MOTHERSBAUGH** (112) Lead vocalist and synthesizer musician with the new wave group Devo.

**JAMES NARES** (169) Artist and director of no wave films including *Rome '78*.

**JERRY NOLAN** (157) Drummer for the New York Dolls and the Heartbreakers. 1946–1992

**KLAUS NOMI** (135-136) New wave countertenor opera and electro-pop vocalist. Nomi was known for his theatrical style, outer-space costumes, and explosive performances. 1944–1983

**GLENN O'BRIEN** (20) Writer, mostly about art, music and fashion. From 1978 to 1982 O'Brien hosted *TV Party*, a new wave New York City public access cable television show.

**JOHNNY O'KANE** (22) Film actor.

**PETER ORLOVSKY** (27, 37-39) Poet, actor, and life partner of Allen Ginsberg. 1933–2010

**BORIS POLICEBAND (aka MARK PEARLMAN)** (124) Classically trained solo violinist who performed noise music with electric violin and police radio. 1950–1986

**AMOS POE** (201) Independent film director who made the punk film *Blank Generation*, which documented the new wave scene in downtown New York. His other films include *The Foreigner* and *Unmade Beds*.

**IGGY POP** (68, 71) Vocalist, songwriter, charismatic performer, and founding member of the influential punk rock band the Stooges (known for the album *Raw Power* and the single "Lust for Life").

**ROBERT QUINE** (120) Guitarist who recorded *Blank Generation* with the Voidoids and *The Blue Mask* with Lou Reed. Quine revolutionized punk rock with his brilliant, quirky guitar solos. 1942–2004

**JOEY RAMONE** (139-141) Lead vocalist and songwriter for the Ramones, the punk rock garage band that revolutionized three-chord rock in songs like "Sheena Is a Punk Rocker," "Blitzkrieg Bop," and "Rock 'n' Roll High School." 1951–2001

**NICHOLAS RAY** (180-181) Film director known for *Rebel Without a Cause*, *On Dangerous Ground*, and *Johnny Guitar*. 1911–1979

**MARTIN REV** (80-81) played synthesizer and drum machines for the influential electronic proto-punk duo Suicide (with Alan Vega).

**RENE RICARD** (210) Poet, artist, and actor who starred in Warhol's *Chelsea Girls*. Ricard also was an art critic; his piece "The Radiant Child" propelled Jean-Michel Basquiat's career to great heights. 1946–2014

**BILL RICE** (23) Painter and film actor. 1931–2006

**LARRY RIVERS** (206) Artist and jazz saxophonist whose paintings fomented the New York School. 1923–2002

**STEVE RUBELL** (162) Co-owner of the uptown club Studio 54 (with Ian Schrager). 1943–1989

**TODD RUNDGREN** (125) Songwriter, musician, recording engineer, and producer whose pop songs include "Hello It's Me" and "I Saw the Light" (both from the album *Something/Anything?*). He produced records by the New York Dolls, Patti Smith, and the Psychedelic Furs.

**JULIAN SCHNABEL** (170) Artist and film director, internationally renowned for his large-scale neoexpressionist paintings, especially those he made with plates.

**GIL SCOTT-HERON** (111) Poet, singer, songwriter, and author whose politically driven spoken-word jazz, blues, and soul fusion style influenced the development of hip-hop. His album *Pieces of a Man* features the song "The Revolution Will Not Be Televised." 1949–2011

**TONY SHAFRAZI** (204-205) Artist who spray-painted KILL LIES ALL on Pablo Picasso's *Guernica* in 1974 and founded the Tony Shafrazi Gallery, which exhibited work by artists including Keith Haring and Francis Bacon.

**STEVE SHEVLIN** (153) Bass guitarist for the Senders.

**CURTIS SLIWA** (222) Founder of the Guardian Angels, a group of unarmed volunteer citizen crime patrollers in New York City.

**SMUTTY SMIFF** (132) Stand-up bassist for the rockabilly band the Rockats.

**JACK SMITH** (186) Pioneer of underground films and performance art, known for his film *Flaming Creatures*. 1932–1989

**TERRY SOUTHERN** (21, 42, 44) Author of books including *Candy* and *The Magic Christian*. Southern was also a screenwriter whose unique satirical style was evident in *Dr. Strangelove, or: How I Learned to Stop Worrying and Love the Bomb*, *The Loved One*, and *Easy Rider*. He was a friend of the beats. 1924–1995

**WALTER STEDING** (20, 85) Accomplished violinist and figurative painter. He was an assistant to Andy Warhol, who managed the punk rock band Walter Steding and the Dragon People.

**CHRIS STEIN** (18, 20, 84) Guitarist, songwriter, photographer, vocalist, and cofounder (with Debbie Harry) of Blondie, the influential new wave pop band whose hits included "Heart of Glass" and "Dreaming."

**STING** (76) Lead vocalist, songwriter, and bassist for the reggae-inspired new wave rock band the Police, whose hits included "Roxanne" and "Message in a Bottle."

**JOE STRUMMER** (110) Lead vocalist and songwriter for the Clash, the most influential political rock band of its time. Their epic releases included London Calling and "White Riot." 1952–2002

**SYLVAIN SYLVAIN** (116) Rhythm guitarist, vocalist, and founding member of the New York Dolls.

**JOHNNY THUNDERS** (2, 8, 142, 144-147, 149-150, 152-157, 159) Vocalist, songwriter, guitarist, and founding member of the New York Dolls and the Heartbreakers, with whom he sang "Born to Lose," "Chinese Rocks," and "London Boys" (the latter song in response to the Sex Pistols song "New York," a put-down of the Dolls). Thunders's hit "You Can't Put Your Arms Around a Memory" was on his solo album *So Alone*. 1952–1991

**PETER TOSH** (82) Jamaican reggae guitarist who was a member of the Wailers with Bob Marley. Tosh was a promoter of Rastafari and, in his solo career, sang "(You Gotta Walk and) Don't Look Back" with Mick Jagger. 1944–1987

**ALAN VEGA** (80-81) Sculptor and vocalist for the influential electronic proto-punk duo Suicide (with Martin Rev).

**TOM VERLAINE** (94) Guitarist and vocalist for the Neon Boys and founding member of the new wave band Television, known for its album *Marquee Moon*.

**ANDY WARHOL** (18, 47-48, 50-51, 59) Prolific artist who produced pop art paintings and silkscreens, films, photos, records, books, magazines, and superstars. His art depicting Campbell's soup cans, flowers, and famous faces revolutionized American culture. He was one of the most influential visual artists of the twentieth century. 1928–1987

**JOHN WATERS** (164, 166-167) Independent film director, actor, screenwriter, author, and producer. His films celebrated bad taste and included *Pink Flamingos*, *Female Trouble*, and *Hairspray*.

**NICK ZEDD** (230) Musician and film director who founded the Cinema of Transgression, a low-budget underground film movement that espoused the use of rudimentary techniques, shock, humor, and no wave music.

# ACKNOWLEDGMENTS

## MARCIA RESNICK:

I would like to thank Victor Bockris, who was there from the beginning; my sister, Janice Hahn, who played a vital role in designing the book; and all the people in the Cast of Characters who posed for my photographs. I would also like to thank my parents, Sonia and Herbert Resnick; our agent, Robin Straus; Deborah Bell, Susan Herzig, Paul Hertzmann, John Espinosa, Rick Longo Burrows, Anthony Haden-Guest, Anna Sui, Lydia Lunch, John Waters, Richard Hell, Bob Gruen, Amos Poe, Penny Arcade, Max Blagg, Gary Indiana, Kristian Hoffman, Roy Trakin, James Chance, Judy Taylor, Ron Miller, Diego Cortez, Brian Eno, Thurston Moore, Byron Coley, Barry Miles, Marc Miller, Liz Derringer, Richard Butler, Dr. Daryl Isaacs, Allison Berg, Frank Keraudren, Catherine Talese, Agnes B, Roberta Bayley, Maripol, Danny Fields, Dean Lance, Rachel Amodeo, Ann Louise Bardach, Lynda Troeller, Rose Hartman, Anthony Bourdain, Gloria Gaev, Marcia Luskin, Robert Connaghan, Robert and Diane Austin, Anne Wilkes Tucker, Bill Nevins, Hiroya Akihama, and the staff at Insight Editions.

## VICTOR BOCKRIS:

I would like to thank Marcia Resnick for thirty-five years of creative friendship. Thanks to all my unforgettable friends in the pictures and all the contributors to the text, plus Gerard Malanga and David Schmidlapp. Thanks to Jason Evans for teaching me so much about photography and design, to the staff of the Jane West Hotel where I wrote parts of this book, and thanks from my heart to Miles and Rosemary for always being my friends.

*We also want to thank the writers we quoted from in the following books, magazines, and recording:*

## BOOKS

Lester Bangs (Greil Marcus, ed.), *Psychotic Reactions and Carburetor Dung: Work of a Legendary Critic: Rock 'N' Roll* (New York: Alfred A. Knopf, 1987).

Judith Jacklin Belushi, *Samurai Widow* (New York: Carroll & Graf, 1990).

John Berger, *Ways of Seeing* (New York: Penguin, 1972).

Victor Bockris, *Beat Punks* (Boston: Da Capo, 2000).

Victor Bockris, *Muhammad Ali in Fighter's Heaven* (London: Hutchinson, 1998).

Victor Bockris, *Transformer: The Complete Lou Reed Story* (New York: HarperCollins, 2014).

Victor Bockris, *Warhol: The Biography* (Boston: Da Capo, 1997).

Bockris-Wylie, *How I Learned to Like Myself* (New York: Warner Books, 1974).

Anthony Bourdain, *Kitchen Confidential: Adventures in the Culinary Underbelly* (London: Bloomsbury, 2000).

David Byrne, *How Music Works* (San Francisco: McSweeney's, 2012).

John Cale and Victor Bockris, *What's Welsh for Zen: The Autobiography of John Cale* (London: Bloomsbury, 1998).

Ann Charters, ed., *Tarantula by Bob Dylan: The Portable Beat Reader* (New York: Penguin, 1992).

Jim DeRogatis, *Let It Blurt: The Life and Times of Lester Bangs, America's Greatest Rock Critic* (New York: Broadway Books, 2000).

Ralph Ellison, *Living with Music: Ralph Ellison's Jazz Writing* (New York: Modern Library, 2002).

Steven Gaines, *Simply Halston: The Untold Story* (New York: Putnam, 1991).

Allen Ginsberg, *Collected Poems 1947–1997* (New York: HarperCollins, 2006).

Allen Ginsberg, *Deliberate Prose: Selected Essays 1952–1995* (New York: HarperCollins, 2000).

Richard Hell, *I Dreamed I Was a Very Clean Tramp: An Autobiography* (New York: HarperCollins, 2013).

Richard Hell, "Johnny Thunders and the Endless Party," *Hot and Cold: Essays Poems Lyrics Notebooks Pictures Fiction* (New York: powerHouse Books, 1991).

Lee Hill, *A Grand Guy: The Art and Life of Terry Southern* (New York: HarperCollins, 2001).

Phoebe Hoban, *Basquiat: A Quick Killing in Art* (New York: Penguin, 2004).

Jack Kerouac, *On the Road* (New York: Viking Press, 1957).

Greil Marcus, *In the Fascist Bathroom: Writings on Punk, 1977–1992* (Cambridge, Mass.: Harvard University Press, 1993).

Greil Marcus, *Lipstick Traces: A Secret History of the Twentieth Century* (Cambridge, Mass.: Harvard University Press, 1989).

Legs McNeil and Gillian McCain, *Please Kill Me: The Uncensored Oral History of Punk* (New York: Penguin, 1996).

Barry Miles, *In The Seventies: Adventures in the Counterculture* (London: Serpent's Tail, 2011).

Thurston Moore and Byron Coley, *No Wave: Post-Punk. Underground. New York. 1976–1980* (Brian Eno interview) (New York: Abrams Image, 2008).

Marcia Resnick *Re-visions* (Toronto: Coach House Press, 1978).

Simon Reynolds, *Rip It Up and Start Again: Postpunk 1978–1984* (New York: Penguin, 2006).

Anne Waldman, ed., *Out of This World: An Anthology of the St. Mark's Poetry Project 1996–1991* (New York: Crown, 1991).

John Waters, "Sort of Famous" and "The Most Beautiful Woman in the World," *Shock Value. A Tasteful Book About Bad Taste* (New York: Dell 1981).

Bob Woodward, *Wired: The Short Life and Fast Times of John Belushi* (New York: Simon & Schuster, 1984).

## MAGAZINES

Lester Bangs issue (*Throat Culture Magazine*, #2, 1990).

John Belushi issue (*Rolling Stone*, April 29, 1982).

Max Blagg, "Iggy Pop: Losers Leave Town" (*Traveler's Digest*, March 1978).

Victor Bockris, "The Life and Work of Basquiat" (*Gadfly*, May–June 2000).

Victor Bockris, "The Mystery of Terry Southern" (*Gadfly*, January–February 2000).

William S. Burroughs, "Time of the Assassins" column (*Crawdaddy*, late 1970s).

Liz Derringer (Mick Jagger interview) (*High Times*, June 1980).

Allen Ginsberg, Beatles Essay (*Rolling Stone*, No. 415, February 16, 1984).

Kristian Hoffman (Klaus Nomi obituary) (*East Village Eye*, 1983).

Gary Indiana, "One Brief Scuzzy Moment" (*New York Magazine*, December 6, 2004).

Barry Miles (Willy DeVille interview) (*New Musical Express*, November 1977).

Glenn O'Brien, "Glenn O'Brien's Beat" (*Interview*, mid-1970s).

Joey Ramone, "The State of Rock" (*High Times*, January 1980).

Glenn Rechler (Biography of John Lydon) (musicianguide.com).

Rene Ricard, "The Radiant Child" (*Artforum*, December 1981).

David Shepherd, "Slippery People (Talking Heads)" (*Mojo Classic New Wave Special, 1978*, February 2008).

"Sixty Best Songs About New York" (*Village Voice*, November 2014).

Alan Sondheim, "Marcia Resnick's Bad Boys" (*Art Papers*, May–June 1986).

Roy Trakin, "Aargh!" (James Chance interview) (*New York Rocker*, February 1979).

## RECORDING

Psychedelic Furs, "Only You and I," by Richard Butler *Forever Now* (New York: CBS Records, 1982).

INSIGHT
EDITIONS

PO Box 3088
San Rafael, CA 94912
www.insighteditions.com

Find us on Facebook: www.facebook.com/InsightEditions
Follow us on Twitter: @insighteditions

Library of Congress Cataloging-in-Publication Data available.

ISBN: 978-1-60887-601-3

PUBLISHER: Raoul Goff
CO-PUBLISHER: Michael Madden
ACQUISITIONS MANAGER: Steve Jones
EXECUTIVE EDITOR: Vanessa Lopez
PROJECT EDITOR: Dustin Jones
ART DIRECTOR: Chrissy Kwasnik
PRODUCTION EDITOR: Rachel Anderson
PRODUCTION MANAGER: Jane Chinn

Design Consultant: Janice Hahn

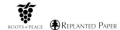

ROOTS of PEACE    REPLANTED PAPER

Insight Editions, in association with Roots of Peace, will plant two trees
for each tree used in the manufacturing of this book. Roots of Peace
is an internationally renowned humanitarian organization dedicated to
eradicating land mines worldwide and converting war-torn lands into
productive farms and wildlife habitats. Roots of Peace will plant two
million fruit and nut trees in Afghanistan and provide farmers there with
the skills and support necessary for sustainable land use.

Manufactured in China by Insight Editions

10 9 8 7 6 5 4 3 2 1